Moving On & Up

Intelligent women will not be intimidated!

The Whistling Girls & Crowing Hens Series
Book 6

Jan Anthony

This is a work of historical fiction. Names, characters, places and incidents are products of the author's imagination, and media articles are used as fiction and are not to be construed as real. Any resemblance to actual events, locales, organizations or persons, living or dead, is coincidental.

Copyright © *Jan Anthony* 2025
All Rights Reserved
This book is subject to the condition that no part of this book is to be reproduced, transmitted in any form or means; electronic or mechanical, stored in a retrieval system, photocopied, recorded, scanned, or otherwise. Any of these actions require the proper written permission of the author.
ISBN: 979-8-3492-5288-4
Library of Congress Preassigned Control Number 2025903269

Published by
Mother Courage Press
Editor/Publisher Jeanne Arnold

Moving On & Up

The Whistling Girls & Crowing Hens Series

Jan Anthony

Mother Courage Press
Editor/Publisher Jeanne Arnold

A creative nonfiction series based on personal letters,
prose, poetry, journals, diaries and imagination

Two straight, married women risk families and careers, leave society's compulsory heterosexuality in 1972, and boldly thrive in an unchartered, intimate relationship. Jan and Bea experience historic events in the women's movement and gay/lesbian world in their 39 years together. Each book presents deeper levels on major topics and adventures.

The Whistling Girls & Crowing Hens memoir series will appeal to:

- •readers to experience straight and lesbian lives,
- •young adults to appreciate what has come before them,
- •adults and elders to remember what they've survived and
- •women-loving-women who've defied society's rules.

Dedication

Dedicated to the women in my life,
especially Bea for her love and her poems
and journals,
and to those who love her and them.

Prologue

Grown up now,
rational at last,
We have the intelligence
to make crystals out of chemicals.
The purely chemical reaction
that burst between us
is growing now
into a lovely
multisided
crystal,
pure and translucent,
warmer than ice,
harder than rock,
more durable than
one lifetime.

by Bea Lindberg

Chapter 1

Bea on January 2, 1983

I didn't keep a diary last year. It seemed too negative. We'd worked ourselves to the bone getting Jan's deceased father's properties in order. After we remodeled and rented the downstairs of his house, we finished the upstairs apartment and rented it, but we don't know yet what Wisconsin will claim from Barney's estate to pay for the years of Jan's mother confinement in a state or county mental institution.

And we're tired.

We inherited his cluttered, run-down old building with our bookstore on the first floor. Our Mother Courage business plunged from $20,000 to $7,000 in two years. Jan's always promoting the store because we can't afford to advertise. She submitted a story about our shop to Lakeshore Bay's weekly Holiday newspaper issue, but shoppers didn't rush in to buy last minute gifts from us when they can now go to the new mall with its B. Dalton and Walden bookstores.

The newspaper story that filled a space in *The Lakeshore Leader* included a photo of the two of us posing together on our library ladder with our books all around us.

It read:

The Mother Courage Bookstore and Art Gallery, 214 2nd Street, has a uniquely appropriate symbol—a figurehead from the prow of a ship, a proud woman.

Bea Lindberg, co-owner and store manager, describes Mother Courage this way: "It's a full-service general bookstore specializing in books for women."

Mother Courage offers the usual range of best sellers and self-help books, plus a wide variety of books on politics, jobs, divorce, widowhood, mothering and home-making. The store also sells hard-to-find records by companies run by women and featuring female artists.

Lindberg and her partner, Jan Anthony, were inspired to start Mother Courage after seeing a woman-oriented bookstore in Madison. They then founded their own bookstore with three functions in mind: it would be a bookstore, an art gallery, and it would provide what Lindberg terms "creative services," that is, her own freelance artwork for advertising for local businesses.

Mother Courage's art gallery features women artists on an artist-of-the-month basis. "We're always looking for new women artists to feature," Lindberg notes.

Mother Courage's activities actually extend beyond these three goals. Lindberg and Anthony also run Mother Courage Press, which first produced Lindberg's set of Women of Courage note cards featuring political and literary women. Their next book production was *Something Happened to Me,* a therapy book by Rachel Sandler to encourage children to talk about their abuse and get help.

In addition, Lindberg and Anthony have participated in numerous book fairs and have been guest speakers at many area conferences and meetings.

Lindberg seems surprised as she recalls all of Mother Courage's activities, which also include poetry readings, skill demonstrations, NOW meetings and book club events.

"Running a business can be difficult. Sometimes you forget how much you've already done."

Jan on January 4, 1983

Our Mother Courage Bookstore isn't paying off like we'd dreamed. I try to find a different professional direction through increased involvement with my Lakeshore Bay businesses and Wisconsin hospital PR colleagues. I must sell myself for for professional reasons: to prove that, despite being a lesbian, I'm a great PR woman.

Randy told me during one of his interrogations of me that I have an inordinate need for recognition and approval. In my whole life—in fifty-one years, I've never received his brand of negative feedback. (Well, maybe when I was a toddler and my relatives told me that I whined a lot. Or when my ex-husband, Alex Carnigian, was jealous of my loving other people—especially my women friends like Marge and Bea.)

Randy is pathological with negative projections of what could happen if, when and whatever. He's the only person who criticizes me for my every move that he knows about, the only one who called me "tacky" or "stupid." He is the only administrator to evaluate me negatively in writing. (I wonder where he files those documents?) Other supervisors have thought me qualified and creative: my principals from my teaching years, my newspaper editors from my journalism career, even Mr. Clark Young appreciated me when he was Lakeshore Med's respected hospital administrator.

Nick Dixon did too when he hired me while I was a newspaper reporter, a Unitarian church friend and an outwardly stable, socially acceptable married woman. It's hard to believe in all these years, all those bosses were only being nice to me. What a strange ratio to have hospital administrators be the top scoundrels among them all.

Bea and I probably could survive if Randy fired me, but would we lose our house? I've lived through tough times before, but this is scary. I've never been the sole economic support person of another person and our mortgaged home.

I must keep my cool so Bea and I will be financially OK. But what if Randy King demotes me. If my incorrigible administrators continue to make me miserable until that forces me quit, I must get by with a little help from my friends, try to stop aching and find peace in a lesser role. Meanwhile, I will quietly collect my salary, medical benefits and vacation time, carry on with my workload, and continue to do my best while I network for another equitable job—or until I'm forced to leave.

It's management based on fear. For two-and-a-half years the pervasive atmosphere of this hospital has changed from Administrator Clark Young's benevolent leadership to Nick Dixon and Randy's paranoid power with Randy micro-managing and following Nick's orders and Chuck McCarthy, Randy's clone, following Randy's style like a puppet. Of course, intense hospital reimbursement problems caused by federal cutbacks on Medicare payments; increased healthcare competition, especially with the new St. Agnes Medical Center offering patients only single rooms; and increased government red tape all factor into administrative insecurities; but rather than enlighten and inspire the proven and positive support of Lakeshore Med's managers and employees, those three transmit paranoia while Nick stands above it all, looking in another direction by pandering to physicians, needing them to refer more patients to Lakeshore Med.

To try to make up for negative forces, these men have started a Quality Circles cost-savings campaign run by an expensive contract consultant who offers motivational seminars and cheap awards for employee ideas. Also, "Meet with Mr. D" invites employees into the inner administrator's boardroom for a half-hour information exchange between Nick and staff. It may be some time before I'm invited.

Carolyn Schafer, my office colleague, several nursing managers, Laura Williams, Pat Holmen and I team up on various projects, including a second year of promoting and producing local cable *For Your Health* TV programs. Ironically, our first program this year is "Depression: Moody and Blue? What to Do?" featuring Lakeshore Med's psych staff.

Bea on February 5, 1983

Jan spent long winter nights sorting her family's photo boxes to create a slide show for her kids and mine when they came last Sunday for Matt's birthday party and farewell supper. Jan's dream of having him employed locally at Jefferson Medical because of his Indonesian trip and language knowledge isn't going to come true. While he was in Lakeshore Bay, he took computer classes and now he's headed for Reno to find a job and commute over the mountains in California part time to finish his master's thesis. He'll stay with his father until he can support himself. Alex certainly can support them using his computer skills working for the government.

After our big dinner and birthday cake, it was time for the show. Jan combined two projectors and carousel trays that alternatively showed Matt and Jenny's growing-up photos, ending with photos of Jan's dad, Jenny and us together in front of our new Mother Courage and, finally, Matt's graduation from UW-Madison. She synchronized three audio and slide machines to work with tapes with music to match the mood using songs from the Beatles, the Monkeys, Carole King and Judy Collins.

She wanted to remind Matt of what he's leaving so that he'll come home again soon. A few tears were shed for these memories of their youth—and now Matt's leaving. Good thing Jenny's staying here.

My daughter-in-law told me the show was moving with Matt leaving. She may have picked up the emotional sadness of seeing so much of their lives together when Jan and her kids were part of a nuclear family. That's not what Jan meant to happen, but I cheered them up by showing the slide show I'd made about my kids.

Also, after much research, I bought a color TV to enjoy and a VIC-20 computer so I can learn about computers and play PAC-Man.

Jan on February 6, 1983

I'm starting to plan for Lakeshore Med's totally renovated hospital open house for April 17. We added our Unitarian artist friend Rita Van Allan a UW-Oshkosh sculptor and mix-media art student and our hospital dietitian's aide. Rita and our part-time photographer, Bob Haban, will help us create "Arts & Facts" collages representing hospital services areas not available for public tours.

Our "Caring for You Open House" goals are to educate the community about our expanded and newly remodeled hospital and services and convince them to choose Lakeshore Med over the new St. Agnes across town. Our enthusiastic atmosphere and staff will show them what we do so well that the public will talk about how well we do it and raise us all to new levels of excellence and increased patient census.

Our office has been moved to the fourth floor in the old hospital area. Now we have more room and freedom to spill out into the hall and we can make some noise while our team works on projects. Ideas and far-out options written on note cards and colored paper decorate our corkboard wall, brainstorming concepts to be rearranged in an outline tour plan with on-sight guest activities, displays and visual aids. Its scope will be the biggest public event Lakeshore Med has ever attempted. Our hours will be long.

Jan on February 7, 1983

I drove Matt to the airport for his next adventure. This time he may be gone for a lot longer. So many of life's events and changes have happened since he was born in 1959. His birth brought great change in my life too with choices made by others until I identified my true lesbian self—and left his father.

Matt doesn't have to worry now about his mother being a divorced feminist who's in a highly visible partnership with another woman. I don't know if he even thinks about it anymore. Now, with his father, they can be out west and "out of their closet."

Chapter 2

Jan on February 15, 1983

Movies have always been healing therapy for me, even if the movie made me cringe like Robert De Niro's *Taxi Driver*. Your life couldn't end up being that bad. Nowadays, it's hard to find a feel-good film, except for last year's movies like *On Golden Pond* and *Raiders of the Lost Ark*. Bea and I stood in line to see Lakeshore Bay's first showing of *ET* in June, and to prove it, we were given a souvenir pin saying, "I was the first to see *ET*."

    Meryl Streep has become a favorite of mine since I could empathize with her roles where, first, she leaves her husband to be a lesbian in Woody Allen's *Manhattan*, and then her husband and child in *Kramer vs. Kramer*. With great expectations, we went to see her in *Sophie's Choice* as soon as we could. I had no idea what it was about, never read a William Styron book and I went.

    That night we saw dear old friends the Shannons as we walked near the front where Bea likes to sit, and we settled in to find more UUs, Rita Van Allan and her sweet, new gentleman friend Tim sat right behind us.

    I immediately identified with the young male character Stingo who left his southern home to begin the writer's life in Brooklyn like Thomas Wolfe, to walk across the Brooklyn Bridge at night, to live "at the crossroads of a million private lives," as the "Grand Central Station!" radio show drummed into my youthful brain, "…Gigantic stage on which are played a thousand dramas daily."

Stingo found a cheap Brooklyn boarding house to live in and became the third party to an unsettling relationship with Sophie with her secret and her Nathan with his obsessions, perfectly playing bipolar by Kevin Kline. Like Sophie, I was enchanted with Nathan's romantic charm and genius—and their complete love. I know that love—the love I have for Bea.

It was divine watching the couple at night dancing in the park and drinking champagne, then the happy trio sitting on the porch roof drinking beer on a sunny afternoon. Dancing in perfect joy, drinking to oblivion, writing to capture that love, laughing in trusting friendship together, until Nathan's strikingly violent mood swing reveals his anger with manic exaggerations. When Stingo rescues Sophie, she tells the naive young man her secret of her guilt, her choice at a Nazi death camp. Then she slips away to look for Nathan. When broken-hearted Stingo returns, he finds them in bed—at peace together, dead from a drug overdose.

The exhilaration of happiness and love shatters into the overwhelming agony of reality.

Swept away by heartache, I couldn't stop sobbing. Bea tried to comfort me; she told Rita and Tim that I'd be all right so they'd leave us alone. The theater lights went on and the ushers started sweeping up the popcorn around us. I couldn't stop weeping and I couldn't move. Sophie's combinations of devotion and bliss, then sudden despair shook my soul from as far back as my memory—perhaps even to my prebirth state.

With Bea driving, I cried all the way home. I think that I will never be able to tell her how or why the meaning of this movie has such a profound impacted me. How my love of her, my family and my mother run in parallel paths along my unstable life—paths not chosen and some that were.

Jan on February 18, 1983

Dear Matt,

I hope you received my Valentine on time. I sent it at the last minute because my mind's been so crowded with events that I lose track of the days. I'm always planning far ahead, meeting an instant deadline, or thinking about something that happened in the past. But mailing you and Jenny a Valentine is certainly my top priority.

And as I've said before, your Indonesian slides and your master's thesis materials that you showed me are terrific.

I'm having new adventures taking eight scuba lessons at the YMCA pool. Bea came to my first class to watch me, and our instructor remembered her and her three sons in his class in 1971 and invited her to join the class as a guest. She is now able to help me with all the skills and equipment: the mask, fins, snorkel, tanks, regulators, weight belts and the BC—the buoyancy compensator. I hope I can pass the written test and then pass my open-water outdoors test in a gentle little lake somewhere.

I hope that you're feeling as good as I am and finding positive solutions to advance your goals.

Much love,
Mom

Carolyn in the employee *letter* on March 3, 1983 "Emphasis on New Lakeshore Med on April 17"

Lakeshore Med has a block-long parking lot, 142 private room accommodations, a new Patient Registration, Admitting and Outpatient area and much more. In fact, Lakeshore Med is a new hospital!

To educate the community about the new Lakeshore Med, an open house is planned for Sunday, April 17.

In addition to Lakeshore Med's new image, the emphasis will be on Lakeshore Med's quality care and excellent medical technology, educational orientation, health maintenance and all of Lakeshore Med programs and services.

A steering committee headed by Director of Communications Jan Anthony has worked on initial planning and implementation. Committee members have begun seeking advice and assistance from individuals and departments.

Displays are being planned along with free screenings and demonstrations.

A pre-open house for employees, volunteers and their families will be held shortly before April 17.

Bea on March 17, 1983

We saw Jessica Lange in *Frances*, another powerful movie like *Sophie's Choice*. Frances Farmer was a beautiful, independent, intelligent, combative movie star whose tragic story forced her into mental intuitions where she was brutally mistreated. The movie revealed horrible psychiatric malpractice plus the details of her lobotomy. We didn't realize what a bleak movie it would be. Jessica Lange was funny and touching in the gender-mixing *Tootsie* movie, but this tragedy had Frances ending her career as a vague but still talented middle-aged woman dying of alcoholism and throat cancer. Except for alcoholism and cancer, the whole movie reminded Jan of her mother's life. Her mother had every potential for a successful and happy life until her first nervous breakdown that descended into chronic mental illness. I worried about Jan's response to the movie, especially after her crying jag after *Sophie's Choice*. But she was OK this time, I guess. We didn't talk much about it.

Good News! After trying and failing to sell Jan's dad's old building for less than peanuts, I negotiated with the upholstery store neighbors to rent the downstairs near their exit. They'll start in June for $125 a month plus utilities. Yeah! That solves some cash flow problems for us.

Jan on March 18, 1983

I typed and submitted our "Caring for Your Open House" outline today for administrative approval. Our steering committee members represent all hospital staff levels, including the Auxiliary volunteers. The four-page outline proposal offers three tour route maps with thirty-nine activity stations including three-dimensional wall displays representing psychiatric services plus the major four-part collage series representing Lakeshore Med's diagnostics, treatment, rehabilitation services, health career education and community support programs.

Jan on March 22, 1983

Miss Judy Collins
c/o Milwaukee Performing Arts Center
Dear friend,
    You are one-hundred percent correct about the power of song—one of the greatest forces on earth. The power that your songs have generated in my life is great, but added to the combined energy that others have gained from them, has resulted in immeasurable positive awareness and a peaceful stimulus for change.
    I have a song that should be added to those with power like yours; only this song is for the earth—for Mother Earth. I hear it in my heart as a universal message, an international anthem of praise and awe to the earth.
    My friend Bea Lindberg wrote it in 1976, and when I submitted it to your agent to have it forwarded to you to consider, I received a form letter response and was frustrated about advancing the song at that time. Life goes by quickly and

when I saw the clipping about your coming to Milwaukee, I sensed that the song's time has come with a new opportunity to be reviewed by you. Hopefully it could join your repertoire of songs than enrich our lives and our environment.

Bea and I and other friends from Lakeshore Bay will be part of your appreciative audience tonight.

Jan Anthony

MOTHER EARTH
By Bea Lindberg

Mother Earth, Mother Earth. Nurture me for I love thee.
Lake and hill, can't get my fill of your sweet land,
Your sea and sand, your trees and sky, your mountains high,
I love them all, your spring and fall, your warmth and snow.
All these I know are mine, my Mother Earth.

Mother Earth, Mother Earth. I in turn will nurture thee
To keep you free for all to see, for all to share,
preserve with care, my precious Mother Earth.
My precious Mother Earth.
My precious Mother Earth.

Chapter 3

Jan on April 4, 1983

April 1, our nine-year anniversary and five years of living in our home. I couldn't sleep through that night so Bea decided to read tarot with our cards spread on the sheets of our double bed with the light of the moon falling through our windows and onto our nude bodies. A flashlight helped us read the cards' interpretations from our favorite *Feminist Tarot* by Sally Gearhart and Susan Rennie. The future looked good for me as we toasted to it with wine we brought upstairs for the occasion and, while we continued our pillow talk, we celebrated our love and all that we've accomplished together with enthusiastic desire to please and to be pleased. I calmed down then and we fell asleep together.

We usually sleep later on Saturday, but I had to work on that open house project. Too many interruptions during the weekdays disrupt my thinking about media releases, advertising and brochures that we're creating for the event.

At least I could take off on Easter Sunday. We were delightfully laid back after our breakfast and shower ceremony that lured us back to bed again for playful surrender to spring rituals of planting joy in our Goddess-given gardens—in the hills and the valleys. It's fortunate that we don't have to be concerned about fertilization. Our way of rejuvenation is much more fruitful for our earthy harvest.

We went outdoors later to burn our dry and brown Yule wreath in our firepot and planted our living Christmas tree in the hole we dug for it last October. I also planted sugar snap peas and spinach seeds in our compost-rich, gentle soil and woke them to grow with their initial water blessing.

Bea on April 10, 1983

Robin Witte's *Women's Network Newsletter* came to the bookstore today. April's two speakers will be "Empowering Ourselves" by Sister Brenda, a Dominican nun, and "Marital Property Reform—An Even Break" by Attorney Judy Hartman, another UU friend. Robin also included an invitation to invite your supervisor or boss to our Network meeting on Boss's Day, May 11. Hell. Everyday is Boss's Day and I'll bet Jan won't be inviting Randy. And that reminds me that I'm blessed not to have a boss.

Jan's not been feeling well but she continues to work long hours and comes home late to eat a warmed-up supper after I eat alone. She and "her team," as she calls them, are working long hours too, but they earn overtime. Jan compensatory time adds up but she's always too busy to take it.

Talk about adding up hours, Carolyn described their absolutely unnecessary art collages, according me, in their damn newsletter. The story explains the collages to those who read the newsletter and it also tells me why Jan's spending so much time at work.

Carolyn in the employee *letter* on April 2, 1983
"Lakeshore Med is Detection, Education, Treatment, Rehabilitation and Service"

The "Lakeshore Med is..." collage display, created for the hospital open house, visually communicates Lakeshore Med's unique atmosphere of quality care, excellent medical technology and commitment to education in its completely renovated and remodeled environment.

Its intent is also to keep the collages in place after the open house as a beginning of a series of health education displays to inform, entertain and educate patients, visitors and employees about the medical center. The display is located at the main hospital entrance in the front entry corridor used by all patients, visitors and staff.

Currently, visitors carefully look over each collage, and employees are still stopping to look them over and point out something to others. Several departments have requested collages of their own to educate patients using their services. Plans are underway to build more of various sizes, the beginning of a hospital-wide health education display system.

Jan on April 11, 1983

We all were working in our office, in the hall, and on tables set up in the nearby day room until 10:30 p.m. when my desk phone rang and the switchboard operator told me that I had a visitor, Bea Lindberg, and should she come up.

I said yes. Bea made her way up the elevator and through the darkened hospital halls, poking her head into the chaotic mess within my bright office. Everyone had been talking and laughing while working on projects that were due on Sunday, and when she stuck her head in the door, they shut up. After greeting her and inviting her in, she said, "No thanks. I guess you *are* working." Then she turned and retraced her steps out the front lobby and to her car.

I was concerned about her driving under the influence, but that wasn't the first time for either of us, and I wasn't going to fawn after her and leave my loyal, hard-working team, even though they advised me to quit for the night and go home.

Randy stopped by several days ago to see what all was going on, found himself in the midst of our production crew, asked a few questions and left.

Carolyn in the employee *letter* on April 18, 1983
"Caring for You Presents Lakeshore Med Stars"

"There's no business like show business…" sounded from the Academy Awards TV show Monday night. The spectacular song and dance routine drew my attention from reading a newspaper article about the elaborate preparations for the show itself. The stage crawled with dozens of production workers, set painters and stage managers.

Of course, one couldn't help but think of our open house this Sunday and all of the people performing together to make a little bit of "show business" an Academy Award success.

It is show business on Sunday because it will show others Lakeshore Med's excellent services and what a quality hospital it is. There may not be a chorus line, skimpy costumes and flashy dance routines, but there will be an audience and the cast will be putting their best feet forward to entertain as they educate about health and excellent hospital care.

No Steven Spielbergs here. But this production has involved many people in the planning and in the fast-paced production. Tension mounts as the opening approaches. Some performers practice their scripts for their part. Others in less structured scenes will use more extemporaneous dialogue.

A sneak preview is planned before the main performance. All volunteers, Alumni members, employees and families are urged to attend the dress rehearsal from 11 a.m. to 1 p.m.

What size audience is expected? It's difficult to predict how the public will respond. In addition to the many excellent health-oriented demonstrations, one extra motivator will attract parents and children. It's the Ident-A-Kid fingerprinting for family records.

After a journey through the most modern medical technology, young visitors will be intrigued with the reality of having a small cast applied to one of their fingers.

Many employees and Lakeshore Med volunteers will be pulling this spectacular together by using their educational skills and a variety of hospitality charms. And there are still opportunities for more extras as performers.

Everyone from the volunteer running the elevator to the professional staff members describing the most complex instrumentation in a few words adds a vital element to the audience's impressions. Lasting impressions of Lakeshore Med are developed every day, but on Sunday, April 17, this is especially true.

The memories lasting beyond that day will benefit everyone. Though no one will win an Oscar for his or her efforts, more people will know first hand about how great Lakeshore Med staff and facilities are and they will tell others of the award-winning excellence they have.

Carolyn on April 18, 1983

In another story, I explained the meaning of all of the banners that have evolved since I started working for Jan. We designed the logos and I created the banners with sewing skills and some press-on Stitch Witchery so that I could use my comp time to visit my lover when he was scheduled to be near me. Jan always says that she loves lovers.

I listed the twenty-six banners and the department groups we combined or those large enough to be a single banner as Lab, Nursing Service, OB/GYN, etc. For our Communications team, I picked ten bells in blue and yellow, Lakeshore Med logo colors, and green for contrast on white with blue edging plus five golden ringing bells. We included our department, the switchboard, messengers, office services and word processing among our banner team.

We also devised a two-sided foamcore panel that has a cut-out shaped to fit over the hall handrails. Each had a large, typeset number pasted on it to match our tour guide, and Bob Haban posted his many photos of each department that the banners represented so each was a significant part of the open house, even if the public couldn't tour Maintenance, Medical Records, Finance, etc. Rita Van Allan made a dramatic artistic display to represent the Psychiatric Unit.

The long halls between areas that could be visited were filled with museum quality banners, photos and displays.

Jan created the 16-page guide and included it as an insert in Sunday's *Bay View Times*. Unfortunately, in a cost-containment effort, she picked a grade of paper that didn't do justice to several photos, and the ink rubbed off when the visitors toured the hospital. Their hands left smudges for the Housekeeping and Maintenance crews to rub off. She learned she should have been at the printers when the magazine was running off the presses to check the results—or that she should have hired an agency or a printing rep to watch out for the magazine's final production, but she was so bugged by costs that she didn't consider all of the reproduction details. Otherwise, the guide was an inclusive masterpiece covering all the quality aspects of the hospital, whether its readers came to the open house or not.

Over 1,200 visitors took a good look at our collage display "Lakeshore Med is …" as they waited in line along its length before getting on elevators and being escorted in small tour groups. Comments after the tour indicate that the collages and tour reinforced each other. In many instances and through demonstrations, visitors saw live what they previewed while looking at the collages. They came away impressed with the "new" Lakeshore Med.

We never received any comments or evaluations from three administrators.

Chapter 4

Jan on May 9, 1983

Everything's swirling around me, including that damn Blue & Gold Run and Walk on Saturday. Everyone is rushing in and out of our office to solve their problems or to vent their frustrations. Carolyn and I already completed the promotional media releases and advertising, t-shirt production and signage before I left, but we have more responsibilities to complete.

The preparations for St. Agnes Health Fair next month are intense. We've saved last year's foamcore theater marquee and Mark Bertini and Laura Williams have been editing the twenty-minute presentation from our *For Your Health* TV programs, but what's going to be this year's gimmick? "You gotta have a gimmick!" Pat Holmen volunteered to be Miss Piggy last year. Now, because I acted the part of the tall and feathered "Yellow Bird" with Laura Williams narrating the outpatient knee surgery TV program, I was conned into being it in full body, feathered costume at St. Agnes on the first Sunday in June.

In my TV part, I needed a new procedure called an outpatient arthroscopic procedure, or Band-aide surgery. "Big Bird" wrenched her knee while crossing the road too many times. The script ended with, "I'm in fine feather, all things considering." (We couldn't use the same name as the Sesame Street character so we wouldn't infringe on its copyright.)

At least I won't have to make tons of free popcorn for the audience this year.

<<<>>>

A bright spot, yet one leaving me with mixed emotions, was Matt's Mother's Day letter. He has his first job, earning $20,000. Good for him; but that's almost what I make after all these years.

And coming forward after lurking in back of my mind is the final realization that Mother Courage Bookstore will no longer be open on a regular basis after May 27, the beginning of the Memorial Day weekend. We'll plan to have special sale events until Bea finds another job or she can't stand to be there any longer. I've repressed my anger and frustration and grief. I can't quit my job that supports us both to manage and staff the store that means so much to me. I cannot force it to be successful. Bea calls it "a storefront missionary for feminism" and she's tired of it all.

It was her store anyway.

We conceived the bookstore at the women-owned restaurant Lystrada in Madison after visiting the women-owned bookstore Room of One's Own. Bea hadn't been able to find a job after she surprised me by admitting herself into Milwaukee's St. Paul's alcoholic inhospital rehab program—and then Randy made me tell her—at St. Paul—that she was let go from Lakeshore Med because we were buying a house together. Supposedly there's a rule that I've never seen that a supervisor and a subordinate in the same department may not live together.

(And I've recently heard that Randy and Chuck, Randy's subordinate, are living together in a bachelor apartment at the Marquette Manor on Main Street, the same venerable apartment complex where I kept my room of my own for several years. I can't believe they're so supremely immune and irresponsible as to flaunt their double standard of living together after they punished us for loving each other and living together. What arrogance! What hypocritical treachery!)

If I don't vent my frustrations, I'll lose control, and that, for me, is serious and scary.

Bea and I moved into our house and I kept on working under Randy as my boss at Lakeshore Med. Soon after, Bea and I went to Madison's feminist bookstore where Bea hung her nude and headless paintings of me. To celebrate her show, we walked around the block to the women-owned Lystrada for an early supper and I asked her what she'd like most of all to be and she said a bookstore manager. I told her I had a storefront. She could be the bookseller and manager and I'd be the partner and PR person. She conceived Mother Courage's logo right there on a napkin. It was an idea conceived in love.

We approached my dad and he agreed.

From the beginning, Bea selected all the books; I was to stay out of the way. It was to be her success and I wasn't to be involved in what she wanted to control. In spite of her bodaciousness, she doesn't take financial risks. She argued that she took enough financial risk when she advanced her inheritance with the $8,000 down payment on our house mortgage before my divorce settlement was finalized and I could then repay my share. She frets when business lags. If I spent money to promote it, I'd feel guilty if I couldn't prove it was worth it.

I never thought the retail part of the business would support her completely. She could have promoted her creative and artistic skills, but Mother Courage Creative Services never got off the ground. Because I hoped we could sell Bea's skills creating brochures, art and writing to small businesses, but those expectations never happened, and then there'd be arguments. She'd scold me, "Don't tell me what to do with my time. I don't want to be rejected anymore."

Mother Courage was relatively successful for two-and-a-half years and then we stopped our programs and mailings and I couldn't fight anymore. I ran out of energy. Bea was doing only what she wanted to do, in the confines of the bookstore. She got bored and frustrated and thought about all that could go wrong. No wonder she was depressed.

When my dad died, we continued to clean and empty my dad's house and the remaining part of the shop, both of us working together

The shop could be an artist's studio. Fantasy. Impractical. If we had rented the basement earlier, we could have had that income, but her boat had priority. Holy Cow! We'll be getting some rent now so the bookstore could sustain itself a bit longer. I've talked about programs down in the basement like an underground women's movie series. And then we'd sell more books upstairs. I could never make her—I didn't want to nor could I make her do anything, so nothing happened and it petered out. And the last couple years have been sad with pain and disappointment—and anger.

Whew! I guess I needed to release some of that pressure from my mind and heart.

Bea on May 14, 1983

Jan was up at five a.m. to do her Lakeshore Med run stuff after working late last night to be sure everything was ready. Honestly, it's like she's still decorating floats with her father and family for Lakeshore Bay's 4th of July parade.

In addition to filling twenty-six orders for *Something Happened to Me*, I'm cleaning and moving stuff to set up an office for Mother Courage Press in the back where Jan's dad's offices were. I move boxes of *Something* from the basement to store in the upstairs front hall. Those boxes each weight over forty pounds. Jan painted those pre-WWII dusty walls before I piled the boxes there.

Jan on May 16, 1983

The soggy weather had little effect on the 390 runners and walkers who crossed the Blue & Gold Lakeshore Family Run/Walk finish line in their new Lakeshore Med T-shirts. They and our volunteers, who arrived to help near dawn, were not intimidated by Saturday's rain and fog with both of the two- and five-mile routes starting on the lakefront past some of Lakeshore Bay's best scenery. They finished at the hospital with awards and refreshments plus free health services like blood pressure checks.

Our own Laura Williams and Larry Duke, with the help of the runners' Midland Striders, made this year's event a success, but Carolyn and I, who designed logos and t-shirts, wrote promotions, media releases, forms and ads, were still finishing up the details until 4 p.m. when I went to help Bea at the shop.

Someone wrote an encouraging letter to the editors at *Bay View Times* and concluded, "Looking forward to next year, Lakeshore Med, but hold the rain!"

I'm not looking forward to another run next year, next month. Not ever!

Bea and I were so tired that Saturday that we skipped supper after cocktail hour, showered and both passed out in bed. But—And—How I love waking up with her bare body touching mine. I shake and shudder like I've been electrocuted. Honestly. That first touch in the morning jolts me—always. Goddess Bless! We didn't have to go to work 'cause it's Sunday, and we didn't have anyone coming over, so we figuratively returned to our Nellie's Nest mode from Key West to our own bed, breathing, stroking, tasting, sensing until we achieved a gigantic simultaneous, joy-filled orgasm as if bonded as one being—a single soul spirit.

Bea on May 26, 1983

Jan and I chopped and cooked most of the weekend preparing food for Jill's graduation party. I did take a couple hours to ace a civil service exam to qualify for a booksellers' job in Milwaukee.

Jill's taken my example of earning her college degree and I love it. She graduated cum laude and all my family came to our house to enjoy her accomplishment, including Jill's in-laws and my ex- and his wife of three years who was my best friend since all our kids were toddlers and many years after that. The food, cake, champagne and a quarter barrel of beer helped us celebrate. Fortunately they didn't stay too late and I passed out after.

On Monday, Matt came back home and came for dinner with Jenny but Jenny had to leave early because she works for St. Agnes Hospital Food Services on the early breakfast shift and begins the day's food preparations. Matt and Jan talked until 1:30 a.m., but I'd had it and went to bed a lot earlier.

Everybody was high for full moon on Wednesday, my fifty-third birthday party and my Croning ceremony. I read that you're supposed to be about fifty-six and have passed your last menstrual cycle for a while, but I couldn't wait. The ancient concept is that post-menopausal women hold their blood within, therefore they become wise elders, but I'm pretty wise now and I'm ready to become a crone.

I started thinking of the concept last March when we had nine-and-a-half inches of snow. I drove Jan to work after shoveling out the driveway as best as we could. School's closed so I decided not to open Mother Courage either. Instead I stopped at the shop to blow away the snow and picked furniture clamps and an old wooden compass that Jan's dad used when he needed circles or arches to paint his signs. Then I headed home to work on making an eighteen-inch pentacle etched into a wooden circle to be the center of our moon circle altar.

I'd been reading about sacred geometry and was fascinated by the pentacle's geometrical function. The pentacle's been connected to the Goddess and pagan worship and is often condemned as the devil's cross or a witch star. It's simply a classic five-pointed star formed by a continuous line. Some even suggest that the Catholic custom of crossing one's self was copied from the pagans who made the sign of the star across their forehead, arms and chest for self-protection.

Jan prepared the opening and closing ritual for my croning ceremony, and I used my knowledge and my lacquered wooden pentacle tray to give our circle members a lesson in sacred geometry and the continuous drawing of the pentacle line to lock out harmful forces. Everyone was quiet during my lesson and when they croned me with Z Budapest's words and set a crown of flowers on my head with rainbow ribbons flowing through my hair, I truly felt like the first authentic crone in our area.

We sat down to feast after the ritual and that's when we had some fun with two new friends, Robin from our church and Naomi, a young UW-Oshkosh junior who had a crush on Robin because she so admired Robin's confidence and feminist ideas that she expressed in their classes. Robin had teased Naomi about being afraid to come to our group and the young woman blushed a flashing pink face but took it in good humor saying, "Now that I found out I wouldn't be eaten alive."

In pagan ritual celebrations for being a crone, we diffuse the contemporary negative aspects of being an old witch—the third and wisest of the Triple Goddess of Maiden, Mother and Crone.

Now with her twenty-some years, Naomi is our true Maiden, Robin, a married Mother with two children and the others are waiting to become Crones. We have a complete triumvirate of Goddesses celebrating our bodies' abilities to menstruate, give birth, nourish our infants and be respected as a wise elder. Now with my being true Crone whose "wise blood" accumulates within, I am honored for having even greater wisdom.

I'll go for that!

<<<>>>

Bea on May 30, 1983

Jan's been working so damn long on all the stuff she wants to get done, and I'm left alone all day at the store. She doesn't come home until all hours. Then before she wants to eat the supper I've prepared, she says she has to have her martinis to wind down from all her stress. In the meanwhile I've had a few drinks myself.

She's got stress! Ha! What's going to happen to me and the store and the rental property she talked me into buying and our home if she has to find a job elsewhere? What will happen to me?

It seems as if all I do all day is to keep alert by plowing through all the books and publications that come to the store. They range from A for abortion issues to Z Budapest's *Themis, a newsletter of the new Women's Religion.* It's dated not by months but according to the equinox and solstices and wheel of the year sabbats in the year 9980 ADA (After the Development of Agriculture). Feminist newspapers and *The Lesbian*

Connection come to us in bulk for distribution to our customers, even though we don't have many of those.

I don't know where these women get their energy and their money to produce all this, especially the newspapers because they probably don't get much cash for what they put out and get no support from the establishment press. Like us, we publish and mail out our little *Courier*. And what return do we get from that!

The subjects they print now were never to be spoken of years ago. We never talked about "periods" except as "the curse." Now they're writing Goddess rituals to celebrate women's bodily functions.

For example, if one article from a newsletter in Oakland interests the volunteer journalists, typesetters and women's presses in New England, it's reprinted there, circulated around to bookstores, and we all learn more and more about incest, endometriosis, PMS, abortion, civil rights, the war machine, support groups topics—and lesbianism.

It's a new world of alternative publishing now filled with lesbian energy and feminist ideology. It helps support an "out" culture leading to a paradigm shift. Only a few years ago, it seemed that the only conversation a woman could have about her lesbian feelings and sexuality would be with her psychiatrist. To hell with psychiatry! Now with open and available resources and support groups, she can find herself in a culture built on positive publications and books with happy endings for the lesbian characters who don't commit suicide or die as in *The Well of Loneliness*, one of the few well-known lesbian books written generations ago.

I've saved a clipping from one of these papers to show to Jan on "Premenstrual Syndrome Action" or "It's all in your head."

We've been advocating for years that feminists are so strong and deserve equal opportunities that we've also ignored or disguised our menstrual-related irritabilities, pains—or whatever. Until now, no one even heard about PMS! And I think I've got it with my severe monthly depressions. The Madison woman who wrote this article said she could get no help here, but when she went to London, England, to begin a course of hormone treatment, she started feeling great and began a counseling program for other women with PMS in Madison that's now going nation-wide. It took an English woman physician to study and treat women who experienced symptoms similar to hers.

I wonder what I can do? Sometimes my depression lasts about two weeks out of each month and ends just before my menstrual flow. I get tired, I crave more alcohol, have joint pain and I put on weight. What's new? That's been happening for years.

The docs offer Valium, but I saw what that does to women when I was in rehab for alcohol in 1978. Valium addiction is worse than alcohol. One doc told me to learn to live with my menstrual problems.

Naturally I'm past pregnancy-related symptoms, but I do have terrible mood swings. I know that when it happens, but I don't remember it because I use my favorite medicine, brandy, to get me over the worst of it. When I'm in that mood, I don't want to see a doctor—actually, I never want to see a doctor. Then when I'm feeling better I hope the damn thing won't come back.

And I don't want to take any hormones. "If it ain't broke, don't fix it," my mother used to say. Ha! The contact person for this condition is Carol Kay, a lesbian friend and coordinator of health education and advocacy at Milwaukee's Bread & Roses. Jan says we know her from our Milwaukee contacts. But I don't think I'll go for therapy. We'll just wait and see.

Chapter 5

Bea on June 1, 1983

The bookstore is closed, unless I'm there to clear out the shop and the building.

Jan on June 2, 1983

The first time I met Mindy, Randy's new snippy little snit of a secretary, I sensed that she felt superior to me. She sent Randy's memo asking for the same old busy work to the fourteen of Randy King's "subjects" who manage the volunteers and almost half of the hospital staff, including Nursing, Laboratory and Radiology. We will have a week to "develop personal and department goals." Hell! I've been submitting goals and plans and weekly work sheets for over two years and he's seldom responded to them. Now we all have to stop our immediate deadlines and type more bullshit that probably won't be acknowledged. And I don't know what the hell he means by "personal goals!" Who wrote that memo anyway?

The reorganization of clerical staff centered in the new Word Processing Center leaves only Nick and Randy with personal secretaries. In the past, I've had excellent rapport with Randy's secretaries. They couldn't help but be supportive of me when they saw me leave Randy's office with tears welling in my eyes. (I'd never cry in front of him.) But I'm going to be extra cautious with Mindy. She'll probably feel self-righteous when she sees how he pulverized his managers with his abusive power to intimidate them, especially the women who work closely with me.

So while Carolyn holds down the fort again, I pulled out my piles of file folders of our proposed public relations goals, provide efficient and cost-effective options, etc., etc., etc., The report that I typed and turned in on May 24 filled five pages.

"In conjunction with Mindy's arrival," said the next memo, I am to forward Mindy the answers to a questionnaire relevant to spring and fall holidays, casual and vacation days, etc. I didn't even think we had other days-off options than vacation days. How do you plan compassionate days? And how do can you measure public relations variances in start/stop time?

One office time "variance" that I can't list involves a full-size canoe paddle where Bea painted, "Never be up Shit Creek without a paddle." We keep it standing in a corner with the words facing the wall, and it's available for any colleague to run into our office, grab it and start paddling the air to burn off frustration and anger. I didn't list that among my "start/stop time."

Start/stop: does that also mean forty hours a week, 2,080 hours a year plus evenings and weekends for media emergencies, open houses, physician and volunteer parties, TV programming, health fairs and runs?

The fill-in-the-blanks questionnaire repeated much of what I'd just turned in. I was able to include Xeroxed copies of past reports to send to her.

Bea and I went out for a belated birthday supper and after we came home, we started talking about my concerns and our options. She told me I was trying to start an argument and asked me—no, told me to stop. I did, but what I want to talk about is still inside me.

Jan on June 3, 1983

Carolyn showed me the cover letter written by her daughter that's printed in this year's program book from the National Women's Music Festival in Bloomington, Indiana. Carolyn's daughter, Jane Schleishman, is one of the founding forces in keeping the music festival alive after the all-women music and arts event left its original site of the college campus in Bloomington, Illinois.

Carolyn's daughter writes "National Women's Music Festival, June 3-5, 1983"

Dear Mom,
    There's lots going on here, with final preparations for the festival and all. I sat down to write the "Welcome" for the program and felt completely overwhelmed. Can something be magical yet solid? Divided yet unconquerable? Organized yet serendipitous? Chaotic yet healing? Can we simultaneously verge on insolvency and euphoria?
    Got to thinking about traditions, "Foremothers;" the strength from which we come, so many women like you who live your lives and raise children with conscience, social commitment, creative coping; who strive to set spirits free; who revel in self-discovery, new adventures, progressive ideas; who quietly work with integrity and a sense of individual dignity and worth; who ceaselessly insist that reality respond to your dreams; in many ways this festival is a tribute to our past, and a promise to the future. We're not the first and we're not the last.
    So many stories converging here. I want to string up a huge, gorgeous banner saying simply, "Welcome Women!" Will that convey all the warmth and power and spirit and joy?
    For some, this is a rest stop; for others, a place of discovery and a point of departure; for still others, it's simply part of our work—to join in wherever we gather as sisters, mothers,

daughters, lovers and friends to share and expand visions, re-energize, regroup, communicate the news of our individual struggles, and share the wealth of our collective expertise.

'Much more than music,' we keep saying of the Festival. The music lights the path, and lightens the load. This whole culture is weaving new ties. So much yet to do—for the Festival and for life.

With love, gratitude, admiration from a daughter and a sister,

Jane

After reading that, I promised Carolyn that we'd go next year and take her with us. Carolyn's lesbian daughter Jane and other women, mostly lesbians, picked up the gauntlet from the Illinois organizers and have so far survived the move through hundreds of hours of legal and financial maneuvering. Jane obtained permission of her own campus where she graduated from law school after completing her first degree at Oshkosh. She's an attorney for Bloomington's Legal Services Organization and is in private practice, specializing in women's issues and domestic relations. Her love of women's music led to her involvement with the first group of thirteen women who revived the festival in 1982 on the University of Indiana campus.

Carolyn has never said out loud to me that her daughter is a long time lesbian, although we've talked about Jane many times. Maybe Carolyn thought Bea and I knew. Maybe that's why the Goddess sent Carolyn to me—because she'd understand more than most what my personal life is like, although sometimes I can't even understand it myself.

Chapter 6

Jan on June 6, 1983

AIDS. What do I know about HIV and AIDS? Margo Wilson, a *Bay View Times* reporter called me about writing an investigative story on HIV and AIDS in the Lakeshore Bay area.

All I know is what I read in the news or hear on TV. Last year *The Wall Street Journal* reported that gay-related immune deficiency disease also occurs in non-drug using women and in heterosexual men. When gay men were dying, the general reaction was "So what!" This year three thousand cases have been reported; one thousand men have died. Until Ronald Reagan dared to mention AIDS, the Acquired Immune Deficiency Syndrome, last September, the government had ignored the tragedies.
Trying to send her away from us, I told Margo I'd have to get back to her and suggested she refer to Lakeshore Bay's Health Department and to ask around in Milwaukee's public health centers and infection control medical specialists for information. Then I warned administration and our infection control people about what may happen and asked for advice about what to do. Could I release the names of experts as qualified spokespersons—and who would they be?
So far no one has responded and nothing has happened, but it's scary to contemplate. Many think that Lakeshore Med is the abortion hospital, but clients are sent to Milwaukee. Perhaps that's what we do if and when we have any HIV or AIDS patients.

Bea on June 6, 1983

My kids, their wives, friends and I started our Wolf River camping trip on Friday, driving north for miles in the rain, setting up the camping trailer and reserving spots for the others coming later. We played cards in our trailer as it rained all Friday night.

Joel woke us bright and early for breakfast and all eleven of us piled into two rafts to begin the treacherous and totally awesome trip down the river. We were falling into and out of the rafts, losing paddles and being swamped and wet for five hours. Joel's raft split open and ours leaked. What a wonderful time! Saturday evening was memorable with a giant bonfire, jokes and "pain killer" being passed all 'round.

We drove home Sunday with me in pain after banging my knee and right ankle that's swollen now, but I had a terrific time with my kids!

Jan was Big Yellow Bird at St. Agnes Health Fair and missed our fun.

When I got home Sunday afternoon, I poured myself a drink before starting to put my gear away. However, I decided to take a nap and slept until Jan came home from being Yellow Bird. She headed right for our bar and made herself a well-deserved double martini with three olives, plopped herself in her recliner and put up her feet. Her ankles were swollen. She's been walking around most of the day with big, yellow-bird feet and could have tripped and fallen many times when she walked about St. Agnes, or was swamped by little kids, or stepped on her own splayed-foot costume.

Her voice was worn out too after talking all day through the top of her cranium. "It was like I was talking out of my eyeballs," she said, "and some remarked that this Yellow Bird had bigger boobs than Sesame Street's real Big Bird."

Of course she woke me in my chair, and soon I was high on the rafting fun I enjoyed with my kids. We forgot to eat, but Jan ate popcorn from their exhibit and wasn't hungry anyway. As we drank our second or third, we decided if one of us got hungry, we'd graze through the refrigerator for snacks.

"We have a big job to do tomorrow at the shop," I reminded Jan. She rolled her eyes as if to tell me that I shouldn't ask her to do more work. Hell! Do I have to do everything myself?

"Jan. I see all this work that has to be done so we can rent the building. I've done a lot all ready."

"Yes, you have."

"How do you know? You haven't been there for weeks. You don't even know what work I've done."

"Bea, I've volunteered to paint and clean up any time for months, but you said it wasn't time.

"I've been so angry, I'm incapacitated! I felt you'd help me. You've leaked out on me and I have to do everything myself."

"You say I never help but there's no way to please you, Bea. And I'm tired of your old scripts, throwing up the same old issues. You choose to accent the negatives while I choose the positives. That's always been the way. And I'm fed up with being screwed by you every time Lakeshore Med pressure is intense. You always blame me, and when I try to get us to a therapist or a counselor to help air out the different way we look at what's wrong, you refuse."

"I don't believe in that therapy shit. Besides, you'll find someone who will say that you're right. Righteous, too. And I don't trust anyone. And I'm tired of Rachel Sandler always phoning me and telling me what to do with her book, send it here, send one there, raise the price, print a Spanish edition. I'm not her secretary!"

"We don't have to have Rachel as a therapist simply because she knows so much about our lives and can cut through the past and help us get through all this tension, especially about your closing Mother Courage."

"*I'm* closing Mother Courage! You don't have to sit there, alone for hours, waiting for someone to come in, and then if someone does, it's usually to talk to me instead of buying a book or two. I've become the therapist, and I hate it."

"I feel terrible about the store closing, Bea, but I hope life will be better for you. I know you're not happy there. But I'm also tired of your hating my work that I must do—and the long hours, and the rage that I bring home with me because of the emotional abuse I endure from Randy who's trying to make me so miserable that I quit. Shit. I can't win and I'd go crazy if I didn't have help from Carolyn and Laura and Pat and Donna Durand and many others who help me survive."

"Don't you think I feel sorry about having to close the store? It drives me into a rage to think of all that I have— that we have—tried to do to make it a success. How many hours am I alone. And then I come home and am alone again, damn it!"

"No matter what I do, Bea, it's wrong. I'm always to blame. Yet we need a referee to help us sort this out. We're on the same team, yet we fight each other. Then you act like nothing has happened, you never apologize—and I'm still in shock, sometimes for days. I always lose. And still I love you so much! We need a referee, Bea. But now, I have to go to bed and try to get some sleep."

I called Josh to tell him that I'd been nasty to you. And I think I'm going crazy. I told him I was afraid Jan would lock me up and I asked him to make sure she wouldn't do that to me. Boy! Did that shake him up. He offered to come over. I said no.

Bea on June 8, 1983

Jan took Monday off and we cleaned the bookstore, even mopped the floor. She rolled paint the two-story-high downstairs walls that night, and on the way home her Toyota conked out and left her stranded on Washington Avenue and West Boulevard's busy intersection. She thought she was out of gas. She forgets to fill the tank unless it's almost too late.. Fortunately it was Henry, one of Matt and Jenny's gang from Jan's old neighborhood who stopped to help a stranger. When he saw it was Jan, he hollered, "Hey! Mrs. Carnigian!" and he pushed her disintegrating Celica to the Shell station where they replaced a shredded fan belt.

Are my legs sore and swollen! I wasn't moving much on Tuesday, taking it mighty slow. When Jan came home from work she wanted to "play war" by fighting over silly stuff again. I think she's pissed off because I went rafting on the weekend and had such a good time, but she says she isn't. Mixed emotions, I'm sure.

I'm still out of commission today but Josh called to borrow some tools to rewire his house. I went over, sat near him, handed him stuff and gave him moral support.

In the evening when I was in pain, I passed out. Jan went and called our friend Joanne who came over, and when I saw Joanne was there—and that Jan had called her, we proceeded to have a big fight in front of her. Jan wanted Joanne to see how unfair I fight—and all I need is to heal, not fight. I'm really pissed at Jan for bringing someone in the house like that.

**Carolyn for the hospital's *letter* on June 9, 1983
"Accolades for Lakeshore Med at St. Agnes Health Fair"**

A tall Yellow Bird entranced young visitors and beguiled elderly ones while freshly popped popcorn filled St. Agnes Hospital with its aroma.

It was all part of Lakeshore Med upbeat production at St. Agnes Health Fair;.

For the second year, Lakeshore Med Video Theater via an oversize TV screen inside and a blue and gold theater marquee outside a meeting room wowed and informed visitors for five non-stop hours. Lakeshore Med crew invited people in to sit, eat popcorn and watch a lively, informative *For Your Health* videotape.

It featured Big Yellow Bird coming to Lakeshore Med for arthroscopy of its injured knee, the CT-scanner, DSA and streptokinase plus excerpts from the "Four Your Health" TV series that demonstrates Lakeshore Med quality health care.

Excellent! Interesting and informative. Excellent film. Good popcorn! Wonderful idea. Wonderful information. Wonderful display. These positive responses mingled with occasional, "Why this is Lakeshore Med!" from people surprised to find us at St. Agnes and who then went inside to see the show.

RN Laura Williams, host of *For Your Health*, answered viewers' questions.

Accompanied by RN Lucy Keller, Jan Anthony as Big Yellow Bird toured the fair, gave out yellow tickets to the theater and lots of hugs to Big Yellow Bird admirers of all ages.

Besides filming and editing the tapes for the show, Mark Bertini set up the equipment and then put on his red and white blazer to become chief popcorn popper and photographer.

Carolyn Schafer built and painted the display and once again handed out more than 800 bags of popcorn to viewers.

Bea on June 22, 1983

Jan went to the hospital's volunteer party where a record nine hundred persons raised over $30,000 for the Lakeshore Med Auxiliary and many of them attended, ate gourmet food and drank champagne, wine and other beverages at Hemstead Hall, the Victorian mansion that the hospital bought years ago for a student nurses' dorm. These parties started in 1972 and Auxiliary members, the hospital's food services and other departments work all year to draw fancy-dressed patrons in for classy food and an elegant evening. Of course, Jan's had to go every year, including those years when her husband escorted her.

Since then, Jan goes alone to take pictures, but she meets up with her pals from work. Of course, I can't go with her. What a disgrace that would be to have an outted lesbian couple at the party. Ha! How many nurses are there with their partners? Not only nurses but all gay persons are especially closeted because they know what happened to Jan and to me.

And she stayed out until after midnight. When she came roaring up to our bedroom, she grabbed me by my painful ankle to wake me with a cheerful jolt, "Hey Bea, I brought you some shrimp to eat!"

Sheesh!

Betty volunteered her husband Hank to fix Jan's Toyota. He's built himself a fully equipped automotive garage onto Betty's little house near Lake Michigan towards Elmwood on Hwy. 32. That means we will have only one car until he decides what's wrong with it, and I'll be the one stuck at home or have to drive Jan back and forth to work. And he'll never get it done. I don't trust him. Yet we can't afford to pay for work done in a regular shop. And Damn! It's such a rustbucket, it's hardly worth fixing.

Even though we fought about Jan's hustling me to go to dinner with her mother's old friends at Dave and Rose Robsens' house, I had an OK time. Eva Martengale and her daughter Pat were visiting from Kalamazoo. It was a pleasant time for Jan reminiscing with old friends who loved her mother and father, and Jan too when she was a teen—and now.

Meanwhile I've been working my buns off at our properties on North Main, 13th Street and at the shop, and lots of items are being crossed off our list—including those at our house and garden.

Jan on June 23, 1983

Dear Eva, (with a similar letter mailed to Rose and Dave)
What a warm and wonderful evening we shared with Rose and Dave, a truly beautiful opportunity to see you and Pat and to have my friend Bea see what strong, dynamic and fun women my mother had for friends. It was also somewhat scary to have some of my childhood characteristics revealed.

What an excellent opportunity for me to evaluate again my youth and to know again the positive elements that were there for me to gain strength, independence and maturity; the positive role models I admired among the women my mother loved, worked and played with during those stressful times of the 1940s; the valued projects and accomplishments you shared together for us, for me to emulate whether I remembered them specifically or had them ingrained into my ethical self, into my goals and my personality.

Thank you again for a shared evening of remembering the friendships we've had for many years even if we've not seen each other for so long.
Jan

Jan on June 24, 1983

Because of the success of our open house displays, Laura, Rita, Pat, Carolyn and I formed an Art n' Facts committee to plan our goals and budget to create informative health displays for our waiting rooms. Pat Holmen always says, "You can't educate if you don't entertain," and I remembered how entertaining the TAM woman's transparent body health exhibit was in Orlando so I connected with the Chicago company that created her. In turn, the company invited us to tour their facilities and take us to the Robert Crown Center for Health Education in the Chicago suburb of Hinsdale. It sounds like a productive and fun outing.

Bea on June 27, 1983

It was a 100-degree Sunday when we installed an air conditioner in our bedroom window. The one that was to cool the whole house hasn't worked and we can't afford to buy a new one.

This morning's welcome rain cooled everything off and I recorded my new song in honor of our first woman astronaut, Sally Ride, plus five original songs to send as an audition tape to the Michigan Women's Musical Festival for stage time during our trip next month.

Rita Van Allan and her Tim, Carolyn, Marian and Sharon and Josh all came over at various times to see our trip slides. Rita and Tim asked me if they could use my song, "I'm Trying to Say that I Love You," at their wedding out east next month. Tony Logan will perform the ceremony and sing the song so I recorded it and another song for good measure. The songs are from my musical comedy, *Senior Citizen*. It's about taking my aging father to a warehouse-type nursing home but it's also about my fear of him finding out about Jan and me being lovers. Plus, it's fun too.

And Jan talks about her office being hectic.

Bea on July 5, 1983

As usual on every 4th of July, we left the house before 7 a.m. to get a parking place for the parade and met all of our families and friends who join us on the front lawn of Jan's father's home now rented to upstairs and downstairs tenants.

I laid new tiles on our kitchen floor today. I spent eight hours on my knees and I did a beautiful job, but am I tired.

Chapter 7

Jan on July 18, 1983

I almost barfed right on the sidewalk while walking into work this morning. I couldn't believe my eyes. Someone approved mounting a metal cross surrounded by pink neon lighting on front edge of Lakeshore Med's roof. To "market" our hospital as Christian, compared to St. Agnes' new Catholic "Medical Center," we've had to listen to Bible and Christian-based inspirational messages over the loud speaker system every morning, endure the newly installed wooden crosses that hang in every patient's room, and now we have to endure tacky pink illumination outlining Lakeshore Med's cross as it competes for attention among a clump of TV and other service antennae.

And my dear friend Laura Williams will no longer report to Donna Durand in Nursing Services. When she came in to our office to grab the Up Shit Creek paddle and flailed away, she gave us the printed memo announcing, "Because of the interaction of Community Services programming with hospital long range planning and marketing, President Nick Dixon announces that Community Services Coordinator Laura Williams will now report to Director of Planning and Marketing. It was signed Chuck McCarthy! I gave my friend a sympathetic hug. She now has to report to Randy's clone who may be less polished and more blunt than his mentor in their abusive management style.

It's interesting that the women with strong feminist leanings who may have defended me seemed to be singled out by one or two administrators' complaints of petty grievances, yet these women accomplish their objectives with extraordinarily high standards.

Jan on July 21, 1983

Our Arts & Facts committee planned a day trip to tour the Chicago company that created TAM, the female robot education tool, to learn about creating future educational displays. Someone suggested that we bring our Auxiliary director and she, in turn, suggested we bring the Auxiliary president along to understand what we may propose to create for the hospital. Rita's Tim drove his van with Rita, Pat, two volunteer leaders, Bea and me on our outing.

It was 105 degrees as we piled into Tim's non-air-conditioned van and rode sixty miles into Chicago to tour the medical display manufacturer. Body parts in piles and pieces explaining all our functions filled display cases, and total plastic bodies stood, looking almost alive, as aids to teach health and wellness concepts as well as diseases, depending on a customer's request.

After a delightful lunch, paid for by the company, the tour director told us to follow his car with our van to the Robert Crown Children's Health Museum, the first children's interactive health-learning center for all ages in Hinsdale. Pat Holmen stopped the group and read somewhat smugly from the museum's brochure, "With high-tech displays, 3-D models and lots of touchable exhibits, it fuses education with entertainment!" We explored these uniquely fascinating displays and demonstrations of bodily functions, cells, even how babies develop in the womb.

Our excitement was high with what we had discovered, and we brainstormed ideas of how Lakeshore Med could adapt these concepts, in a simplified format, of course. We laughed at wild ideas that we blurted out without censoring, as brainstorming sessions are supposed to do. Considering the heat, I'd packed a cooler with sodas and a few beers to quench our thirsts on the way home. All together we had a great day.

Yesterday my phone rang and Mindy summoned me to come to Randy's office immediately. A board member, the husband of the volunteer, called Nick and told him how terrible and unprofessional we behaved on this trip—and who gave me permission in the first place to involve volunteers on money-spending projects—and the hospital could be sued because we were on a trip in a private vehicle and didn't have proper insurance—and that I was drunk on the way home after drinking beer—and that I wore unprofessional clothing—shorts.

I can't believe it. Those exaggerations. True, I never thought of the insurance factor, and I was exhilarated at what we had experienced, but I was not drunk—nor did I wear shorts. We were all well behaved while on our tours and were appropriately dressed. My trip to "the principal's office" was unfounded. Defending myself only made it worse. I endured Randy's contempt for an hour. Doesn't he have anything better to do than to chew me out?

My colleagues gathered in my office and couldn't believe it when I told them what had happened. Pat and Rita said no one questioned them about my behavior or clothing. We were on a mission to enhance the hospital! How much more do I have to do to prove my loyalty to Lakeshore Med.

And I thought everyone in the Auxiliary loved me. Ha! I did nothing to cause this fiasco.

This is it. I need help, and before I left work, I called my psychotherapist friend Nora Carpenter at Lakeside Therapy to learn how to qualify for insurance coverage for her help. She said she'd arrange for me to be interviewed by her group's psychiatrist to justify insurance and counseling with her. Bea was stunned when I told her what happened and that I'd called Nora for therapy. Bea was immediately on the defensive, especially after I asked her if she wanted to join me. She refused.

The next day, the hot weather finally broke and the horrible humidity let up. Thank the Goddess. And we had our full moon evening where we talked about what age we'd pick when our lives were going well. I picked the years when my mother was at home and well.

Jan on July 22, 1983

As is my custom, I walk our guests to their cars after our full moon sessions, especially when they're alone and when it's a pleasant evening. Last night, Nora left a bit earlier than the others and when I walked her to her car, I was able to unload some honest feelings only with her.

"You don't have to walk out with me, Jan. I can find my own car, especially by the light of this moon."

"I like to give and get extra hugs and be sure that you leave here feeling affirmed."

"Jan, in our circle when you picked an age for yourself, you showed that you were super responsible early in your life."

"To defend my own well-being, I've forgotten a lot of the bad times."

"Your life theme is to select the good."

"That's me, a Pollyanna. And I've found the job that's supposed to do that, to accentuate the positive. Yet sometimes at work I have to confront my problems when the opportunity is right. And that's what I'll have to tell Randy: to get off my back. But I need to acquire strength and security before I'm brave enough to tell him that."

"Get off my back? Is that what you need to tell him?"

"Yes. So far. Get off my back. The way he's treated me and some of my colleagues! Except for Carolyn—she supports me all the way but is clever and stays out of the conflicts. Nora, he doesn't have to love me in order to work with me and if he can't work humanely with me, that's his problem."

"It's his problem but it's yours too, Jan. And when you're stronger it will be easier. When everything is hurting, it's hard to gather the energy to say 'Get off my back.'"

I started to tear up but was able to say out loud, "When Bea is stronger and more normal, when the bookstore closing is completely finished, when I can afford a better car, when I manage our rental property without going to small claims court or force an eviction notice on our tenants, when we can stop stressful situations at home, then I'll be able to challenge him at work."

We both leaned against the car as if I were carrying a heavy load. Nora asked, "What else are you going to say to him besides Get off my back?"

"Oh, thank you, Nora. It's so good to say these words out loud. I've been practicing for years. I'll tell him what an unjust, demented person he is to me, to other women, especially my friends—and some men, too—and that I almost feel sorry for him. He's pitiful."

"He's dangerous, Jan, and can do a lot of damage."

"He abuses people—and he's wrong. It's a male-power management style that's counter productive, and it's sick."

"Sounds toxic. It is toxic."

"I see him as Oscar Wilde's Dorian Gray and imagine Randy's grotesque portrait hidden in his closet. I see his toxic influence throughout the hospital—perhaps more than most because I work with so many people, and I'm always on the defensive with him. It's bad, Nora, really bad—and Nick isn't much better. Nick is abrasive on the outside, but Randy is abrasive on the inside. Randy strives for power and he knows what he is doing. Nick could feel sorry when he does something wrong. I've observed that while in Door County when we were families visiting together. Randy, in his opinion, never does anything wrong and would never apologize even if he did acknowledge his abusive actions."

"What's the relationship between the two men?"

"Nick was Randy's mentor, but Randy teaches Nick some tricks. Nick needs Randy to be dedicated to him and to the hospital and for his ability to anticipate all the intrigue that could happen. Nick tends to be impulsive. He's made mistakes so he sometimes is able to tolerate mistakes or differing points of view from others—but not often. Those two complement each other. And Randy—he is so involved in every detail and looking for errors that you often make decisions based on fear. I don't fear Nick as much as I fear Randy."

"When and if you do confront Randy," Nora asked, "can you be assured of Nick's support?"

"No. There's no guarantee of that. Nick would fire me too in his anger because I presented him with another Unitarian troublemaker like Bea, admitting herself into St. Paul for rehab after getting plastered on our Las Vegas hospital trip. Ha! But she's only one of two Unitarians who've committed social blunders working at the hospital. And who knows how many other employees have behave badly, including Randy."

"What do you do with your anger, Jan?"

"I'm afraid of losing control and I swallow my anger. But I've been losing it and doing dumb things at home where it's safe."

"You could always scream to release the pressure," Nora said with a smile.

"Yes. After I divorced Alex and started buying a house with Bea, I could imagine Nick becoming furious and probably screamed at Randy to get rid of the both of us. "Get them out of here," I can hear Nick holler. And Randy—as a good company man—has been dedicated, almost delighted, to try to do that. We embarrass Randy. I imagine him as a closeted person who has complex sexual feelings and appreciates same sex relationships.

It's like he has to punish Bea and me—and, ironically, then has to live a life where he's afraid of the same punishment."

As Nora, hopefully, would be my future therapist, I confided in her a bit more quietly before the rest of the moon group started to spill out our door to leave.

"Nora. When Randy and I were office partners ten years ago, he expressed confused feelings when he went to college. So many guys there were gay, he told me. I remember then my young friend Randy saying that, and he felt comfortable talking with me—until he performed this horrible act that we've never spoken about but is always between us—when he screwed Bea after a party at her apartment. He hung around until I had to go home. I left him alone with her. I left her when she was drunk—and he fucked her! And then later he fired her while she was in rehab! I'm going to confront him on this too—sometime. I heard someone quote him saying, 'I have to have intercourse with five or six women a week in order to prove I'm a man.' That's the problem of having your boss work in your office early in his career. I know too much about him."

"You're a real threat to him, Jan. I'm happy we've had this private time together and am looking forward to hearing your issues after you get past the psychiatrist's interview."

I leaned down to give Nora a big hug and she responded.

"I love you, Nora."

"I probably shouldn't say this as your future therapist, but I love you too, Jan. We've been friends for a long while."

"I'm sorry if I laid my bad trip on you."

"I'm fine. You have enough to think about without worrying about me. Good night, dear. I have to get home and check on my cats.

Chapter 8

Jan on August 5, 1983

Again, a *Bay View Times* reporter called to ask me about the number of HIV/AIDS-related cases that have been treated at Lakeshore Med.

A joint AIDS policy meeting with our Laboratory director, our infection control nurse and their St. Agnes counterparts met again today. Priorities established a myriad of protection gear and rubber gloving to be used by every staff member treating every patient. Another was questioning the source of blood for transfusions. Yet almost everyone seems quiet about the threat of this new disease reaching the Midwest. Most of the menace described for the layperson in the media was about its being spread through gay sex, especially among men's indiscriminate, anonymous sexual contacts in gay bathhouses and "boxcar" orgies in highly gay population centers.

Yet fear is growing here because of rumor and vague unknowns. Medical news sources write that AIDS is spread through "bodily fluids." Can you catch it from sneezing, kissing, touching? Using the word "semen" is taboo in mass media and "blood" makes everyone nervous, especially staff handling or patients needing blood from blood banks. The average American doesn't seem to care to know about intravenous drug users sharing needles and the details of gay male sexual practices. The average American only wants to know how avoid this disease or being identified as an HIV/AIDS person.

Little has been in the local news that I have access to, but I'm sure the reporter—and our medical staff—read about it in their journals. Despite the increasing sense of urgency into finding methods to treat the disease, I've heard that political leaders are ignoring the problem. Do they think it will go away?

I was told to tell the reporter that no HIV/AIDS related cases have been treated at Lakeshore Med. She should call Dr. Jeffrey Davis, the state epidemiologist at the Wisconsin Bureau of Community Health and Prevention in Madison.

I also noticed that the latest party at the Shannons had the hot tub covered with a wooden lid, but their swimming pool was open for their guests.

The Sexual Revolution seems to be ending. No one was immune to this fear of the unknown.

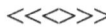

Bea on August 5, 1983

There's a part-time job at Gateway Technical Institute and I fulfill all of the qualifications, including darkroom knowledge and experience. I dare them to find anyone more qualified than I am. Jan composed an exceptional reference letter for her "exceptionally talented writer and interviewer—intelligent, perceptive, flexible and dependable—a good sense of humor." And much more.

I've applied as a social service agency office manager and machine tool bookkeeper. Those didn't come through.

When I get a chance, I stop at various businesses and stores like the dive shop in Elmwood to see if they're hiring. I think I'd like to work in a dive shop. Friday I dressed up in my western outfit for Western Days and did some politicking at the Camera Store, but no bites for a job there.

Jan came home late from work. After cocktails and before she served supper, she came to set the dining room table. I said one wrong word about her trying to get a cheap fix for her rust-bucket Toyota. She threw the wooden salad bowl she held in her hands up towards the ceiling and, of course, lettuce, tomatoes and all came floating down. I got dressed and left for Gerry's gay bar. I didn't feel comfortable going to any other bar, and at Lakeshore Bay's only gay place, I enjoyed a pleasant chat with a cross-dresser in a blonde wig and high heels—the entire punishing feminine regalia from head to toes. I came home to find mess still there. I made her get out of sulking in her chair and clean it up. Then she went to bed. When I went to our bar to pour a glass of jug wine, I saw an interoffice memo to Jan from Randy King.

> Jan: This memo is to formalize an important element of our discussions of 7/20/83 and present a proper procedure for you to follow.
>
> Nick Dixon is the only employee of Lakeshore Med authorized to initiate discussions with the Auxiliary concerning the use of their funds.
>
> When the committee involved in exploring visual displays of patient education material is ready to make a recommendation on how the hospital should proceed, I would be happy to consider that proposal. If accepted by myself, I will make a recommendation to Mr. D. He will then be responsible for contacting the Auxiliary.
>
> RK/mjt

No wonder she was pissed. And those double martinis before supper always light the fuse to whatever rage she's holding inside.

Jan on August 7, 1983

Yesterday's annual tour of Lakeshore Bay's Summer Artists Fair turned into a day of despair when Bea berated me for some unexplained flaw of mine, being too nice, I guess. A pain in the ass again. I turned away from her embarrassing outburst in the crowd and when I turned back, I saw her car flash down the street without me. I've not only been incredibly shocked and shouted at, now I'm abandoned with hundreds of people around me.

Seeking a place to take cover, I trudged the three blocks to my hospital, waved weakly at the front desk clerk who wasn't surprised to see me on a Sunday. I made it to my office and fell into my chair. The air-conditioning made me shiver and then I began to cry. What if someone walked by and looked through the window and saw me there, without lights and work before me—in a painful state of tearful confusion? I wanted to remove myself from society, rip myself from this unpredictable person and the love with so much distress.

I couldn't run away; all my resources were here. If I chilled out with martinis, I'd still have to face another day in order to survive. Suicide was never an option for me; I've feared that with Bea and my mother for too long. Could I rid myself of the one who causes me pain? Her absence would be worse. I do nothing but hope and wait for better times.

Wait. Where? And I crumpled to the floor, gathering myself into a fetal position under my desk, pulling my chair close to hide me—an intelligent adult woman, coiled up, hoping for refuge, for peace, for understanding. Why am I so vulnerable to her unpredictable behavior? The contrast from our joy to despair shocks me into being helplessly irrational. And here I am so pathetically regressed that my next move would have been to put my thumb in my mouth and feel even more sorry for myself.

After a while, I regained my intelligence. I must live in this world without expecting my lover to be gentle and kind to me. She's having a hard time herself. I must face up to these absurdly unstable times. My dreams and my reality, my need for stability without boredom and subservience, my grand illusions of being forever happy are merely that—illusions.

I unwound myself from under my desk, phoned home to let Bea know to pick me up at the hospital's front door. I decided that I must live each day with what is hard to accept and make the best of it.

We never spoke of the incident, ever.

Bea on August 8, 1983

Jan was livid when she came home from what she called an inquisition by the psychiatrist who heads Nora's agency. Jan said she had to prove to him that she was crazy before she'd qualify for insurance coverage.

"After he grilled me for an hour, he patronized me by asking what did I expect as a professional woman working in an atmosphere of powerful men? I could have blasted him with my litany of injustice, of sexism and abuse, but I kept my mouth shut so I wouldn't compromise the chance of having my insurance pay for the help I need. I didn't reveal my bosses' homophobia either. I acted cool, but I feel demeaned and degraded again—just like at work. But I think I passed the failure test. Maybe Nora put in a good word for me before my interview.

Chapter 9

Jan on August 19, 1983

Dear Matt,

I've been thinking of you often and hope that you're all right with your job and conditions in Reno. It's been a while since we've connected so I'll let you know quickly what's going on.

I've decided to take better care of myself and I'm going to see a therapist on Saturday mornings, starting tomorrow, to help free me from some of this stress related to work, etc. I've "passed/failed" a psychiatric interview with the group's top shrink. I guess I proved to him that I'm emotionally exhausted with increasing frustrations levels. "Burned out" is another qualifier. He said that my stress level qualified me for care and that makes it possible for me to get full insurance coverage. Thank Heavens or I wouldn't be able to afford to pay for the help that I need.

My therapist is an exceptionally skilled feminist woman friend who trains counselors at St. Paul Alcohol Rehabilitation Hospital and is a friend/member of our moon group. She works full-time at St. Paul and part-time in private practice in Lakeshore Bay. She's perfect for giving me the perspective that I need to better understand my problems and stressors.

Jenny called last night and we had a long talk reflecting on her life and her future. We've had some good talks in the past couple months and I hope we can be closer through greater perception about each other's lives.

The tenants in Grandpa's house are interested in buying it. It needs a new furnace, storm windows and wiring. Looking at all that needs to be done, beyond the cosmetic but hard work and long hours we spent repairing it, I'm not averse to selling if the price is fair.

I also owe the State about $9,000 for my mother's years of hospitalization, so that's another reason to sell the property.

Have to close for now, dear. Take good care of yourself.

Love,

Mom

Jan and Nora on August 20, 1983

"Your sighs come one after another, Jan. I'm so happy you're here so we can talk."

"I'm so happy to be here, Nora. (Chokes back tears. Clears throat.) I took your advice and screamed."

"You sound hoarse."

"Yes." (Clears throat. Sighs make it hard to breathe.)

"What happened?"

"Before we begin our sessions, I want to ask a favor."

"Of course, Jan. What is it?"

"I've been in therapy with Rachel who tapes our sessions. I didn't ask her not to or why, and she didn't offer to tell me. But I brought my tape recorder and I'm asking you to let me tape our sessions. And I'll tell you why. Bea refuses to come with me. Perhaps if I tape what happens, I will be better able to remember what I've learned. Otherwise, I'm too hurt and emotional to come away with concepts that can help me. And maybe I can explain to Bea what I'm experiencing."

"No one has ever asked me to tape a session. (Pause.) I guess it will be OK. It's quite unconventional though, to have a client tape a session, but who's conventional? (Pause while taping begins.) Tell me where you are now."

"I think I'm going crazy. No matter how successful my long hours and hard work are, I'm losing it more and more. And I can't let that happen. I lose control and do stupid things. I even screamed like you said I should do. Well, the latest. We arranged for Hank to patch my Toyota's rust in his garage and I needed to pick up the car to drive to work on Monday! I suppose I could have taken a bus to work, or asked Hank or Betty to bring it over. Bea knew I didn't have my car and I waited, anticipating a quarrel over asking her to drive me there. Finally after about six hours at home, Bea started dozing off. Before she fell asleep, I told her I had to pick up my car or I'll call Hank that I'm not coming. And she started getting mean, telling me that I'm kissing Hank's ass and why do I have to do that to fix the damn car. It's not worth it anyway—going on and on and on."

"Does she do that a lot?"

"It's not fair. I asked one favor. This is so typical of my frustration when I've held back and then suddenly I get an emotional jolt and lose control. Finally when Bea did drive me to Betty's, she blamed and berated me. I can't afford a new car because we don't have money for lots of reasons—including drinking. We spend more money on booze than we do on groceries."

"That's a fact?"

"Well, maybe an exaggeration. Anyway, when we were passing the onion fields on Newberry Road, I started hollering. It was wonderful. I found my 'under the trestle' release like Lisa Minelli's *Cabaret* movie in Berlin or like in *Last Tango in Paris* where Marlon Brando screamed out his anger and grief. And I screamed and screamed, 'You're not always right, Bea. You're not always right.' It's so hard for me to argue with her. She overpowers me—especially when she's drinking or when she leaves me fuming. When she's like that, it's impossible to talk. And that's why I do crazy things to make her stop being mean to me. So when we got to Hank and Betty's—as if they haven't had enough crazy experiences themselves—I went in and shook his hand, gave him his money and said, 'Thank you, Hank, but I'm not supposed to kiss your ass for helping me fix my car,' and I went out the door and started to back away in my Toyota. And he asked if I was mad at him, and I said, 'No' and pointed to Bea. Bea was standing there and I don't know what she said or did, but I took off in my car."

I shifted my weight in the sofa and took a deep breath. "I sat in our back yard. We hadn't eaten, but she picked up some chicken that we'd agreed to do. I was outside, right? I turned and looked into the window and she was eating the damn chicken while watching TV. She hadn't even offered me any. So I turned over and slept outside, bundled up in my lounge chair until about 3 a.m. She blames me saying I push her. She tells me I'm crazy and doing irrational things. It takes so much out of me."

"These are more frequent?"

"It goes in streaks; sometimes four months without any problems, sometimes once a month. We had a horrible weekend around Lakeshore Med's Patron Party in June. And before we went to Florida we had a big fight because I was working such long hours. In between, everything seems caring and wonderful. Well, not all the time. We have problems, but it's these explosions—like she lights a fuse in me. Once we had the fight and I threw the salad bowl in the air."

"Enormously painful, Jan."

"In addition, I get all this shit at my work. It's terrible. I was sitting at work with the people I trust and we're trying to solve problems with our bosses, and I broke out and cried—in front of my colleagues! At work! Fortunately, they understand and are supportive. I just collapsed."

"This is being identified as crazy behavior?"

"When I scream like that? But oh, it felt so good."

"That's your style—turning the pain in on yourself. Even the sore throat felt good."

"There's lots of crap I'm barely keeping inside—just to hold on."

"That's why I want you to learn about co-alcoholism—people who try to help and are frustrated by dealing with a lover who's an alcoholic."

"I remember St. Paul back during Bea's and my interviews. When someone labeled me co-dependent, I almost punched him."

"No one likes labels, but some of the literature makes sense."

"What is 'co-dependency'? Am I the problem with alcohol in our lives?"

"I don't think so, but in the past few years I think it has to do with PMS and alcohol. That combination makes any depression much worse, and blood alcohol doubles before the period and after with twice as much craziness. You have a wonderful love together but the behavior that you see isn't Bea's or your behavior, it's the alcohol."

"I made up my mind I wasn't going to get sucked into her program anymore—and I wasn't going to blame her. I don't drink as much as she does. I don't feel the need to drink as much. I'm not going to get sucked into that irrationality. I used to say, 'Shit. If she drinks up all of our money, I might as well drink that up too.' Well, that's stupid."

"It's not unusual for couples to do that."

"Why should let myself do that. It's shit."

"It's easy to do when you love someone. This is a role you've been into all your life—to provide responsibility when others lose control."

"Well, I don't feel responsible for others. But I have to feel responsible for behavior that I fall into."

"It's easy, when you love somebody, not to separate what that alcohol does to the one you love and what that loved one is all about. Alcohol is crazy-making."

"There are other factors. I don't want to be simplistic about blaming her drinking. She has an incredible amount of emotional investment in her kids. She's vulnerable and so thin-skinned that anything they do jerks her around, whether she's drunk or sober. She may be getting stronger about her kids, but also, she doesn't have any of her own income."

"That has to be hard for her."

"She wants to be acknowledged as a productive human being. She thinks she's just like a housewife, but she's not. She takes care of all of our properties, our finances, our *Something* book orders. We had a long talk and she said she's not proud of our book. She hates doing the clerical work, yet we can't afford to hire someone. And she hates it when our author bosses her around. Lots of mixed-up thinking. And then instead of solving problems, she uses alcohol to escape. And I'm so sensitive to her that when she hurts me emotionally, I explode or get so hurt that I can't get over it for days, weeks. And often she doesn't even remember what she did—and never apologizes."

"I fear you don't explode soon enough, Jan. You hang in there until there's no other choice."

"This week I could have picked up my car by asking Betty to come and get me. But why should I? I'm living with this person that I love. I should be able to ask her for help. So when she turns on me because I ask her for a favor, I explode."

"That makes sense to me. I advocate getting it out rather than pushing it down."

"I'm so crushed by holding back that it's hard to breathe."

"So you're holding everything in. The explosions only occur when you're overwhelmed?"

"Yah."

"Otherwise your control is almost exact. You don't even want to talk about alcohol."

"I guess that whole St. Paul rehab business in 1978 was too traumatic. Not only St. Paul, but because of the shit that Nick Dixon and Randy King laid on us. And Bea thinks Marge ratted on us too. There's still so much pain—especially (Chokes.) when I had to tell Bea that she was let go as my PR assistant."

"What I see, and you know how I feel about labels, but this amount of drinking is toxic and you don't get it out of your system. It builds and builds and the toxicity creates more toxicity. Jan, I've never known a co-alcoholic who hasn't felt like she was going crazy and/or ended up cracking up."

"I'd once thought of going to Alanon."

"Would you be interested? I will go with you."

"I think it would blow Bea's mind."

"If you talk to others and see what's going on in their homes, each would have fully believed they were going crazy."

"I don't know if I need to do that if I talk with you."

"It's an alternative option that deals with people who are too damned hurt. There are impaired professional Alanons in Milwaukee, and for spouses, too. (Pause.) You know, I've often thought when I met you two at St. Paul and we cried together when Bea said she admitted herself for treatment. I was as surprised as you. I should have counseled her to go to Minnesota where they treat more professional clients. It all happened so fast that I didn't have time to change her mind or to advise her to go elsewhere other than where I worked."

"I didn't know we had other options either. I'll consider your Alanon offer. I haven't wanted to walk into a local group because I'm so vulnerable. I'm still somewhat closeted as a lesbian, of my work and the bookstore, and I'm afraid of having to defend myself about that."

"That would be tempting for you—and the timing for that is wrong. No more taking care of other people. The emphasis has to be on Jan."

"I can imagine my going there and seeing some people asking me for help. I'd just explode."

"That would be the typical scenario. You'd need help and ten others need help, and you'd help them."

"I've always done that."

"And you have since you were a small child. I'd guess before your mother was hospitalized you took an enabling role for her. You didn't have a choice. You were cast into that."

"It's not fair. (Expels deep breaths.) I think it's working, Nora."

"What you're going through is totally irrational, so destructive. Without chemicals it may not be destructive. Remember, Jan. It's not Bea who's talking. It's the chemical."

"That's what Betty told me once."

"That behavior is so induced by that chemical, and we have new research for physiological and gender factors in alcoholism."

"I lose control when I'm badly hurt."

"When you say you lose control, you express pent-up feelings. I sense of no loss of control in terms of craziness, but yes, in terms of anger, sadness."

"When I was married to Alex, I'd often feel a loss of control, yet I had control on the surface."

"What does 'loss of control' mean to you?"

"One time Alex was in bed next to me. We had another terrible fight about continuing my relationship with her, and he lay there, seething with rage—and I'm supposed to lie next to him. Just when I'd begin to fall asleep, he'd move or make some comment, and I'd be angry again. Then off I go again. Finally I made my hands into two fists and beat on him. I said, (Cries. Sobs.) 'I want you to fall in love with somebody like I've fallen in love—and you try to give up that person. I dare you! I dare you!' And I beat, beat, beat on his chest—and he just lay there looking at me. Then I realized what I was doing—Oh my God, all he had to do was to hit me once (Sighs. Laughs.) and I'm dead. Or thrown right out the window. But I almost wish he had hit me because then I'd divorce him on grounds besides boredom or mental abuse or lack of love or patriarchy or whatever. But pounding on him was a loss of control.

"I hear a strong expression of feeling that you've been mistreated, Jan. Nothing else."

"There have been times, Nora, when Bea's behavior changed almost within minutes."

"That can drive you crazy."

"I arranged her birthday dinner and spent a first-class evening there. Of course, lots of couples were on dates, but also people other than couples were there. Here we were, two women on a Saturday night, and I'm sure that suddenly Bea's mind clicked. She's without a man. Why isn't she wining and dining with a man and thinking, 'Why am I a lesbian?' Within the difference of one course in our meal, she turned into a cruel dinner partner and I almost threw up with painful emotions. But I didn't lose control then."

"You have strong control, Jan. You are physically aware of your body, your stomach, your chest. I still have to hear about loss of control."

"Our lives are so intense. I'd wait for Alex to go someplace so I could be with Bea. I wasn't happy with Alex and I wasn't happy because I'd have to leave Bea. We'd spend our time together and then the tearing apart— (Sighs. Sobs. Chokes. Breathes.) And the whole Las Vegas trauma—it goes on and on."

"I have yet to hear any craziness or loss of control. You could have pulled it together any minute that you chose to do so."

"I suppose so."

"Jan. You define loss of control differently than I do. The steam builds up where you can't tolerate any more pain and you've got to erupt to survive. It's like breathing. That's not pathological. There's no indication except for a strong expression of feeling that you've been keeping down."

"Why should I have to go through this? I'm so tired of pain. How long—"

"I don't want to scare you by doing anything drastic. Better times are possible and I have a strong feeling that we're going to have to abstain from alcohol for a while and then better times are possible."

"Thanks, Nora. You've already given me some hope."

Bea on August 22, 1983

Each Saturday, Jan looked pretty raw after Nora's therapy session. Nora actually let her tape the sessions and Jan left the tape player on the dining room table. After Jan left for work today, I couldn't resist finding out what happened on Saturday with Nora and I listened to the entire tape. Shit! How evil am I? Everything is my fault! And why does she dredge up all this shit from as far back as St. Paul. Alcohol! Alcohol! That's all she and Nora have to think about. It's all my fault. Always! Get over it, damn it! But I'm not going to let Jan know that I listened to the tape. That would start another nasty quarrel. Boy! Does she need help!

Besides, I got a period again after not having one for almost a year. I guess I'm not quite an official crone yet, even though Jan calls me our moon group's High Priestess.

On Sunday we brought presents to Jim's family at the farmhouse they've rented with lots of room for the two kids to play. It's much better than their trailer. Once when Jan and I were baby-sitting at the trailer, I got thirsty and went to their refrigerator for a drink. I thought my son would certainly have some beer in it. Hah! Nothing—except for a plastic pitcher of water. I started pouring a glassful and found a goldfish swimming in it. Jan went to buy a six-pack of beer. On this visit to the farm, Jan and I noticed that the *Chainsaw Massacre* video was playing on their TV, which the kids watched when they weren't chasing or tormenting each other.

Chapter 10

Jan on August 27, 1983

Ironically and paradoxically, in this session I released almost every painful wound that I've been holding inside of me. I remember saying to Nora as I turned on my tape recorder that there's nothing left of me. If I don't heal, there'll be nothing left, nothing to give to anyone else. It's all used up. Well, maybe not all. I'm still hanging in there, but I'm running on empty.

As my hour with Nora progressed, I moved from my chair to front of the tape recorder, shouting, grieving and crying out my woes, especially the loss of Mother Courage Bookstore. I spewed out my hurts and screamed into the speaker the disappointments in our relationship, our missed or bungled opportunities, frustrations, anger.

I wanted to purge myself now so I can move on with life and heal the wounds, the physical and mental pain that my love for Bea has caused me. The loss of my family and home, the alcohol-induced blunders when she worked with me, especially letting Randy King screw her after an employee party in her apartment, our Las Vegas fiasco, admitting herself into St. Paul, her being dismissed as my PR assistant—and my having to tell her about it while she was in St. Paul. All those acts initiated my problems with Randy. But what did Nick Dixon actually know about that? My trusted old friend Nick hated the feminist-based commentaries that I wrote to the *Bay View Times*, that I divorced his friend Alex, and in the gossip, I was "outted" within his inner circle as a lesbian involved with another Lakeshore Med employee and another Unitarian.

All the hostility that festered inside me spewed into that tape.

I knew Nora would help me after I burst my lungs and my heart. I cried it all out where I was safe, in a protected place where I wouldn't lose Bea—or my job. I counted on the tape to help me analyze the poison or the parasite that existed inside of me. I held nothing back.

After a long, quiet spell stretched out on the floor in front of my recorder, Nora gently helped me back from my personal exorcism so I could restart my life.

Ironically and paradoxically, true. When I found strength between my therapy appointments and a quiet time alone, I rewound the tape to review it.

It was blank.

Jan and Nora on September 3, 1983

"Thank you, Nora, for making this appointment during Labor Day weekend. I need to talk things through some more, especially after my outburst last week."

"I've been thinking about you all week."

"You won't believe this, Nora, nor can I. The tape didn't record a thing I said last week."

"No kidding. Isn't that weird."

"I guess it was meant to be. I threw up a noxious pile of pain—and now it's out and I hope I'm over it."

"Tell me, Jan, how's it going?"

"Well, we've cut back on alcohol. Yet I feel as if I'm like the battered housewife when she's asked, 'Why do you stay home?'"

"You're involved in this relationship."

"I love her." (Sobs.)

"I know you do and she's a lovable person, a talented gifted woman who has loved you like no one else."

"If we'd get off the God damn booze."

"Yup."

"Our lives are so rich and our evenings are so close—and we do so much even if we only sit and play a games of cards, read books or watch a good TV program."

"The two of you have enough going for about ten other couples in terms of interests and energy, brains and talent."

"When we went to Florida, (Sighs.) we both agreed not to drink. I cried so hard when she told me she'd made some resolutions and we weren't going to drink and we'll have adventures and lose weight. I felt so relieved. And when we'd return from our trip, we made resolutions: we'd eat as soon as we got home, we'd eat in the kitchen, have beverages—wonderful coffees. As soon as we got to Florida, that stopped. We started drinking again. Bea uses brandy for medicine, and when she's hurt, feels trauma or is under stress, she'll go to the bottle and then it gets worse. And I get stuck—sitting, waiting for her to recover not only from her bruises and her trauma but from her alcohol—and I'm alone."

"That's right. You experience the effects of alcohol and not Bea herself."

"Oh!"

"It's not Bea."

"And when I say something, she just drinks more, and probably my explosions are becoming closer together because I can't stand it as long. She has to get in gear and stop hurting herself because she's hurting me too. And I have so much going against me at work."

"She's killing herself, Jan."

"I know. She's been killing herself for a long time. She told me this weekend that she wasn't going to commit suicide. (Sighs.) That's always a concern of mine—from my mother and my worrying about all that shit. I'm so tired worrying about whether someone's going to commit suicide! WHEW! I said it out loud."

"It goes hand in hand with depression, and alcohol greatly emphasizes suicidal thinking."

"Alcohol is an easy way to go, Nora. Just drink yourself to oblivion and death."

"It's a miserable way—and it takes a long time. You lose all your friends and your support system. You lose your brain and your health. You lose yourself."

"It's such a waste."

"What do you want to do about it, Jan?"

"Well. I can go off the booze."

"What do you want to do to save Bea's life?"

"Am I responsible?"

"If you love her."

"No doubt about that!"

"I'm also convinced about what a beautiful woman she is. But there may come a time. And I want you to think about this. There may come a time when you'll want an intervention."

"It's up to her to decide. I will never do that again."

"Who did the intervention before?"

"At St. Paul?"

"No, I did not say 'treatment.' I said 'intervention.' It's to help people to stop drinking. We used to say that's the only way to get an alcoholic to stop drinking. Pardon my labels. I don't like them any more that you do. It's that you can't do anything until the person's ready. But there's a process developed years ago and it's carefully planned out."

"I don't think she'll go for any intervention, Nora."

"Well, what happens is that group of people start planning together on how to confront the individual in a loving way. It could be people like Tony Logan and myself and you and Betty and people that you chose, people who believe that Bea is killing herself. An intervention is set up and each person, in a loving way, says something like, 'This is what I see happening to you. I've been watching you kill yourself and—I want you to stop drinking. I love you very, very much and I can't stand watching you kill yourself and I want you to agree to such and such,' and usually there're some consequences. It will be hard for you."

"Aha. (Sobs. Sighs.) Yes."

"I'm introducing that as a 'down the road' idea because I don't think you're going to get out of this without addressing the alcohol issue."

"I called Joanne Zekas one time because Bea would never go to see Tony. When things got bad, I said we've got to see someone. 'OK.' she'd say, 'We'll make an appointment to see Tony,' and then she'd get better again and back out. This June when she came back from rafting on the Wolf River, she had hurt her ankle and was drinking. I was so furious with that whole process and under stress myself, I was afraid of what I'd do. I needed to talk with her and I was afraid that she'd get in the car and drive away or that we have a blow-up again, so I called Joanne. She came in five minutes because I needed to talk while Bea was sound asleep in a stupor. I'd gone out to the yard to turn off the sprinkler and before I knew it, Joanne appeared in the house. Bea woke up and there was Joanne. Then I came in—Bea has incredible pride."

"Aha."

"And to have Joanne there while I confronted her, or to even have Joanne see her sleeping made her furious."

"Yup."

"But I was able to talk to Bea, tell her some of the things that I'd probably screamed about under a bridge—and Joanne was a facilitator. Later, Bea commanded, 'Never ever do that to me again. Never ever do that to me!' Of course she said it when she was drunk."

"Interventions are never done when people are drinking, Jan. It doesn't reach them. She was drinking when that happened, and when it's on a daily basis that toxicity never ends. It's there: the desire, the craving, the preoccupation, all the craziness. So what I hear is that you'd be most hesitant to do an intervention."

"I think so. (Sniffs. Sighs.) Yet I don't know if I can do it myself."

"The reason for the intervention is because the person closest to the alcoholic cannot do it. Do you have enough time for me to show you more about the process? You can keep it in mind that it doesn't have to go on. (Goes to get literature.) I've been on intervention teams in Boston, Chicago, and many places. One person cannot do it, Jan."

"I've been in denial so long myself. To justify myself." (Scans and reads from "Information on the Denial System.") 'Shields anyone from the consequences of alcohol. Denial. Depression.'"

"And the socialization of women especially is a factor, Jan. Being responsible for everything. I'm not going to pressure you. My presenting this to you is that there's hope—for a beautiful life—and it's no fault of hers, no fault of yours. It's a tragedy."

(Sighs. Chokes. Sniffs. Sighs.)

"Why don't you just cry, Jan! There's nobody here. You can cry and scream. I have no concerns about any 'out of control behavior.'"

(Augh! Groans! Pause.) "Betty said something about antibuse. She actually sticks those pills down Hank's throat (Laughing together now.) and strokes his neck to be sure he swallows them."

"She does things uniquely."

"I told her, 'That's what you do to a dog,' and she said, 'Yup!' Jees. That's terrible to have to do that."

"Well, do we dare to read some more?"

(Augh!) "I'll read some other time."

"Are you too timid to bring about change?"

(Pause. Reads. Sighs.) "What does CD mean?"

"Chemical Dependency. What happens when the condition is not something the individual can handle. Lost of control."

"Oh. Loss of control. Somehow Bea and I pull it back together again, Nora?"

"For how long?"

"How long. If I could only eliminate some stress in parts of my life, I can deal with it in others."

"One way of eliminating stress is to learn about what's contributing to it—like chemistry."

"When Bea was in St. Paul, she said she was in jail, yet she had a support system there. I was alone."

"No one at St. Paul offered you support?"

"No. I was alone."

"You should have had a full support system."

"In fact, not only was I alone, but I was the one who had to tell her that she was being fired from Lakeshore Med. And then I'd go to work and everyone treated me as if I had the plague—that Bea and I were lesbians. And driving alone to St. Paul and back again, walking alone—with my history of going to the state and county hospitals for decades to see my mother, and now the disillusion of my choices and my relationship. (Sighs.) It seems as if you chose to love someone to help you heal from your parents' weaknesses, and then you're angry and disappointed when the person you love has similar faults. I never knew what to expect or what my life would be like almost every day. And that apprehension has never let up."

"And that's where you're at right now?"

"On all fronts. At home and at work."

"Is it safe for you? Is Bea going to be offended if you take this literature home with you?"

"I don't think she'd even look at it. I'm at a point now that I'm going to do what I want to do to help me get what I need. There was a point in my marriage where I couldn't even read *Ms. Magazine* because Alex would get mad at me. Shit. I'm not going through that again. I'm an intelligent person and I'm not going to be intimated by anyone."

"That sounds wonderful, Jan. I hope to hell that's on the tape. I'd like to have you say it over and louder."

"Well, I'll say it for myself. I'm an intelligent person and I'm not going to be intimated by anyone."

"Tell me again one more time."

"I'm an intelligent person and I'm not going to be intimated by anyone."

"Tell me who you are. (Pause.) You're intelligent—"

"Well, shit. I'm an intelligent person and I can do what I ought to do. I'm not going to be intimated by anyone. I'm sensitive about other people. I save arguments and give in on fighting about TV shows and crap at home—and when I have to kiss ass as work, I should be able to do what I want to do at home. I hope that cooperation and understanding can be arranged so that I can have some of my needs met. And I'm not going to be intimidated!"

"It's appropriate that you meet most of your needs."

"Absolutely! I don't think I'm a bully. Shit. I'm getting old. I deserve something better."

"You had marvelous experience in taking care of people. You were given that assignment—so early, and you've done it so well. There's nothing wrong with it, however, it's important to be aware of it."

"If I don't heal, there'll be nothing left of me. Our lives were so beautiful when we were chemically free and we opened the bookstore—and on our opening day, we had our first drink and that was fine. My dad brought out his brandy bottle from his desk drawer and offered to share our success with that. I never told him about St. Paul. That was our first drink—but that was it. Then on Thanksgiving, we were invited to old traitor-friend Marge's who encouraged Bea to have more and more, and the booze started to flow after that. On that day and afterwards."

"And the behavior changed after that? Can you think of anything terrible that happened at your house that wasn't associated with alcohol?"

"I thought about it. (Augh.) Well, there were reasons. The terror and the trauma, like Bea's kids leaving her after her divorce, her Learning Center closing, and her losing her Lakeshore Med job working with me."

"But there wasn't the accompanying craziness."

"Nora, there hasn't been much time when we've been without booze. I drink as much, even more as she does because she passes out and I may keep on drinking."

"But she has a different psychology and chemistry—her enzyme system from birth—her genetics. More new evidence is coming out about genetics, enzyme chemistry and physiology of alcohol that does different things for her. But I will say that it's not good for you, either."

"No, it's not good for me."

"But it's not killing you."

"Well, I feel better talking with you, knowing that insurance is covering more sessions. This is going to get a lot out of my system."

"Take time to think and pay attention to what is happening and how things change when the alcohol starts. If you can not drink yourself, or drink minimally, that's going to make you a better observer."

"I've already made that resolution. Anything can happen when the both of us are drinking."

"And I'll go with you to Alanon if you like. The only purpose of this organization is for individuals to help themselves, not another person. There is no way, Jan, that I'll ever force you into any kind of action. I've worked with alcoholism for fifteen years and I do know about the destructiveness and the heartbreaking tragedy of it. I know that part of it."

"Plus Bea and I have extra pressure of being lesbian and working under that all the time. That's getting better for me 'cause we've built some support systems and our kids seem more accepting. But there's always that defensive tension."

"The defensiveness about lesbian?"

"Yes. But we've talked about enough stuff for one day. I hope I haven't kept you over for your next client."

"It's a privilege to be here with you, Jan. We have covered a lot."

We hugged each other and I left for home—exhausted.

Bea on Labor Day, September 5, 1983

We golfed at Rolling Hills Country Club by renting a cart with both of us using Jan's clubs to play nine holes in three hours of fun, and we enjoyed a drink in the bar with a pleasant view. We've been drinking less, playing pool and canasta. I even had the bike tires pumped up to take rides. Last night, Jenny and her boyfriend came over and we cooked up a meal, ate it outside and enjoyed a fire in our fire pit.

On Friday, we went out for a lobster dinner, saw *Risky Business* and then to Lakeshore Bay's new Sheraton for music, but we came home to dance together to our records. After Jan's Saturday session with Nora, we played golf, and in the evening we played two Scrabble games and exchanged delightful massages that Jan especially loves.

Jan on September 6, 1983

When Nora Carpenter called me to get addresses to mail her wedding and reception invitations, she told me she tells others that we have—Bea and I have—the best marriage in town. Little do others know how challenging it is for me. And how vital and satisfactory it is for us—for me—when it truly is the best marriage in town. Of course, Nora thinks hers is the best, and I hope it to be. She met a big name guy in psychiatry circles at a workshop and they're getting married around Thanksgiving time.

My body's stiff, but from golf this time. We did our last of at least ten golf outings for this season. I say "ten" because we invest in a book of twenty and then share, and I'm happy we worked in these games in our busy schedule before the fall leaves hit the ground to hide our wayward drives into the woods.

In our lives together, we share so many good things. I shouldn't complain. Compared to almost everyone, we are the tops. That was what everyone thought about my heterosexual life with Alex was too. My drinking friend and neighbor Adelle told me we couldn't part. Society was such a mess after Vietnam, Nixon couldn't be trusted, and if Alex and I would break up, what would they have to believe in?

I think of that story when times get bad with Bea and me. Fortunately, I don't see that break-up ever happening. So what's wrong with an explosive argument once in a while? What's wrong with my seeing and thinking negative things and thoughts about my lover, wondering how her ego can be so big, or thinking that she's not even aware of how she comes across, or being reminded of how difficult her alcoholic, bombastic father must have been to live with.

My perceptions and my responses are what's vital to our relationship and to me. But I give in.

Adelle often comes to mind as another image of what life can be. Her only option was to endure. "Endure" is such a tough concept.

I am grateful. My health gives me enough strength to pursue an active life. My mind is absorbing new concepts and celebrating old memories with my writing. My emotions are positive and spirited. My soul is enriched by my faith in myself and in the All There Is, the metaphor of the Goddess.

And when Bea and I are both on that balanced mark, life is supreme.

It is happening more and more as I become more of my own person and accept Bea as the person she is. No more scary disappointments, right! But we both created new ways to deal with ourselves in a society/culture that barely knows what to do with us.

Thinking of what my life would have been if I hadn't fallen in love with her brings me home happy with joyful anticipation in a calm sense of appreciation. I truly enjoyed another day of our "vacation" activities this week—one day after another of pleasure. I'm indifferent to my golf score. It's just a game. The weather, though hot, had cool breezes and we came prepared with ice water. There was no stress because the women behind us were cool too about waiting for us and all our extra putts. We moved along quickly in our little cart, but we seemed to have to travel back and forth, crisscrossing the course.

We would never compete against others. We two have set our own rules of the game. And Bea's bravado of her good strokes and absolute forgetfulness of her bad ones would unnerve other players—and herself, because she wouldn't be likely to do what she does.

Anyway. Fortunately, and with great thankfulness, we found each other in this life. Found each other and love each other now as we are. I will, I know, become more of "as we are" in my own right. With practice on my sense of humor to soften the edge of her—what's its name—bravado? Bravado based on insecurity? Ego. Bravado Ego. I'll try and find a better name, and with practice and after all these years, we'll continue our commitment to grow old together and to enjoy the process.

Chapter 11

Jan and Nora on September 10, 1983

"My goodness, Jan. You look five years younger. How are you doing?"

"When I got back from our session, Bea was in a blue funk. As usual, I thought, 'What have I done?' She withdraws as if she's getting even with me. She's off the booze but sullen and silent. It ain't no fun. And I'm off the booze, too. If I suggest we do something, entertain friends, folk dance, a movie, she'd say, 'No. No money.' Finally I pleaded, 'Please tell me it's my fault so I can find out what I did wrong.' She said she felt depressed. I was going to call you, Nora, but I didn't. I have to discipline myself not to use you for a crutch."

"Oh, no, Jan. I'm around. I'd say that you've been through a lot. Someone should listen to you."

"It wasn't the end of the world. What behavior should I expect when someone withdraws from chemicals? She deserves to be depressed. The jobs she applied for aren't getting any responses. (Sighs.) Then I realized that I hadn't created her depression. Sullen and silent—I've lived with it before. That's what my ex-husband always did to me. But when I ask for clarification from Bea, I expect a genuine response. I argue and fight more with Bea than I did with Alex—until he found out about us. Her sullenness reminds me of those bad times with Alex with quiet, abrasive negativity. It's like breathing toxic air."

"You created none of her depressions."

"I know—when I look at this intellectually. And usually I love to come home, in contrast to my life with Alex when I happily left for work to get away from his oppression—and boredom."

"How did you take care of yourself as a little girl? You didn't have any brothers or sisters to support you. How did you manage?"

"I don't know."

"Of course you had your dad."

"He was supportive."

"You were taking care of him?"

"World War II was scary when my dad was in the Seabees and I lived alone with my mother for two-and-a-half years. Dad felt he had to enlist. He sucked in his hernia and pulled up his fallen arches, and left me alone with her and with very little income. Then when she was losing control of herself, I felt I had nobody to help me, but I guess, looking back now, I wasn't alone. I had the counsel of social workers, some of her friends like my "Aunt Edie" and Rose Robsens. Her dear women friends loved my mother. My grandmother, my dad's mother, was there for me, but I never talked to her about my mother. I'm sure Grandma never wanted my dad to marry her."

"How did you take care of yourself with your mother?"

I told Nora the stories when my dad was away, how she built us an attic apartment, wrote poems and letters to the editor, fought with the downstairs renters, held on to her frail sanity by having me placed at summer camps, a foster home—and I felt safe at my schools, except when I questioned the Lutheran's rigid dogma.

"I guess I could say that Mother was seriously ill. She was not always aware of what was happening. And when my father was home, he and mother would argue. I took care of myself and stayed out of the way. I remember Lakeshore Med E-Ward. I was ten. I remember her being treated in a fancy residential home in Milwaukee for five weeks but my dad couldn't afford it, so she came home. Next, I think, it was St. Catherine's Hospital in Milwaukee for a while with all the nuns bustling about. On and off she was ill from the fall of 1941 until my dad was discharged before the war ended to come home to take care of us. Then she went to the Winnebago State Hospital for several months—in and out, hospital or home, ill or well. I seldom had both parents at the same time. He was in the service or she was gone: years of her shifting, going away, coming home—painful for my dad and me every time. Last time she was taken away to Winnebago, I was a new junior at UW-Madison. I can't remember all of this now."

"But Jan, how did you take care of yourself?"

"I'd adopt families."

"Describe your life to me, one age, one day in your life in the first person. Be a little girl."

"Which age would I pick? (Pause.) I'll pick a happy day when we lived upstairs at North Main Street when everything was going well between my mother and me, before I got too old to be sassy."

"Are you choosing an age?"

"Twelve."

"Become twelve. Where are you going today?"

"I am an independent person. My bike, my cousin's hand-me-down boys' bike—I jump on it in the morning and head for school. I don't like the teachers—all men and most of them are mean, but I liked being with the kids."

"Tell me what that means."

"I like most of my grade school friends, but I don't trust all of them—except for the Green Street Girls. The others are relatives of the ministers and they think they're pretty superior, but they like me 'cause I'm fun—and I'm a good athlete."

"What kind of things do you do?"

"Once I invited them over to my house for clubs and stuff."

"Hum. You make clubs. Any special clubs?"

"I stopped that and kicked everyone out. Kicked them out the front door."

"Kicked them out?"

"They took fingernail polish and colored my mother's beautiful nude lady statue, marring her breasts, painting red in her pubic area, and laughed that I'd have a statue like that in my home. My mother was working at a nearby luncheonette. I'd walk there for one meal every day. It was fun eating hamburger steaks, mashed potatoes, gravy and pie at the counter."

"You're mom's working?"

"She seemed to be pretty happy earning an extra $10 to $20 a week. Our government allotment was $21 a month."

"You seem to be pretty concerned about your mother's happiness."

"Well, if she's happy, I'm happy."

"So you do have to worry about her happiness."

"Because if she's not happy, my life is miserable."

"What are your responsibilities?"

"I play a lot—tennis, basketball, going to the beach. I wrote a Letter to the Editor to get us a night for girls' basketball at the City's recreation building on our corner."

"How old were you?"

"I was in seventh or eighth grade, and I wrote my letter because girls were being unjustly treated. The center had a night for dogs' obedience school and for boys basketball, but nothing for girls until I wrote that letter."

"Well, the power of the press—and doing a little social reform for women's rights. In the 1940s. Incredible. What did your friends say to you when you pulled that off?"

"Well they all came and played and we had a good time. It was a big ugly building, but I loved it and that's why I was hired later as the playground leader."

"Well, yes. No wonder they hired you."

"On Sundays, I sell peanuts and popcorn at the zoo. I was too young then to work in the popcorn stands so the manager and I filled a basket of snacks to carry to the people watching the bears and seals. Ten cents on the every dollar would be mine. "

"Did you arrange and negotiate that."

"Of course. A network of kids did that when I graduated to work in the stands. I worked the stands at the park's night baseball games. I was always making money. I never had any financial stress. That didn't mean we had money, but I always had what I needed. Twinkies only cost seven cents. I hung around the corner store where we girls danced to the Andrew's sisters' 'Rum and Coca Cola.' I loved ice-skating at the zoo pond. Every night there was something to do with my good friend Bev. She went to St. John's and we used to fight about being Catholic vs. Lutheran. Her mom was awfully nice to me. They had lots of kids living upstairs in a little flat like my mom and me, but her dad hollered at them. Bev's mom was afflicted with polio and had a tough life. I liked Bev better than those cousins and relatives at Martin Luther's. I could trust Bev."

"I'm not hearing much about what goes on at your house."

"You can tell I wasn't there a lot."

"Lots of activity elsewhere."

"I'd go home, run up the steps and hope that everything was all right. Maybe I'll go back downstairs and play with our tenant's little boy and his baby brother."

"Jan. Rest for a second and imagine going up those steps."

"I cleaned and painted that hallway only two years ago." (Chokes. Gasps.)

"What are you going to find? (Pause.) Up the steps?"

"When things are good, they're really good; when they're bad, they were bad. She'd sit at the table for days and days, typing letters and sending them off. She read them to me and I didn't understand them. (Sobs. Chokes.) But I never knew what I'd find, going up the steps, holding my breath—especially when I anticipated problems."

"Did you ever check the basement?"

"When I couldn't find her, I'd go down the basement to look for her. I had a friend whose mother was released from Winnebago. My dad and I would ride with them to Winnebago and when their mother was released, my dad and I were so happy for them. Then, soon after she returned home, she hung herself in the basement. It was scary, but I was always relieved, of course, to find my mom in our little apartment. Mother never talked about doing herself in. I probably was the only one thinking about it because of my friend's mother. Many times my mother went somewhere. It was a fear I brought on myself."

"It didn't come from out of a clear blue sky."

"No."

"Plenty of evidence around you."

"It was the uncertainty of everything. (Augh.) We had one little bedroom and I slept with my mother then. It was good for me. I could get nurturing and I could snuggle very close!"

"How could you get nurturing?"

"By holding her and she holding me. She needed nurturing too. She didn't have her husband there and we would both curl up next to each other. And I could feel her heart beating. (Sobs.) And when I was born I know nurturing was something I didn't get. She lost her son, and I'm sure that I never got that mother/baby bonding."

"She lost a son just before you were born?"

"Yes. She was five months pregnant. He was killed by a car and she almost died. She had had several abortions while married to her first husband and she was a wreck. My delivery was cesarean. Snapshots taken before I was born show my brother, Richard, standing with my mother. She's so happy and had married my dad. She was divorced from her first husband—with guilt too, I'm sure, and then having Richard killed in June—and being pregnant and then I arrive in November. In those days adults didn't pick up babies much anyway. I probably just waited. And I know, I know I didn't get the touch and love, whatever affection that any infant would need."

"Anything. Anything would have been OK at that time. You've said all the right things—'whatever affection.'"

"If I got any affection, I'd be like a puppy dog and those times together were wonderful. I felt real bonding then. But we fought—mother/daughter stuff. I didn't do anything right and I left the glass coffee pot on the lighted electric plate and it cracked and smashed to smithereens. It was terrible. We had lots of scenes. I'd go for counseling with counsellors from The Family Center off State Street. Wonderful people helping families in distress, and they also had day care and education for new immigrants. I remember Margaret Wheary. Mother went for therapy there, I went there to see why my mother was so unhappy."

"To see why your mother was so unhappy?"

"Yeah. That's what they said. I talked with social workers. I went to a girls' camp on the Fox River so I could get away and so Mother could solve some problems. Then off to Rose Robsens' home, supposedly to help with her kids and to help her clean house. Then I discovered my mother paid her to take me. That was disillusioning. I was often with my mother's friend Bernice and her three daughters, friends from when my mother lived on a farm with her first husband. When I was about eight, I started taking the Interurban to Milwaukee, crossed the street to the Northwestern station and transferred to the Hiawatha train to Columbus, Wisconsin, where they'd meet me with open arms. I was independent pretty early."

"I should say so."

"In my confirmation classes at school I'd argue with the teachers. Mother would be writing letters, revolutionary-type stuff about being angry with men and their power, and the Japs and how the government was trying to subvert civilian defense, quoting Thomas Paine, etc. She'd given me lots of crazy, revolutionary ideas to use to challenge my teachers, and I wasn't popular with them."

"But was that all right with you?"

"Yes, and I still challenge. And now I'm challenging my bosses."

"For sexism?"

"If they don't like the way I live my life, shit! That's the way I am."

"How do you perceive yourself to be, Jan?"

"An outsider—compared to what's 'acceptable.' Even being a UU was good practice to be an outsider, to become a lesbian. I'm an only child and I have to be creative and make my own way. I've always done that."

"Take care of yourself? I didn't hear much of how you were taken care of, more about how you coped and managed."

"I don't remember being taken care of. I was always prepared. My mother told me about pregnancy and childbirth before second grade. I knew what a penis was for. She prepared me for menstruation in case she wasn't around. Her perceptions were right on target. (Tears now. Choking.) But I've felt abandoned many times in my life."

"You were abandoned!"

"But I never felt unprepared for it. It's been worse. It's like what I wrote in my journal last week—that the scar tissue grows deeper and thicker, which is scary because I don't want to be apathetic—like a person after a prefrontal lobotomy."

"Scabs upon layers of scars. Who's causing that in your life now, Jan?"

"(Sobs.) Work, I know; Bea, I guess. We've been through so much strife and mood shifts, unpredictability and devastating affects that wipe me out. And work. Every time I build up greater defenses into a shell that makes me tougher so I won't be hurt so badly. That shell is a scary thing because it diminishes me."

"Become the shell and describe yourself to me."

(Pause. Sighs.) "The shell is strong. What's underneath is vulnerable. I used to be a trusting, open and loving organism."

"Are you being the shell tissue or are you the organism?"

"I'm the organism."

"Well, you're still loving and trusting and open. I want you to be in touch with the scar tissue now. You're purposeful and you're necessary and you're scarring yourself Jan."

(Pause.) "The scar tissue that I am is a barrier to protect Jan from hurt, and what I'm doing is weighing her down."

"Are you heavy?"

"Oh, what a burden I am."

"How heavy are you?"

"Sometimes I'm three inches thick and crusty around the torso, back, chest and shoulders.

"The heart part?"

"Real heavy." (Sobs.)

"Can anybody get through you? Do you provide safety?"

"No. There's still her head that I can't get to and the rest of her skin, her arms and legs. She's a sensuous person and any little bit of love, touch or affection makes me turn into—tissue paper."

"So then you're not protective."

"Only when the chips are down. To protect her, I'm like leather. I visualize a turtle shell, but that's too permanent. I see scales, layers, with every growth getting thicker and thicker, but, like a scratch or a wound, the scab comes off and it's a bloody, painful mess."

"How long will that scar tissue last?"

"Probably not long because I still feel the hurt."

(Silence except for ticking clock.)

"What needs to be protected to save you from more hurt?"

"My heart. It's my heart that seeks a solution. My head has to be clearer."

"Your head has to be clearer. That's a strong silent statement from way back, Jan. 'My head has to be clearer.' It's protection."

"I've taken good care of my body. It's treated me well. I'm seldom sick. But I could take even better care of it."

"Take better care of your body and your heart, too."

(Clock ticks.)

"That's what I'm doing now, Nora. My head has to be clear, but my expectations hurt my heart."

"You need to think about how you're going to take care of your heart. Who else will do that for you and how many hearts have you taken care of?"

"I guess I'm what Bea says, 'Jan's insatiable.' What's wrong with that?"

"Nothing, but I don't think that's true."
"I'm insatiable. I want more."

"Well you have a fine appetite for life."

I told Nora about Florida's dolphin zoo starring the hardest working dolphin, Jan. She jumps the highest, leads the pack, has worked there the longest, and they taught her to pronounce, "I want one more."

"And if that isn't me, I don't know what."

"What do you want one more of?"

"I want more good things. I want more loving, more orgasms. I want hugs. I want more pay, more happiness, and more security. I want to be happy, and I work hard enough and jump high enough. I shouldn't have to jump higher."

"I'm glad to hear you say that."

"And I'm not responsible for urging other people to jump."
(Sighs.)

"Big sigh after that one. Big sigh!"

"I used to run in and rescue people. I don't do that anymore. I want to be friendly and listen to people but I can't risk making decisions for them or helping people with their problems. Well, maybe, but they have to ask me."

"You can't take that responsibility."

"And that includes Bea. I have to support and listen but I'm not going to find a job for her. I can't do that again. She came to Lakeshore Med and the results of that ended up being all my fault. I got Betty a job at Lakeshore Med once. (Laughs.) That was a big lesson for me. She lasted all of four weeks. And

Marge. I used to be her incurable rescuer, but I stand back now. She's part of that shell, too. And a shell is better than a scab. It doesn't hurt. I've gained a little wisdom now. I try diplomacy and tact and allow others to be on their own to gain their own sense of accomplishment. I get in enough trouble taking care of myself—and Bea and me. It's good for me to hit these sore spots. It's like going to the dentist to heal. I'm not afraid to confront anything that's happened to me."

"Your inner wisdom is coming through loud and clear, Jan. Appreciate yourself and take time to heal. Be reasonable and do more of what you want to do and choose very gently. Take better care of yourself, and you may want to review the influence your fantastic mother still may have on your feelings."

"I'm not looking for any quick and easy answers to change. Thank you, Nora. I'm afraid I may have worn you out."

"You're not responsible for me, Jan. I can take care of myself, remember?"

Jan and Nora on September 17, 1983

"Thanks to you, Nora. I stopped drinking, Bea has too and, so far, we stopped having outbursts fueled by booze."

"Don't thank me, Jan. You and Bea are changing your behaviors. It's remarkable that she has the power to quit with you."

"It helps keeping busy and active together. Playing Scrabble, going to our church events, folk dancing."

"Sounds good to me."

"Bea and I have the potential to argue about our many problems, but we're working through them now without the turbulence. We've given up on our dream to sell Mother Courage's building. But we can discuss it now. Our money is leaking out, but Bea didn't get defensive. She knows she's appreciated, I'm sure. Well when she's down she doesn't feel that, but when her senses are all right, she knows how valuable I think she is taking care of complicated accounting, our loses, properties, inheritances. Our conversations could have blown up if we had been boozing it up, but we're able to get through this and be OK. In the past, we'd come home, have a couple drinks and wouldn't want to do anything."

"And that contributes significantly to depression for someone with a tendency to be depressed."

"The first week after seeing you, I felt she was showing me what her personality would be like without booze, and that I don't need to be responsible for her.

"How wonderful?"

"She sold her sailboat. She got her health insurance changed for half the cost and she didn't have to answer questions or lie about being treated for alcohol abuse. That's a big integrity issue for her. And the insurance company didn't check it out. It won't cover everything but will cover what we need. It's too bad that she can't be covered under my insurance from work. Hah! That will be the day! She's been compromised by admitting herself into St. Paul, even if it was five years ago."

"I'm sorry about that, Jan."

"Another help to stay off my martinis is that I haven't seen Randy for two to three weeks. I avoid him because I get angry inside. He doesn't seem to miss me. I keep sending his secretary long weekly lists of what we're doing, and I don't hear anything in return so our gang keeps on chugging along, accomplishing great projects as long as he and Chuck McCarthy don't interfere, but there's lots of tension and stress. I'm always afraid I will be fired and then both Bea and I'd be out of work."

"What could he fire you for?"

"People are let go for incompatibility with management—whatever excuse they think up."

"He wouldn't do that, Jan, with all the visibility of you and your office."

"He most absolutely could. With my visibility as an outspoken feminist and an abhorrent lesbian? Homophobia! But if he fired me, I'd free me to express these injustices in public or even publishing them in a novel—or take him into court."

"You've been there how long?"

"Thirteen years but not full time until 1976. Perhaps they'll give me some kind of separation agreement and send me out the door. I certainly am incompatible with management—and justifiably so. I'm trying but I can't find another job. I'm so desperate I applied for the PR job at St. Paul, but I wasn't even interviewed. Nick Dixon meets with his peers at the Hospital Council in Milwaukee and if PR positions open up, what does he tell them if he's asked about me. I have Mr. Young as a reference and he gladly supports me in my search, but who asks for a former administrator's reference? It's obvious that I'm not in sync with the current one. So I'm stuck. Randy's cut my salary. I make $23,000 and I should be making another $10,000 compared to my colleagues' salary range."

"Your peer group is higher that that."

"The hospital is a $35 million operation. Supposedly I'm the Director of Communications. I work completely in a vacuum and Randy sets me up, finds minor errors or omissions and reams me. He ignores anything good. He says, 'Look. You're supposed to be such a great organizer for all these big events you put on, yet you do something as tacky as posting a story on the bulletin board about a patient dying at St. Agnes. I posted that one clipping to diminish our employees' perception that the paper prints only the good news about St. Agnes and the bad news about us. They're so defensive about Lakeshore Med, its image, and their jobs. But yet, Randy accumulates a list of every petty detail that isn't to his liking, in spite of all our big events and then harasses me for an hour or more in his office."

"And your motives, obviously, are to do the best for your hospital—and from what I perceive, you do so."

"It's obvious, Nora, that he wants me to be so unhappy that I'll leave. He wants me out. I've heard that he and Nick have gotten into some terribly abusive exchanges with some others at administrative meetings. One of my supportive women administrators told me, 'I never thought we'd have to endure that,' or 'Remember the Good Old Days. Mr. Young never used to holler, except at Nick.' She was trembling in our office, a safe place because she knew that I've been in the same situation for five years. It's bad for all of us. I still hope that our managers have enough insight to think that we could accomplish so much more in a better way. Those three men are terrible, just terrible and I'm going mad in the midst of misogyny."

"It's a real world."

"Ha! They're hiring a motivational group to turn our cost-containment issues around with bonus awards and merchandise, but employees are saying that all they need is some appreciation from administration because we all want Lakeside Med to survive. If I have a chance, I may try working through these motivational people to advise administration about what's wrong because most of us don't have the courage or the clout to confront them directly. It's like being the boy in Hans Christian Anderson's story telling the naked emperor that he's naked. But it's naive of me to think these consultants will change anything that's not in their best interests."

"Is it possible to save hospital costs by handing out gifts for cost-saving suggestions?"

"We're told it's self-funding and paid for out of cost savings from putting employees' suggestions to work, as if we haven't been doing that all along. It's a crock. And what about the labor costs of staff writing and submitting their ideas and a committee evaluating suggestions and handing out "credit points" toward funky prizes and certificates—and all of us attending motivational lectures? I suppose it's one of my responsibilities to communicate those concerns to administration, but of course I can't. In addition, Marilyn and I have to promote the damn program."

"When will your next communication with Randy be? Will you seek him out?"

"Two years ago he told me that I should see him every week. Weeks go by and I can't get in to see him. Then of course it's my fault—the onus is on me. My memos and phone messages aren't returned. It's an avoidance issue."

"You must be participating in that too."

"Oh, absolutely. We're both busy persons but he's avoiding me. His secretary will call, 'Randy would like to know...' and I'd ask why doesn't he call me? 'He's busy.' Well, that let's you know that you're not a person important enough to deserve any of his precious time. It's another 'Fuck you, Jan.'"

"So, knowing that he's in an uncomfortable position, Jan, what kind of action are you going to take so you have the upper hand?"

"I've just stopped talking. That's when the stress was so bad." (Sobs.)

"But you do have the edge with your insight."

"But he has the power. I try to keep a sense of humor—a cynical one. Since he became Patient Care VP, three months could pass without seeing him. In fact, I made a promise to myself that I'd never again go in his office alone. But when he wants to get me, he manipulates it so we'll be meeting with a group and then he'll say, 'Jan, I'd like to see you for a few minutes.' Then when the others leave, he'll chew me out—and what pisses me so much is that when I get out of there, I almost feel that I'm as bad as he says I am. I even wake up at night thinking, 'Well, maybe he's right.' And that's wrong! It's a dreadful erosion of my personhood!"

"Try to avoid it. Help yourself maintain your tolerance of this behavior."

"Salaries have been frozen and I haven't had a job evaluation—other than being ridiculed. (Pause.) He and I keep an evidence file on each other. His memos are all written. I Xerox everything, like we're programmed to confront each other—like it's going to be a cruel disaster."

"It's a real world. Jan, can you give me an example of an interaction between you and Randy? I'll move these chairs to be his office. You describe it, please."

"So you want a psychodrama, Nora? OK. Here goes!" (Sighs. Pauses to think.) "I'm Randy, interrogating from behind my spacious teakwood desk. I have a window and the shades reflect on my glasses. I lean back as if I'm relaxed. That way, when I lunge forward, my body shows more power."

Randy's voice: "I've been working to make you miserable for so long. I'm a superlative bully. If I can do that to you, I can do what I will to anyone. It gives me power to control you even though you know so much about me. It gives me pleasure to watch you squirm. You're a hostile feminist and contrary to my standard for others, especially public relations types. You're hardly a PR person when you ridicule the actions of your administrators. Get out of here and go someplace where you can be happy instead of groveling around here. I enjoy being powerful and throwing all this shit in your face. I've got you under pressure where you're even listening to all this—and I'm winning.

Nora: "We've got to better understand his power, Jan. Where he's getting it and where he's going with it?"

"Nora, the fact that I trusted him in the first place was a mistake." (Pause. Sighs.)

Randy's voice: "You're typical of all the women I know. You try to win me over and be my friend and then you shit on me. I won't ever let another woman do that again. I'll never allow myself to be a genuine person with a woman. And you don't have a chance. You have been around here since I started and you don't have a chance. You're going to hang in here until you quit or suffer to be humiliated until you retire in twelve to fifteen years—and I'm the boss. Be a lackey in the shadows or I'm going to destroy you. This is a two-hospital town and I'm going to be powerful. Who knows, someday I could be a politician. I've got all this power and I'm not even forty. I'll be bored with hospitals. Once I solve these hospital issues, my career will take off. I'm not going to be satisfied abusing stupid tacky people like you. I'm moving ahead and abusing more important people."

Nora: "Meanwhile, Jan, how are you going to survive? Come back over here as Jan, as the strong women that you are. Here's this thirty-five-year-old, hell bent in one direction. How long are you going to sit there and listen to him?"

Jan: "Randy, it's time for you to get what you deserve. For the last five-and-a-half years you have emotionally and financially abused me. Because of that, the institution that we both work for is suffering, as are the both of us. Why not stop being abusive so we both can function in a professional manner. You've caused pain with almost everybody you've worked with, and you all have to live with that pain. Let's start over and work together for the good of everyone so we can be productive, helping human beings."

Nora: "How are you going to do that?"

Jan: "I have hope—unrealistic perhaps—that things are going to turn so bad that Randy and Nick are kicked out, or Nick will move out and take Randy with him."

Nora: "Until that happens, what are you going to do to survive? What's your bottom line? Certainly it's not listening to more destructive abuse."

Jan: "I want to know what's possible as far as budgets and goals. What are my hospital's priorities? And I want to work with you, Randy, in a professional manner and not from a list of negative, petty details. I want to know what's going on so I can be part of the solutions. You permit me to read administrative meeting minutes, but I know that's only what a secretary interprets. I find no pulse beating there, no idea of what the hospital needs. I want to be able to speak with you without being afraid, and I want to get paid what I deserve. That is a fact that has been unjust for years, and you know it."

Nora: "That sounds incredibly clear and loud with lots of energy. 'I want to get paid what I deserve!'"

Jan: "And I want to be honest and straight forward without being abused. You are the worst manager I've ever seen, yet you have the potential for doing so much good."

Nora: "What choices do you have to take care of yourself?"

Jan: "This negative regard—always negative. Let's discuss and set policy and guidelines. We obviously have different points of view. Let's make our working relationship clear. When something you don't like happens, tell me. Don't wait for six months and have a mile-long list of evidence that you've been accumulating to use against me."

Nora: "Tell him what you're going to do if that happens again."

Jan: "This behavior is counter-productive to what we're trying to achieve. It's bad for you and for me. There's no reason why two intelligent people have to behave like this. Why should I allow you talk to me like this? Because you have power."

Nora: "Why do you continue to sit there?"

Jan: "Because I'm afraid I'm going to be fired, and Bea doesn't have a job, and we (Sobs.) have a lot of—I'm fifty-one years old and—(Pause. Sobs.) If he hasn't fired me yet, it's probably because he's afraid to. Why do I sit there being abused? I don't do it with Bea! I didn't do that—well, I did that with Alex too, but not near the end. I don't have to take it. I've tried so hard to find another job. I've got to survive. I've got to confront this unbearable man." (Sighs.)

Nora: "Look at yourself with compassion. You're taking a lot of abuse but you're used to it. You'll make peace, wherever you can. Is that what you want?"

Jan: "I need your skills, Nora. (Sighs.) I've backed down in the name of peace—and security. I've taken too much too many times. I'm a good person and talented and perceptive, and I'm respected by others. But I've gotten myself in situations where

I've lost control. People that I had cared about have disillusioned and disappointed me."

Nora: "What could you consider doing on these occasions?"

Jan: "I've always thought about running away, but that will solve nothing."

Nora: "I don't think anybody will criticize you if you stood up and walked out. It's merely a statement that says, 'This doesn't make any sense and I'll come back when it does. I don't feel good about this and the best thing for me to do is to leave.'"

Jan: "I don't think I'd get fired for walking out on him like that. I remember now doing it once before. I was in control."

Nora: "Give him a walking-out statement. He's become irrational and that's an insult to your intelligence."

Jan: "I don't need to sit here and take this distorted hostility. I'm not going to submit to this. We can continue our conversation when it reaches a different plane."

Nora: "Wonderful. Come back and be you. 'Jan just walked out on you, Randy.'"

"Standing up was powerful, Nora. I'll bet no one has ever walked out on him."

"You can do it politely."

"My problem is that I react from my gut, not my head. Why do I always sit there? I was afraid of his power. I wanted to run again before as I did from Alex. I used to run away from home a lot when I was a kid. I kept hanging around Randy's tainted office until tensions settled down and he dismissed me. I'm always feeling responsible. That's my job, keeping things rational at home with Bea, with Randy, with Alex, with my mother."

"Don't put yourself down, Jan, because you haven't adjusted before this."

"It would make me mad when Bea would drive away, but I guess it was the smart thing to do until emotions settled down. But I'd feel abandoned and I probably was angry that I didn't run away myself from the craziness and then come back. I don't always have to be responsible."

"Good. Good. Good."

Chapter 12

Jan on September 20, 1983

Our TV series whisks along with its programming and production. Our committee has dwindled to four: Laura Williams, Pat Holmen, Mark Bertini and me. We have working breakfasts where the air swirls with creativity. We're currently doing "Hospital Costs" with Nick Dixon, "Keep Infants Seated Safely" with the new K.I.S.S. Auxiliary program that loans car seats to "Keep Infants Seated Safely," and "Hospice," Lakeshore Med innovative specialty to care for terminal patients.

When we tape, we devise sets and visuals that make our programs more than talking heads. That's where the fun comes in because we access all departments and include more people. I've often grabbed a wheelchair to transport borrowed plants from the day rooms to dress up our sets. Our written scripts and visuals are quite snappy, but our host Laura often improvises while heeding Pat's advice on keeping the program entertaining. Our printed TV promos continue at the bottom TV newspaper programming listings and throughout the hospital.

Jan and Nora on September 24, 1983

"I don't want to short change myself on these sessions, Nora. I feel good now, but during the week, I explored new challenges for you and that opens another wound to be healed."

"You're entitled to whatever you choose for yourself."

"I was thinking today (Pause. Sighs.) that it's the last weekend for Mother Courage Bookstore. We're having a sale and everything left over will go to women's causes. I have (Sighs.) residual grief (Sobs.) that I'd like to work on. I can talk about it here. Like Bea, I had my dreams tied up in it too. I feel grief about the bookstore that's worse than leaving Alex."

"And you're alone in this dream?"

"If I expressed my grief to Bea, she'll say, 'You're mad at me for not making this work.'"

"So you don't talk about your disappointments of the end of your dream."

"I'm always cautious about implying blame on her. Then all hell would break loose."

"Well, Jan, you wouldn't be blaming her! She might perceive you're being negative, but she may—"

"Nora, I'm afraid I must vent my repressed anger and frustration or I'll lose control again, and that's still grim and scary. I need to keep my cool so I can survive at work. Bea's tired of running a feminist missionary. It was Bea and Jill's store anyway. It was never truly my store. I was the gofer and the promoter. I seldom made decisions. Now Jill has her full-time job and Bea wants to be her own person. I have grief and Bea has relief. She doesn't want to work for someone else either. It's an end of another dream—and a beginning of something different—for her at least."

"What is so sad, Jan, is that you had so few chances to develop that dream, because if you could change the circumstances—"

"I was shut out. But yet, ironically, if I weren't with Bea in the first place, I wouldn't have had that dream. It's one of those situations where you have something that's quite obtainable because of the situation; but yet it doesn't come true because of the situation. The economy is a factor, but I did get shut out almost from the beginning. The fact that I had access to the building and would share it rent free made it work as long as it has."

"And it is a big dream. I love it."

"Another part of my disillusionment is because it wasn't supported from others as it should have been. I shouldn't take it personally. If I owned a shoe store and people didn't buy my product, would I be angry? Probably. Still, I feel betrayed. People say it's our location. Shit. We couldn't have had a bookstore if we had to buy or rent. There's no problem parking. It's easy to find. It pisses me no end all the talk about the mall. It's only been there for two years. Mecca. Worship God at the Mall. Small unique businesses are being snuffed out. And I hated stopping our *Courier* newsletter. My pride and political energy lived in that newsletter, and I (Sobs. Chokes.) I risked my job writing letters to the editor on gender issues and the horrific holocaust of our neighboring town's burning witches on Halloween. Imagine what image that made on those children? Imagine Randy's seething when those commentaries were printed. Ha! Nick Dixon fuming! Maple Grove sponsored a Halloween witch-burning bonfire to burn a fake witch. What informed, intelligent person wouldn't respond to that."

"Who are you most angry with—about this?"

"I'm angry at Bea—and a lot has to do with booze! She's alone there all day, yet I shouldn't expect her to do anything else? She's an artist, a poet, a writer, a musician! Yet who am I to say what she should do with her life?"

"It's a joint venture. What do you mean you shouldn't expect her—?"

"I wouldn't have minded if it wasn't all that financially successful, but she just sat there. She's written novels, but she won't even take those manuscripts out of their boxes. Painting! But she's tired of rejection. So we're going out of business and we don't owe anybody anything. And I don't have money to put into the building in new plumbing and wiring to bring it up to code, so I guess being mad at Bea is easy."

"Well, that's one dimension and it sounds—"

"And I'm mad at being shut out."

"Repeat that again."

"I'm angry and I couldn't say anything because she'd say, 'I'm interfering with her and her daughter's relationship.' And I'm disappointed in my daughter for not being more involved with the store. But why should she? It my dream."

"Just got scratched."

"I had dreams of a creative services agency. I could freelance with her and leave my toxic job. Once I was so desperate to leave Lakeshore Med I wanted to start a women's newspaper and shopper with Beth Johnson. But Bea mumbled sullenly during our planning times that made it was a hostile act for me to even meet with Beth. Bea insisted that she wouldn't be involved. Actually, it could have been financial disaster if I left Lakeshore Med to do that with no venture money, no health insurance. (Chokes.) That's another stressor when you're not happy at work and you can't lose your benefits. Everything falls in on top and around you when your alternatives are cut off." (Cries.)

"What's it like today?"

(Sighs. Pause.) "On the last day Mother Courage was officially open, I parked the car. Walked passed it in tears." (Sobs.)

"Don't stop those tears."

"But I did stop those tears because I was concerned about Bea. She's happy about it. (Pause.) There was a time when I wished I'd get fired and then she'd have to go out to find a job, any job, and I'd manage the store."

"You had so much invested in the store."

(Sobs. Long pause.)

"What's it going to be like this weekend, Jan?"

"We're having a rummage sale. This is it. Everything will go. And then we'll probably sell the building. Who knows, this might be the last chance. So it's reality—and I have to accept it.

(Clock ticks.) At least Bea is relieved and that's one less stressor to deal with."

"What's Bea going to do now?"

"I don't know. She'll find a job and if she doesn't? (Shrugs. Pause. Sighs.) Women used to say they would have to walk up and down the street or sit in their car to get the courage to even come into our store. I don't know if they were afraid of dealing with lesbians or learning about women's issues."

"Where did you hear that?"

"More than once. Oh yeah. Joanne Zekas told someone, 'Why don't you go to Mother Courage and get those books' and the woman answered, 'I don't want to go there.' There are myths, crazy mixed-up stuff about the store."

"Lesbian bookstore myths?"

"I don't know. A radical bookstore? Sistermoon in Milwaukee closed too. She had volunteers. She told Bea she lost her lease and didn't mind owing publishers money. They can wait for their payments, she told Bea. Volunteers could go someplace else.

"What are you going to do with the dream? Are you going to put it to rest?"

"No. I'll never put it away. I'm telling myself, 'If you ever want to do it again and if you have the money to do it, you don't have to own a building. If, when you retire, you don't have to be so self-sufficient. You can pay rent.'"

"Lots of stress keeping track of all that property."

"Bea truly has been remarkable with all the details: accounting, taxes, insurance. She's saved us thousands of dollars. I don't pay a bill. She takes care of all our money and is really clever doing so."

"What about Mother Courage Press, Jan?"

"I guess it's not the total end of a dream because if I have a chance, Mother Courage Press will still be functioning and expanding. We're making space in our house for book storage and an office. That's positive. But that's been a battle too. I almost forced her to do those sensitive *Something* illustrations and she hated every minute of it. She's angry with Rachel who doesn't even call to bug us any more. But her book is successful."

"It's such a unique publication."

"After all this, whatever Bea does, she does. I won't push or nudge her or do anything anymore about working on projects for or with me. It didn't work at Lakeshore Med; there's stress at Mother Courage; and then our book—even through it's beautiful and important, she said she isn't proud of it. But I think she was probably plastered."

"She should be proud of it. It's unique. Well done. Illustrations are excellent."

"They surely are!"

"So how are you going to get through the weekend?"

"That's one of the reasons why I wanted to come today, Nora, to get free of all this, to release some of this grief about Mother Courage."

"Would you be willing to do a little role playing with Mother Courage? It's creative. It's more than I can probably ever know or comprehend in terms of saying goodbye to her right now, her importance to you and your love."

(Cries.) "Sure. I don't know if I'm strong enough to do it."

"That's one of my concerns as we talked, that you'd be able to talk about it and report it factually. Now you can allow yourself the privilege of actually grieving. Mother Courage is one of the most beautiful aspects of you, Jan."

"I guess I'm not going to let her die."

"OK. You can be addressing that to her."

"Maybe I'm too close to it. I don't know."

"We can try it out unless it's too hard."

"Mother Courage was in my heart? But Bea had Mother Courage in her heart too."

"But we're talking about your relationship to her."

"I named her."

"Start talking to her directly. She's a real part of you, Jan."

(Groans.) "I have so many unfinished dreams and wishes about you. I wanted you to be a source of strength for other people because I didn't have a source of strength like her when I needed it."

"Mother Courage does represent you, Jan, as a source of strength!"

"But she's not going to be there any more. Why should I feel responsible for other women? Why should I?"

"Let Mother Courage speak to that."

(Pause.) MC: "You've always wanted to try to soften the way for others and provide alternatives for them. I get a real kick out of that.

Jan: "I get a big boost when I can come up with some solutions to help people and give them strength."

MC: "And that's what I'm all about? And there's no other place for people to go that's like me. I give power to people, especially women, and that's a scary threat for women to have power because women aren't used to it. They don't know what to do with it and they look at you and they see how you screwed up with your marriage and all the problems you and Bea have. It's scary for them—and for your children, too. Customers look at you and come in and see me encourage them to do the same—and they're afraid. What you are is scary. You challenge society, you challenge men, and you challenge your children."

Jan: "I guess I'm not important in the light of what's happened. Who am I to be so egocentric that others make their decisions based on what I do. So I helped create you."

Nora: "You created Mother Courage out of Jan Anthony."

Jan: "And Bea. It's our baby. Bea's and mine."

Nora: "Do you want to tell her how you love her?"

Jan: "OH! Oh. I wanted you to survive. (Sobs deeply.) I wanted you to be strong and powerful and to have influence. (Cries.) I wanted you to be as popular as a chain bookstore in every town—the McDonalds of woman's power. Fantasy? True!"

Nora: "Dreams."

Jan: "I had great expectations that didn't work."

Nora: "Is she dead?"

(Inhales. Pause.) MC: "I don't know. I'm still there inside of you and I'm very much alive."

Jan: "I'm not very much alive. I'm just—I have to rest for a while. I have dreams of Phoenix rising from the ashes. (Groans. Sobs.) But it would take a revolution to make that happen. Sell the building. I'll never be able to afford the financial risk of fixing the building and you'll be lucky if Bea comes along with us, and it would be a big problem if she didn't. So much of you" (Ahhhs.) "in here—is me."

Nora: "What a huge sigh. Huge."

(Clock ticks like a heartbeat.)

Jan: (Heavy ahhhs.) Time to rest a bit. (Ugh.) I'm so proud of you. (Ahhhs. Exhales deeply.) And I'm terribly disappointed, terribly. Other people didn't help to make it work and I couldn't make it work by myself. I had the raw material and ingredients to make you happen. I couldn't do it by myself. I bragged about you. Pushed people toward you. Practically wore a sandwich sign on my body all the time. We met with too much resistance or competition or absolute economic facts, but I couldn't manage you because I had to survive with money from a conventional source."

Nora: "Tell her how much you love her and how proud you are and how much you wanted to keep her going."

Jan: (Silence.) "I don't know what to say. (Long pause.) You have other outlets. You can approach people in other ways. You don't have to sell other people's books. Write one for yourself. Why don't you get your ass in gear, Jan?"

Nora: "Believe in her, too. She believes in you."

Jan: "I would have loved, Mother Courage, to be the bookstore manager for a while. I'd have taken better are of you. I would have fought harder."

MC: "And you could have insisted. You could have made your presence felt. You didn't need to give up on me."

Nora: "What do you say to that?"

Jan: "Well, that's a pretty heavy trip to lay on me 'cause I sure had enough other people that have turned on me. Don't you turn on me now!" (Laughs.)

Nora: "That was healthy for you to say."

Jan: "Who in the hell do you think I am that I can make everything survive!"

Nora: "Life's lesson. That's your role. You sit there and pay attention to the craziness and you wait until it's over."

Jan: "It's over."

Nora: "Now Mother Courage becomes one more person who makes excessive demands."

(Laughs gently.) Jan: "That's a different dimension of her that I hadn't seen before. At first I just saw her as a dream."

Nora: "How are you going to say good-bye to her now? Tell her you loved her and appreciated her."

Jan: "You, Mother Courage, are nationally known. Despite the fact that we're out of business in Lakeshore Bay, we're still publishing our little press and are listed in catalogs—and this September's *Ms. Magazine* included your name and address among the seventy-three feminist bookstores in the nation. But then you go out of business. Finally you get your name in *Ms.* Your name was a restaurant in New York City in Rita Mae Brown's *Rubyfruit Jungle.* Your name came from Bertolt Brecht's anti-war play! You've touched many lives and they're not going to forget you. But I am going to resurrect you—somehow! You're mad at me maybe, but you're not dead yet. You're just not living at 214 2nd Street anymore. There! In fact you're going to be stronger. Maybe we'll even start a mail order business."

"Bea's not happy working for anybody, Jan, and she might want to start something like that."

"You're right, Nora. Mother Courage is alive. When we were chopping vegetables at the Michigan Women's Music Festival food tent, someone from San Francisco said she knew about our book. Some people all over the country and in Australia know Mother Courage Press. As time goes by we won't depend only on customers here. We'll go farther. I guess Mother Courage is still here. We just released her—and Bea—from the confines of that building. But Mary Elizabeth, our figurehead on our sign, is coming home with us."

"I think she's pretty neat."

"This hurt a lot, Nora, but it was good. I needed to do this. I never thought of a mail order business, even if Bea got a new job, Mother Courage is not dead!"

"It would be a shame if she were. Mother Courage is you."

"Mother Courage is Bea too! But I'm the risk taker and she's the insecure person—and the bored one. It's easier for me to be a risk taker because I have a job with a regular salary. I hope we can find alternatives that are not as abrasive to the both of us."

"I'm glad Mother Courage is alive—was and will be, Jan."

Jan on September 27, 1983

Dear Matt,

Mother Courage will have its final clearance sale next week when the Downtown merchants have another Octoberfest street party. We're asking $22,500 for the building, but I don't think we'll get that. It was appraised at $16,900 for the estate, but we've cleaned it up. There's no fairy godmother or knight in shining—or even rusty armor to help me create my fantasy of using the building for my dreams. Also, the bridge next to us will be rebuilt and traffic will all but stop for who knows how long.

My financial concerns are decreasing when Jenny helped me find a skillful and affordable dentist, a brother of one of our women friends. My allergy shot series is over and all the tenants are paying on time. My only remaining concerns are for our property on 13th Street that needs a new furnace, my rusty Toyota, finding a new upstairs tenant and replacing the furnace at Grandpa's place—and continue to repay the State on a monthly basis for the years of my mother's care. If we sell the shop, I will have even more ways to solve those remaining concerns and relieve some stress.

But generally, things are really looking good!

Love,

Mom

Chapter 13

Jan and Nora on October 1, 1983

"Good news, Nora. Bea is going to H&R Block today to learn how to prepare taxes, and she could have a job after that. And I'm so pleased that Bea and I went to your workshop on depression and PMS last Saturday. It's amazing how the dynamics of this aspect of women's health has been neglected—or joked about."

"It took a feminist revolution in medicine for researchers to change their priorities. The myths of 'the curse' and that women got mad at menopause persists—and we must change that."

"Nora, it was a revelation when I read about PMS for the first time and I realized how it set off chaos between Bea and me. Your workshop was another helpful discussion that we could talk about and better understand what goes on when this happens. Incidentally, this is my first free Saturday in a long time. I can pick and choose to do what I want to do. I usually do what Bea wants to do. Today I have a whole day of choices."

"A whole day of choosing what you want to do. That sounds like a breakthrough for you."

"Even when I'm on my own, I'm still thinking about work or Bea or my kids or Mother Courage. This morning, Bea and I were talking about our *Something Happened to Me* book. Wow! Was that a struggle to get Bea to illustrate it and traumatic working with Rachel, too. What stress! Those two disagree; I'm stuck in the middle and Rachel would get frustrated with the both of us. And Bea would get mad at me if I didn't support her. But Rachael should have known what she was getting into when she insisted that we illustrate, publish and promote her manuscript. She constantly nags Bea to jack up the price and wants me to change Bea's mind about it. Doesn't she, of all people, our one-time therapist, know how fruitless that is? Meanwhile we're looking for ideas for other books, brainstorming the possibility of a whole line of Mother Courage books."

"There's certainly a pressing need for survival books for teenagers and children. The need for your sensitive approach in your book is desperate."

"Bea hadn't even thought of publishing more books, but why go somewhere else for a job when we can create our own business? I'm sure you could write a survivors' manual for kids in almost any problem-solving situation, Nora."

"Another chapter for Mother Courage. Teachers are desperate. We are desperate in our field. I encourage both of you to publish more in that direction."

"Ideas seem to be coming together. It's the end of the bookstore, but I can't push Bea into anything else now. In contrast, all I need is a nudge. We can work it out so simply—work from home without a building or an office. But it's been a—well, last weekend I was so proud of us. But that quickly changed. We had a bottle of brandy in the house and Monday I had a touch of the flu. The America's Cup sailing event was on TV and we both had a cocktail and I fell asleep. I asked her to wake me when supper was ready. When I woke up, she was completely plastered and asleep in her chair. I was scared. She made supper but didn't eat. She went up to bed. Jill called at 7 p.m., which made Bea more upset with herself when she talked to Jill with that alcoholic slur. The next morning, it's the traditional 'Don't say anything.' I need to talk but not argue or place blame, yet Bea won't talk."

"That's a strong message, Jan."

"That night she poured the third of what was left in the brandy bottle into a water glass. I was brave enough to tell her, 'The last time I saw that kind of water glass brimming with brandy was in your father's apartment after he'd fallen down.' Maybe she thought, 'I'll drink that up and be rid of it.' I don't know what it meant to her. The next day, Tuesday, I was emotionally down, upset, not feeling well. But at 2 p.m., she called me at work. 'I want to apologize for last night. I don't know why I did that because I've been such a good girl.' Bea actually apologized!"

"It's so difficult, Jan. The nasty part for her is that she doesn't have the same kind of discipline. Her body is different."

"We were experimenting. Could we have liquor in the house? Her apology was like a ray of sunshine, but I told her, 'I appreciate what you're trying to do, but you don't have to apologize to me for drinking. It makes me feel like you're not drinking just because of me." Then Bea responded, 'Well, then I apologize for being rude and not taking care of you when you were sick.' That made me happy. 'I accept that, Bea, and I truly appreciate what you've just said.'"

"That's wonderful insight, Jan."

"After Bea's call at work, I told Carolyn, 'I guess I shouldn't have slept through this time.' Actually, who wouldn't fall asleep during the America's Cup. Carolyn told me that it's not right. I don't have to be alert all the time. It makes me angry that I can't take my guard down, even if I'm sick. I was disappointed. Bea was rude. But now her awareness is helpful. On the day after your workshop, Bea and I talked a long time about how we've lived through all our trauma since the late '60s. We didn't know anything about PMS. I was drinking a lot when I was married. Alex would rather have me zonked out on the couch than my going out, working, having a good time and being a productive person. After your PMS talk, we browsed around antique stores, went to church on Sunday and enjoyed the weekend together. And then on Monday, this happened. I was stunned."

"Sometimes it's a shock, Jan, a total disbelief that a person can't have that much control."

'Yet we can feel so wonderfully healthy, so emotionally right with the world."

"That's denial, and you have lots of reasons for that denial."

"How?"

"Alcoholism is a punitive and nasty disease. Sometimes when people are feeling their best and feel strong enough to tackle it, it hits them. Why? I do think we're going to have the answers fairly soon—genetic make-up perhaps. It has nothing to do with being a bad person."

"Bea said, 'Just when I've been such a good girl,' and I said 'You're not a bad girl.' When we were antiquing, we saw a wicker clothes hamper, the shiny, marble-green plastic hamper, and she said it reminded her of the one at her father-in-law's when she and her husband and kids lived with him. She hid vodka there and would sit on the toilet and drink and say, 'I'm not going to let that bastard get me down!'"

"Fond memories of days gone by."

"Monday's a shock. Tuesday is wonderful. We entertained for Jenny's twenty-second birthday supper and during coffee we talked together for a long time. Bea entertained us with her humor and, for the first time ever, Jenny relaxed enough to gossip a bit about her father—his wine and bagel-making parties, various women wanting to take care of him, about dating Marge. Jenny expressed herself in a tactful way, without pettiness or rancor. It was as if we all accepted each other after years of being quiet about our feeling—and it felt good.

"Then I revealed a fantasy to Jenny. Life passages can be nasty. Alex is so angry with me. Bea's Jake doesn't hold a big grudge. My fantasy is to have this big gathering—a picnic, my kids, Bea's kids, Alex, Jake, Marge and her mother and Marge's kids—all coming together in a bunch. And we have a great time. Jenny responded quietly, 'I don't think I'll go to that. Leave me out. It won't work.'

"Then on Thursday we went to a City Hall meeting about rebuilding the bridge and how it probably will damage our building. Friday was folk dancing and we enjoyed one nice drink and ate pleasant suppers each evening."

"The incident turned positive."

"Then I experience my old imagined fears like, 'Here we go again. I'll be afraid of what I'll find when I come home. It's going to be bad again.' But my fantasy didn't manifest itself, thank the Goddess."

"How's work?"

"It's rough. I've been painfully down at work. (Chokes. Sobs.) Lakeshore Med is going through traumas: cutbacks in government reimbursement, rising costs of materials, administration won't raise room rates and they hold back news. They've worked up a scheme to reinstitute employee step increases that were frozen. It's the carrot and the stick. Three major communications efforts went out that were positive but—I've been treated as if I don't exist. I can't even get any response. News could get in the paper. I was supposed to write a media release based on two pages from Randy's notes that Mindy handed me plus one page of Marge's notes."

"Even Marge? Wasn't that strange for you."

"Yes. And Nick. I've tried to see Nick for ten days. I wrote what I thought would be relevant from what they gave me—and Randy changed my story. In anticipation of a negative newspaper article, I drafted a letter to patients to assure them that no change in their care would result from government restrictions. That floated around Administration for ten days. Nursing Services loved it and encouraged me to distribute it. Four or five more people reviewed and approved it. I gave it to Randy and, like a slap in the face he threatened, "Who are you to say you can hand out these letters?' I'm forced to make decisions based on fear. Do I wait for Randy, Chuck or Nick to approve it or do I get it in the neck for not taking the initiative? I get nothing but support from others who are frustrated too."

"You obviously are covering all your other bases."

"Ha! I read about my hospital in the paper. A new reporter, who has been unfair to us, thinks she's the people's advocate. She called Nick directly. He answered her and she interpreted his comments incorrectly. I read it in the paper! We got bad PR from what he said, and it makes me look like I'm not doing my job."

"The story was confusing when I read it, Jan."

"And that reflects on my salary. I went back through my files. We were to receive a general raise in March 1982, but my position was passed over. Randy's rational is that employees at the top of their pay range will receive no increase at this time, but he could have said, 'You ought to feel lucky. You've got a job.' Carolyn is making now what I made two years ago."

"How does that feel?"

"I'm happy for her but I feel cheated. I can't go to Personnel with Marge there. My last written review was in April 1981. I found my copy and I brought it for you to read. It's the worst performance review anyone could have had, but on the same day I was given a $3,000 raise. I probably was an embarrassment for them when they filled out a district hospital salary reimbursements report because I was paid so poorly."

(Quiet time to read review. Clock ticks.) "Jan. I don't believe it. Of all the years I've known you, I can't believe that anyone would use the word 'insensitive' to anything you've ever done or been."

"I'm such an evil person, Nora? I'm so hard to get along with? I'm underpaid, harassed and emotionally abused."

"It's a sick letter. I'm shocked. Absolutely."

"And at the same time I my salary was raised from $15,600 to $18,600! I should take them to court. I could have argued on every one of these points in that review, but it was so excessive, I couldn't let others know about it or I'd never find another job. It's in my file. Or it could be in Randy's special file on me in his desk.

"Has Nick read it?"

"I don't know. I hurt so much when I read it. 'The market function…demoted to communications assistant as opposed to leading these functions.' I am, in reality, demoted to communications assistant. They didn't even tell me when 'marketing' had begun. My title is 'director.' Under whose direction? I work independently for five, six or more administrators. I serve them, all of them. When Nick wants me, he calls. Fiscal calls. Chuck, now our marketing man, calls. When Randy wants me, his secretary calls. And speaking of calls, a nun chaplain is supposed to fulfill the hospital's spiritual component as part of its marketing plan. Shit. She reads Bible verses over the loud speaker. That's not a spiritual component. That's Big Brother. I have concerns for those patients who don't want that assault on their lives. They've even installed wooden crosses on patient room walls."

"That's part of the hospital's marketing plan?"

"At least they didn't post crucifixes with Jesus hanging from them. And that doesn't factor anything about Randy's womanizing with hospital employees—and all that shit that we've lived through with what he did to Bea."

"What do we as women do?"

"Go home and have a drink!" (Sniffles. Chuckles.)

"That's not possible. We can bond together."

"But look at what happens. Beth and Joanne are fighting court battles because of job discrimination and sexual harassment for over a year and they haven't gained any victories yet."

"I fired a man who worked for me. The V.P. entertained the man I fired. Do I get invited? What would I do even if I went to their party? I would have to talk with his wife and I don't even embroider."

"The system is hopeless. Where do we go?"

"Creative places like our full moon group."

"But what can we actually do? I know I have to address these injustices stacked up so high, write them down in my own words and confront the situation."

"Respond in an open and honest way?"

"How could I do that? I am prepared to justify my existence, protect Carolyn and her salary, and I need someone say, "No, Jan doesn't deserve what's happening to her.' But I know they'll say, 'If you don't like it, you can go somewhere else.' You suck cock and you eat shit and they make you feel that you deserve it."

"You're immobilized. There's no space to move. Can't talk and can't act."

(Sobs.) "If I don't get input and I don't act, they say, 'Why didn't you find out about it?'"

"How are you supposed to do that?"

"I find out things in different ways. I'm supposed to have access to administrative minutes and sit and read them in the board room, and I hate to sit down there because Randy might come in. I get nauseous just looking at him."

"Walk out when he walks in. Be pleasant and pass the time of day."

"I'm chicken. I don't want to be confronted. My only access is reading those damn minutes. Plus, I don't get any answers if I ask questions about the minutes, except from a secretary."

"One more way of getting accurate information you need."

"They aren't accurate, Nora. The controversial issues are sanitized."

"I'm interested in places you have to stay away from because of Randy, that he has that power scares me, Jan."

"I'm a fifty-two-year-old professional and I don't like feeling like a naughty, irresponsible child. That's what he does to me. Once I noticed that I'm taller than he is and I decided to stand more."

"Stand up more. Stand up every time you see him."

"Avoidance is the best thing. I don't want to be scared or put down, fired or miserable. Maybe feeling better at home, I can better cope with being miserable at work. I don't hear the employees' healthy humor now, Nora. Joking and joshing can release stress, but not now. It's not healthy just to bitch. That's despair. When you're sitting at a table with twenty people and somebody's bitching, that transmits despair to everyone. Yet we're in the same boat. I used to be able to buoy people up and I can't now. I'd be laughed out of the room."

"It's a lot different than five years ago."

"Oh, yah. In those days when we had frustrations and conflicts, we all pulled together, especially when we had the strike."

"That was a rough time."

"But, Nora, we got a single message from administration: 'We're all in this together.'"

"How is it different?"

"People are afraid. They need job security and health benefits, especially when their husbands or wives are unemployed. They may have taken on big mortgages in better times. And now there's more government regulations and pressure on hospitals. We have to deal with Randy King."

"Do you have access to files on Bea?"

"I don't know if I dare to find them or not. Remember, I suspect that Randy keeps his own files on us. And it's difficult now for me to ask Marge."

Carolyn in the employee *letter* on October 14, 1983
Lakeshore Med Wins Communications Awards

Lakeshore Med won two top awards at the annual meeting of the Hospital Public Relations Wisconsin (HPRW) on October 12.

Jan Anthony and Carolyn Schafer accepted the awards of excellence for Lakeshore Med cable television series *Lakeshore Med—For Your Health* and the collage display "Lakeshore Med is…" on display in Lakeshore Med lobby.

The TV series, now showing at 7 p.m. on Mondays and Wednesdays on TeleCable 4B, is created and produced by Jan, Laura Williams, Pat Holmen, Mark Bertini and many other Lakeshore Med employees, plus Lakeshore Bay medical and health care experts.

HPRW judges cited the program for its breadth and scope, saying "Particularly noteworthy is the fact that the program was able to harness hospital personnel with appropriate expertise to contribute to the various programs in the series. A first-rate effort throughout."

The collage display was created and produced by Carolyn, Jan, Rita Van Allan, Pat Holmen, Laura Williams, Robert Hanley and Tim Clinton, plus construction and finishing assistance from the Engineering and Paint departments.'

Visual display judges said of the collages, "You should be proud for tackling one of the most difficult challenges—explaining health care terms and technology to the public—which is certainly not an easy task. An ambitious, well-executed project."

HPRW sponsors this annual review to recognize outstanding performance in communications produced by Wisconsin hospitals. As one of the first award programs of its kind in the nation, the program is recognized for its quality and credibility among health care communicators.

Chapter 14

Jan and Nora on October 15, 1983

"Nora, I met the new St. Paul PR man at the HPRW conference. He seems to be an ineffective person. Maybe he only appears that way compared to our hospital PR gang."

"But he has a penis. That's what we're looking for these days."

"I actually applied for that job, and I guess I'm OK about not getting it. Carolyn and I both won top HPRW awards. Randy, surprisingly, allowed both of us to go. Bea drove to join us for the Thursday night awards dinner where our TV and open house projects won awards. We swam while others were at the bar. On the way home Bea told me, 'I liked being there with you, and I wasn't the least bit intimated about going there as your wife.' In the past she'd be defensive about going places with people who knew us at Lakeshore Med. And I was proud to be there with her. (Sighs.) Bea's getting better about seeming as a couple. I'm strong when we can stand together. 'Too bad if you if you don't like us. We're wonderful human beings and it's your problem if you reject us.' I think Bea now feels the same way and that's wonderful!" (Chokes.)

"What's that I hear in your voice, Jan? Is it tears? Being touched so deeply?"

"I'm near tears of joy. I've been waiting so long and finally—from the start, much of our trauma together was because I was a woman and she loved me. I got over that really fast. I don't know why or how, but once I made up my mind that I wasn't going to fight this love anymore, it didn't bother me like it bothered her. I've been afraid of what people may do to us. I was afraid of how nasty our neighbors could be when they found out they had lesbians living next door. But there were no problems over all the years. Or when you go to a new environment, there's always that edge of defensiveness and apprehension. You're under so much stress. It's an underlying concern all of the time. I'm getting more and more involved in Lakeshore Bay community projects. I'll say to myself, 'Who cares! If she's going to be my partner at an event, she's going to be my partner.' Yet there's so much potential for trauma surrounding us, and I can never tell if she's going to start drinking to overcome her homophobic feelings. But it's changing. We've lived through our kids being concerned. We're living through our battering by Lakeshore Med administration. All together, it seems that we don't have to deal with the trauma like we did."

"You're confronting homophobia in others and Bea has some of it inside herself as well."

"We know of women who've lived together twenty-five years. They've taught in the same school systems and nobody knows who lives and/or with whom. They're paranoid—and probably rightfully so. Having Bea with me at this HPRW was wonderful."

"A little hopeful crack in the wall?"

"The homophobia doesn't have to be there all the time. Hopefully, we can be together and feel truly free. We mixed with new and old HPRW friends, yet we stayed out of the drinking and partying after. I had a bit to drink in celebration of our awards. Bea had a gin and tonic. What a good time, and liquor wasn't a problem."

"Homophobia and liquor don't mix well."

"Last Sunday we went to the Holly Near and Ronnie Gilbert concert at Chicago's Auditorium Theater. We drove with Carolyn and her son Ben and we met Carolyn's daughter and our friend Jane and five lesbians. We ate at a French restaurant, La Bastille, and had a grand time.

"That's quite a few lesbians. Did you have any problems?"

"The waitress took good care of us. We left hefty tips. A glass of wine was $10, and the food, though expensive, was memorable. Each of us ordered something different and we fed each other, tasted each other's food. What fun to be playful and feel free. The concert included an older woman, Ronnie Gilbert, one of the Weavers. And Holly Near. Ah! What a role model. When she introduced "We Are a Gentle, Angry People," she said one of the verses sings out for being gay and lesbian. She asked that the audience join in to sing that stanza too, even if they're straight. It may the first and only time that lesbian and gay men may be able to say and sing those words out loud without being singled out, and the words affirm their being. 'And we're singing, singing for our lives.' Wow! When we sang that verse, I started to cry and I put my head on Bea's shoulder with our arms around each other as we choked through the rest of the song. Our first lesbian concert with Holly Near in Milwaukee was liberating too. And when she performed for us in Michigan at the Festival's Night Stage, she walk out on one number on a long platform into the cheering audience of at least 5000 women belted out—I don't remember the song, and held her arm up and toward the storm clouds that started rumbling over us, daring us to be gutsy and brave. Wow! What positive memories! What powerful images that make me strong."

"You've experienced a great deal."

"Last night I asked Bea if my coming to see you is helping the both of us. She said yes. I asked how? She answered, 'I'll tell you sometime,' and added that she was reading my horoscope and it said not to talk of family matters now."

"She's feeling much better? Good!"

"We go out and can buy a couple of drinks, have fun and socialize, but drink isn't the main reason and it doesn't take over. On the way home from HPRW, Bea and I drove north to see the geese fly in at the Horicon Marsh. We got there before sunset. In the bar and restaurant where we waited at a vast window overlooking the horizon, we had two beers, felt really close and had fun talking. 'Gee,' she said, 'a person could actually hang one on waiting for those birds.' We can even joke about it. I'm so relieved that we don't have to go through the grief that we went through in order to straighten out our alcohol and relationship ordeals. That is a ton of shit off me, considering how scary everything was this year.

"I'm delighted for her and I admire her strength."

"Isn't that something, Nora?"

"Yes."

"She's a wonderful, wonderful person."

"I understand her depression problems. Immediately after the cessation of alcohol, there's a physiological period that's extremely difficult. But she's survived."

"Now that woman is determined. When there's something she wants—"

"And to be able to joke about it."

"We were watching an HBO movie where Peter O'Toole acted so drunk in one scene, he was strapped onto his trunk being wheeled to his room. I remembered that most devastating night on Lakeshore Med's Las Vegas trip, and somehow I knew to stop looking for her and return to our room. I found her stretched out on her back, completely passed out. Someone dumped her there. I was afraid she was dead! She could have been dead because she could have vomited and suffocated. It's such a devastating memory. Later she told me security guards picked her up, put her on a luggage cart and pushed it to her room. And, of course, the scene in the movie may have been funny to most, but it wasn't funny to us. I don't know how she felt because she didn't say anything. And I didn't ask."

"That was wise, Jan, not to remind her of that humiliation."

"Now to have the future look so bright after all that. It's so much better now."

"I don't know anything more devastating, Jan, than alcohol is to the person whose system isn't able to handle it."

"Bea's very proud and I'm sure it hurts to have those memories. It could be part of the motivation to never to do that again. And Nora, we're so close after all these years. After a while you reach a tolerance level, yet we're getting closer all the time. Sometimes I want to celebrate wherever I am, but I hold back because I don't want people to think that the lives we've survived were so messed up. For example, woman has plastic surgery and someone says, 'You're so pretty' as if she wasn't a beautiful human being before."

"Both of you are aware that alcohol really makes a great difference. Every bit of research now in genetics, biochemical makeup, certain psychological factors contribute, but not everybody has similar psychological factors and responds to alcohol the same way. My strong belief is that there should never be any judgment that so often creates a vicious circle: I need something to relieve that pain. I know best what relieves that pain; and it's alcohol. So much for judgment. The more we know about this, the less willing we are to turn our backs on it and the easier it becomes to confront it. I cannot guess how difficult that is for Bea. I'm amazed. She's a strong woman."

"(Sobs.) "Stubborn, too. Cause when she makes up her mind—"

"It serves her well. I don't mean to lecture—"

"I feel so helpless, Nora. What was condemning us intellectually and emotionally was scary and only recently is the whole genetic thing being analyzed."

"And biochemical. You were at the point when you came in here where you had to make a decision that 'I'm not going to go back. I can't!'"

"That screaming passage I made down Chicory Road."

"That was the last straw. You looked so sad."

"But I'm stronger now. Now I'm seeing a time coming quickly—Appraisal."

"Coming up."

"Tactics—of response. (Long pause.) Nora, I need some money first. I've got to do something for myself at work this week. One—read the Administrative reports. A bunch of bull shit. A loose-leaf folder full of bull shit. Two—I went to Personnel and asked Marge to show me the last time I had a raise. I also saw my file. Going to the Personnel office is something I want to avoid. Randy's evaluation was not in my Personnel file. It's in his office. His file on me must be so thick—like an attorney gathering evidence every time his authority is challenged. And I have a huge file in my own office. (Pause.) You know, Marge is short, too. I remember looking at Randy to discover how short he is. I've been looking at people from different perspectives, basically physical perceptions. I look at you, Nora, and I've never thought of you as being short."

"Neither do I."

"The last two weeks I'm just a lackey. Coping with this ever-present battle within me of how to deal with or to compensate for problems so they can't wear me down any more. My personal life isn't going to fall apart now. And I'm not afraid anymore. That's a big relief."

Jan on October 18, 1983

Dear Matt,

We've rented the building's basement to the upholstery guys for $125 a month and they'll enter the basement door. That should cover expenses for taxes, insurance and utilities that the building will accumulate until an alternative comes along.

I've also found a new tenant for the upstairs flat on North Main Street so we'll have to adapt to that with some extra work and change. She is a dog trainer, a show-dog person, and owns a prize Doberman named Damien, of all breeds to be in that little apartment. When we started renovating Grandpa's house, we said no kids and no dogs. Now we have kids downstairs and Damien upstairs.

I have to find better tenants on 13th Street; tenants I don't have to take to small claims court to force them to pay the rent. I'm going to put that investment mistake I made back on the market.

Bea's taking an extensive tax course and enjoying the challenge. Her knowledge will certainly come in handy for us and I'm sure they will hire her. It will also look good on her résumé. She has been accepted as a substitute teacher at Prairie School but hasn't had any calls yet. Lakeshore Bay's school sub list is so long she hasn't even applied.

Meanwhile, our lives together are getting even better. It doesn't seem possible to have our relationship continue to grow, but we've been through so much. There always have been many underlying currents of 'shoulds and oughts' and real mental pain for us. When we break out of this stress at home, at the bookstore, at Lakeshore Med, and stop drinking heavily at home, we will start new projects and make new people connections with confidence that we're not going to be blasted by others. Each day gets better.

I'm rambling about life without editing because it's all so positive that I don't feel the need to be on guard.

Our published book is still doing well. Bea processes about $300 in orders each month. We're also thinking about expanding our line of books.

Our garden continues to give me great pleasure as well as produce that keeps me cooking.

Let me know what you're doing and how you are.

Happy Halloween!

Mom

Bea on October 22, 1983

We enjoyed our first full moon Samhain Halloween celebration last night. What a witchy party we had with Betty and me in black robes and pointed hats, Joanne with her witch's black outfit cascading with rolled and ribboned diplomas to signify her as an educated witch now that she's completing her degree as a therapist. Jan was more colorful as a rainbow witch. Carolyn came as a bag lady, something she fears she will be, she said, and needs to face that option head on. Beth came with a full-blown sense of humor and mischief and wore one of several of our extra witchy hats. Robin brought her young friend Naomi with her young face flushed from nervous laughter. What did she think we would do? Lure her to bite out of a poisoned apple or dance skyclad around a fire ring?

Our thoughtfully quiet Halloween ritual around the little altar on our living room rug empowered us to be liberated even when we become fearsome old hags and witches who dare to challenge patriarchy. Then we gobbled up Bea's pumpkin soup to cackle, drink and chatter until 2 a.m.

Jan and Nora on October 22, 1983

"Nora, dear. I'm sorry you missed our full moon ritual last night. Bea read from Z Budapest's 'Hallowmass and the Time of Hecate,' the sacred hag who returns to her sisters to give wisdom of the ages, to protect, to revenge."

"I like that idea, but did it get too serious? I could see how we could take out some revenge on our enemies."

"It's more like our realizing that we can ask the wise Crone Goddess to remove those who are troublesome from our paths."

"I wonder what 'remove' could mean."

"We're not into serious hexing, more like finding support and safety together."

"Hmm. Jan, do you remember that I've asked us to be sure we don't talk over our time this morning. I have a new client coming in after our session and I don't want to keep her waiting."

"Yes, I remember, and this gives me the chance to thank you for giving me extra time because I know how I've talked longer than I'm supposed to."

"That's no problem, Jan, because it's Saturday morning, and I usually have my tighter schedule on weeknights after other people's working hours—and my working hours too. (Sighs.) How's your Lakeshore Med support system doing?"

"One of the Tradition of Caring committee women told me that things are so bad now, you might as well make the best of what you can. She shut our office door while we were talking, but she trusts Carolyn and me. If my overall attitude is bad, why would she and others trust me?"

"You have an important job to do, Jan. You've demonstrated that you can and want to do it. You have proven that consistently over a number of years."

"Otherwise I'm criticized—and that's harassment."

"You need clarity."

"I know in my heart that when Carolyn and I disagree on a project, I don't attack her personhood. Yet when I ask Randy about budgets and goals, he says he doesn't have time for me, after he wastes our time calling me stupid and tacky over a minor point. (Pause to grab a pillow and twist. Ugh!) I may have to hang in at the hospital for another ten years to get any retirement or to have him move on to another job—but that sounds like a life sentence. Still, I can continue to my job and enjoy working with my team. I can survive."

"Can you?"

"I would be smarter."

"How?"

"I wouldn't let myself be scolded. I'd be proactive rather than reactive."

"You're giving up?"

"I'm being tolerated! I lived with Alex for twenty-five years of being tolerated!"

"So we know you can do it."

"A hanger-in-there, that's what I am. I could work it out. But then my heart, my insides, will have to tell me that's what I'll have to do."

"Pay the price. Compromise and accommodation, Jan. Those are not bad. They're skills."

"I would like to turn off the voice that's inside of me telling me that I should take on all of these battles and solve them. I'm not responsible for people's low morale. I'm not responsible for administration's malfunctions; and yet I want to make it better and turn off that consistent, droning voice in my head about what's depressing at work. I hear those noises in my sleep. It would be so wonderful if Randy would go away."

"But that doesn't mean they can't hire another browbeater."

"I fantasize putting a bomb in his desk—and I'm not a violent person. But I heard that thought in my mind. I once had thoughts about Alex's dying."

"What? How did you work it out with Alex."

"I left him. I'm in the same situation."

"If you'd change the way you handled it with Alex, how would you do it? What demands would you have made?"

"Equal rights as a human being. And I would have wanted him have fun and to stop being so heavy, always wanting to 'work on our relationship.'"

"You can't change Alex and you can't change Randy."

"My management style—my joy of life—everything is different from theirs. They must have changed or I wouldn't have had anything to do with either of them in the first place. And I don't have their win-or-be-a-loser ego. I don't pretend to know all the answers."

Chapter 15

Bea on October 31, 1983

We met Tony Logan and our UU gang at church to ride to Milwaukee's vintage Oriental Theater to see *The Rocky Horror Picture Show* at its best night, Halloween at midnight!

When Robin's husband pulled up in his van, he told us Robin had decided to stay home. Rita Van Allan and her Tim were prepared to compete in the costume contest wearing the Adam and Eve outfits she created. Kim as Eve wore long underwear with grapes and cherries on her boobies and pubic area with a huge snake wrapped around her, holding an apple, of course. She was matched by Tim as Adam wearing another long underwear outfit looking quite naked with a formidable jersey penis and testicles embellished at its base with grapes for pubic hair. Tim also wore Groucho glasses and moustache. Until it was time to buy tickets for the every-Saturday-night midnight movie classic, we chose to patronize the German tavern across the street from the Oriental, and a wave of shocked chatter rippled across the tavern until the surprised patrons realized our nude refugees from the Garden of Eden were indeed fully clothed and it was Halloween and almost time for *The Rocky Horror Picture Show*.

Tony told us to buy or bring popcorn and spray water bottles and other props to use during the movie. We didn't know what we were getting into, but we loved joining the fun with our gang of our four gay guys, one straight couple and Robin's husband, the van driver navigating us to the weird Transylvanian world of the longest-running, 1975 ultra-campy midnight cult movie. Tony and others recited the script word-for-word and song-for-song. They danced in the aisles, sprayed when it rained, threw popcorn on cue and performed other strange routines in sync with the gender-bending fantasy. Of course, Jan and I never knew what was to come next—and that included the entire evening's activities.

The best costumes were chosen during intermission and most of them duplicated the outfits worn by Susan Sarandon, transexually-garbed Tim Conway and other weirdoes in the movie plus movie patrons in Halloween get-ups. We cheered as they lined up on the stage. But when our Jill and Tim finally made their way through the audience and up the stairs on the side of the stage, the audience roared as Adam and Eve emerged into the spotlights holding hands and embracing. They won the prize, a gift certificate to an adult sex shop for edible underwear and other toys.

We made it home at 3:30, laughing all the way.

Of course we slept late until we got a call from Robin that she and Naomi had to come over right away. Now we know why Robin didn't come the movie with us last night. She had Naomi over to her house and when Dave came home in the wee hours of the morning after dropping all of us off at church, he found the two of them drinking coffee, all rosy and warm. When he said goodnight and headed for bed, he discovered that the sheets and pillows were also warm on this chilly October pre-dawn morning. And the aromas were overflowing with sweat and estrogen.

By the time he came down to confront the two of them Naomi had slipped out the door and Robin confessed what her husband had suspected. That's why they had to find a safe haven, our house, to meet again. Holy Cow! He could have come home a few minutes earlier and found them in bed together. Didn't the two of them have any sense of time?

After they shared their dilemma with us, we cleared out of the family room and got busy elsewhere in the house so they could talk. Hell! They weren't talking. We could tell by how quiet it was down there and by the sheepish rosy looks they gave us when they finally left. They didn't think we would judge them. We know how they feel, except that Robin has young kids and is a decade older than her lover who hasn't even graduated from college. And, of course, now that Robin has been outted, what about closeted Naomi with her large Catholic family? Who knows what Robin will do?

In the midst of this all, my Jill came by to borrow our witch hats. Ha! Everyone knows where to find those.

Chapter 16

Jan and Nora on November 5, 1983

"We're getting properties ready for winter, Nora, especially on 13th Street where I've paint three sets of outside stairs and did my circus high-wire act balancing tools, sealant, tar paper rolls and ladders to keep the outside gutter system from rotting away. And for comparison, I've organized administrators' talks with our admitting physicians, new and old.

"How can you produce so much?"

"By working long hours—and being fair, I guess. A little humanity produces so much, unlike my boss. Beth Johnson told me that she and Randy are both on college alumni committees. She said he makes everyone feel depreciated and he picks away at minor details so nothing gets done. 'It's counter productive—and pitiful,' she told me with a sympathetic snicker."

"Anything but to solve the real issues by frustrating so many desperate people."

"Well, Nora, I'm not desperate anymore and I've come to the decision that I'm becoming immune to this toxicity. After the last five years of being surrounded by it, I'm completely re-conditioned, just like having my allergy shots. Although I may have a relapse every so often, I've risen absolutely above it all. It finally clicked: a lot has to do with not feeling responsible to offset their gross management errors."

"Good! I like the idea of allergy shots."

"I was watching PBS and 'The Seasons of Man'—and in spite of the gender title, I watched this guy—a motivational speaker like Leo Buscaglia but with a charismatic Southern accent. He talked about guilt. Bea almost makes me feel guilty because I don't feel guilty. I may have been embarrassed about some things I've done, but it's not guilt. This speaker used the word 'toxic.' Finally, the concept hit me. I realized I'm getting immune."

"You've risen above it."

"The whole concept crystallized for me. Now I'm even singing when I'm hopping up the steps in the hospital stairwells."

"Wow! That's marvelous to say this place is full of toxicity and then be singing in the stairwells."

"I don't have to get sucked into the toxicity caused by three men—while watching others suffer. I'm the longest sufferer, five years with current power struggle, and I'm still there. I could have come home frustrated and thrown the salad bowl in the air again, but I haven't. I'm now more of a witness than a victim—and I'm not going to be a victim. A recent meeting that included Randy's clone Chuck focused on my media draft about not raising hospital rates in January. Randy didn't abuse me verbally. His attitude could have, but I didn't get sucked in. He questioned my heading. OK! Change it. I didn't say it but I thought, 'Now it tells half the story, but if that's what you want.' Randy and Chuck scratched around on the pages. Randy made a copy for Chuck but not for me and gave me verbal commands. I'm supposed to write down all his changes, do all this mental work, analyze it, and defend myself at the same time. When Chuck got up to leave, I asked him for a copy of 'what you and Randy have worked on.' I caught Chuck off guard. 'Don't you have one?' he asked. They'd been editing for half an hour before I came and I'm supposed to come up with answers to please them in a few minutes."

"How would you advise someone in your position, Jan?"

"It's taken me five years to come to this point—not to feel responsible."

"It's out of your hands."

"This could have worn me down, Nora, and hurt me badly. But I'm not going to play that game, I didn't let Randy jump on me, and I left when Chuck left."

"You took better care of yourself."

"I think I'll bring my tape recorder to his office next time."

"Won't that be intimating to him?"

"Yes, and won't that be wonderful?"

"In my experience, Jan, every thing is revenue. 'I'll punch it out on my calculator—and the calculator is like a metaphor, as in 'A little equipment problem?' (Humph.) I'm going to get a bigger one.' Oh, if this is how we're going to do business, I'll bring in my machine too."

"I want to be sure I can get accurate information—on tape. I use it when I interview people. It's a tool in my trade. I'll set that baby right on his desk."

"Attach a big mike in front of him, Jan."

"I take notes. That gives me half the info I need. I was afraid to ask questions to fill in the blanks. He actually accused me, demanding, 'Why don't you know this?'"

"Sounds brutal."

As Bea says, 'Anyone who wears two pairs of socks has to be insecure.'"

"Anxiety?"

"Yup. Two pairs of socks and long underwear. I know that from when we shared our office when he was a student. And we were in a TA workshop together. (Quiet.) He does wear long johns, but he's so skinny you wouldn't notice it."

"I don't see how he has any friends unless he's different at home."

His latest girlfriend is a Lakeshore Med nurse, a beauty queen. He's thirty-two and has been through lots of women. Years ago he told me stories about relationships with women and having to have a woman almost every night. I suppose it's to prove to everyone that he's not gay."

(Quiet.) "Jan. He's in his thirties. That may be it!"

"I'll punch him! He used to dump his troubles on me about his relationships, frustrations about relatives, pretty nurses, being a sex symbol, not having a true relationship. Pawns. Pawns. Pawns. Using us. The Superstud!"

"Could we dare imagine he's gay?"

"I haven't heard anyone say that. Well, maybe one or two, but people don't suspect that because he always picks sexy girls to date, but when was he on break from college and spent summers working in my office, he seemed concerned about so many gay people in his dorm. I remember stuff like that because I was going through my initial anxiety about my sexuality."

"His sexuality is a big area for him."

"And then he fires Bea because we live in the same house—a supervisor and a subordinate cannot live in the same house—and then, I heard that he has Chuck, an immediate subordinate, move into his apartment. Talk about double standard. Flaunting! How could he fire someone as valuable as Bea because we were living together and then have the nerve to take his immediate subordinate into his apartment. And why was he allowed to do so! I could punch him I'm so angry!"

"That seems more than justified, Jan."

"And now Bea and I are achieving remarkable stability at home and having fun. Last Friday after folk dancing, we went to The Gallery someone had told us about. We were in the midst of hundreds of twenty-year-olds, and a cop asked us for our IDs. We laughed and said thanks. We had one beer and then I saw an opening to escape the young crowd. We went to the bar where Jenny's friend works and found Jenny sitting next to two empty chairs. She's been working through some issues. Usually I've always stayed away from where she hangs out so we won't embarrass her."

"I don't think you'd embarrass her, Jan."

"I'm not too sure of that. Her girlfriend, the bartender, made us a Blood Clot, a first for us. So here's Mother and Daughter together drinking at a bar. That's unusual for us. Bea and I usually drink at home. But now we don't have to drink everyday. Bea's set a new standard on that. If I want a glass of wine and she doesn't, no problem; I'm not going to lead her astray. Each is responsible to make our own decisions to cut back."

"You're sure about that?"

"Nora, you should see all the weekend carpenter work and hard labor we do. You gotta have a beer when you're doing a hot and sweaty man's job. It's not a problem. It's a celebration."

"Rigid rules are dangerous, Jan. Saying 'Never' has done people in who think that they'll never have another drink or be sociable; that if they do, they'll go straight down the path to destruction. You have more control than that. However, when there's a great amount, it's time to get scared."

"We've had our scares. This morning Bea said, 'On December 27, we're going to have had this tumultuous, exciting, tremendous relationship for ten years.' We date our relationship three different times. A lot of the tumult has been around booze and other issues: PMS, leaving children, depression, job security and more, and I don't see those as the horrible Boogie Man anymore. Our lives together look so bright and promising, so positive, even with our ups and downs."

"That's quite a history—ten years."

"And I've only been divorced for five years. Talk about tension and stress and being strung out like a strand of a spider's web—and it's worth it all."

"That's wonderful to hear you say that."

"I could feel secure about feeling immune. My history is that once I've made a commitment, as strong as I feel now—and just as I made a commitment to Bea ten years ago—I won't be sliding back into something negative. I feel competent that I can make it work."

"You sound strong when you say it. You've reviewed it and made a decision."

"I'll stay with Bea, but I'll try for a better work situation wherever I can find one that fits me and my values. I'm taking off next week and will send out more résumés. Mr. Young has written a letter so at least I have some credibility of my past professional life before his retirement."

"It's interesting that Mr. Young writes your reference letter rather than your current boss."

"How do you ask your current boss and keep your job search a secret? If opportunity comes up for a better job, I'll take it. Bea and I are selling North Main Street. The family we rented it to wants to buy it. We'll invest that to help me have financial options that are not tied up in real estate. If something happens at work, I'll try not to have money concerns frustrate me. And we're not drinking so much. We're not making decisions based on that craziness. Still, the decisions that we made not to sell earlier are helping us now. And Bea is gaining new expertise with taxes. We're a good team again."

"That's a lot different from feeling like you did in August."

"I can laugh now and can help Carolyn laugh—and other people too. A lot is falling into place, Nora. What I needed and wanted was to add wisdom in handling my issues. I've identified them and enjoy working to make them better."

"Are only women suffering at work?"

"I don't know much about the men. They're less verbal. One great guy, Barry, we go to him. We can talk with him. He's honest. He's hurting. If he makes a mistake, he'll accept it. I'm sure he's suffering too."

"It's good to have at least one man who understands. You have a lot of information on Randy. Can you see how much safer it will be for him without you there? His fear? 'She knows about me and can she see through it all.'"

"But I'm not having a heart-to-heart chat with him!"

"His irrational behaviors and fears and unhappiness. When you're like that you have to be careful to do people in before they do you in. It's critical for most males to be in that position."

"Well, I refuse to feel sorry for him."

"You're not going to adopt him? And I thought you were a humanist, Jan."

"I refuse."

"I'm so disillusioned."

"Hell! I'll throw rocks at him."

"One of our highly respected women administrators heard me say that going to see Randy King is like being sent to the principal's office. She turned to me and said, 'That's the truth.' Even she gets that treatment. She's doing a great job and yet she can't wait to retire. And Randy at a party, big or small, as soon as he can, he starts playing the piano and all circle around him to sing his songs. The image of him, all of these women, including Marge, is like he's a rock star with his groupies. He plays piano and takes control of the whole situation."

"Beats socializing or having to deal intimately with people—another way of having power over others. He doesn't have to talk to people, to be intimate and he has control of both."

"Well, Randy played Bea's little electronic piano at her apartment until it was so late that I had to go home and leave her alone with him the night she let him screw her."

"His regard for women is pathological. I'm glad you can take care of yourself, Jan."

"I'm going to do it! I'm not going to put up with what I did before. If I get fired, I get fired. I'm not going to be a victim anymore. And what are we going to do about us now, Nora? Are we going to keep on going?"

"Whatever you want, Jan. My presence here is for you and you can choose whatever you like."

"But here's for comparison, Nora, my high-style extra high-finance Business & Professional Association reception that I'm chairing is moving along with some top-flight help from several corporate committee members. It's a big deal and we've invited area media, CEOs, politicians, festival sponsors, volunteer organization reps, every big shot from across the city and the county to meet the new Convention and Visitors Bureau director. It could be the biggest turnout of Lakeshore Bay County leaders since my mother and the Women's Trade Union League hosted a 'Bury the Hatchet' event between local industrialists and labor leaders that helped start the Lakeshore Bay 4th of July Goodwill celebrations in the 1930s. So far, I've earned many affirming responses from Association members, and I feel good about the excellent networking I've earned."

"Is this outside your hospital job?"

"Well, sort of. I'm doing it on hospital time after I volunteered myself to be a member and do positive PR for Lakeshore Med. I didn't ask for permission. Just reported it in one of my weekly reports that never gets read."

"Is that how it works!"

"Months ago, I'd taken on another project for the Association's PR committee made up mostly of men with big PR staffs and budgets. The call went out for someone to produce a magazine touting the benefits of living and working in Lakeshore Bay. No one wanted the job nor volunteered and when the luncheon meeting ended and they went back to work, the director, his associate and I remained at the board table looking at each other. I told them that if they wanted me to head the project, I'd do it. My ego that this lesbian leading this community effort over-shadowed my other responsibilities. Good networking too."

"You're devious, Jan. They know you are a lesbian?"

"I guarantee that with Mother Courage Bookstore and my editorial commentaries in the paper? Carolyn helped me start brain-storming sessions with the Association's PR Committee's free lunch I arranged at the hospital on what is unique about Lakeshore Bay. We settled on a slogan, 'Bravo Lakeshore Bay!' But then a new Lakeshore Bay Visitors and Convention Bureau program director would be named soon, our committee concentrated on fundraising and planning a reception for the new executive and for a rare concept—to spend money to promote Lakeshore Bay as a recreation and convention site and welcome the new director at our prestigious new Sheraton Hotel. A Jefferson Medical PR executive volunteered his art department to come up with a logo. That's a big help. We want to do this up first class."

"Of course you do?"

"I'm truly grateful about coming here and I don't want to give it up."

"You'll know when to give up coming here. It's been pretty hairy. I feel close to you as a friend and I care for you. It's easy to do that."

"If it's healthful, let's keep it up. It's not like going to the dentist where he fixes your toothache, you feel better and you leave."

"No. It's not like that at all, Jan. I'll make your next appointment in two weeks."

Chapter 17

Bea on November 14, 1983

It's Jan's birthday today but it seems as if we've been celebrating all week. Jenny came for supper and I gave them both terrific Tarot card readings to go along with other good news.

I have a job with H&R Block and we've agreed to sell North Main Street to our young couple. Yeah! We've been keeping our fingers crossed, plus I've been buying new dress-for-success outfits for good luck on my new job. I guess we're witches after all—good witches.

On Friday, Jan and I started our weekend attending Milwaukee's annual Woman-to-Woman conference. Each of us went to different workshops at first. After last year's conference, Jan wrote on her evaluation that if this is a real woman-to-woman conference, why is there an obvious and significant lack of lesbian workshops. This year the committee scheduled a couple and Jan went to support the few who were courageous enough to speak and to attend those sessions. I went to writing and business-oriented sessions.

My tax class was on Saturday so Jan went to Milwaukee alone. I joined her again on Sunday when we both took the inspiring double session on goal setting with a dynamic Patricia Durovny who told us how to use her LOG: Life Organization Game ring binder to inspire, energize, organize and reach the goals we've set. She was selling seven-by-nine inch leather-bound binders, but I resisted my lust for leather and will follow her format to create our own. The beginning pages will be collages we create to visualize our strengths, dreams and goals, and she had us write Shakti Gawain's mantra for us to use if we choose: "This, or something better, now manifests for me in totally satisfying and harmonious ways for the highest good of all concerned." She inspired three hundred women eager to live by those words.

But even more important for the two of us was to celebrate Jan's birthday at the Polaris Room that rotates on top of the Hyatt House overlooking Milwaukee. We had two drinks and talked for two hours in an aura of energy by healing the past and visualizing a successful future together. I will never forget our intimate and intense conversation as we circled the city from dusk into a starry night sky.

Jan had made reservations for us at The English Room of the Pfister Hotel where we had to wait for over an hour but we talked even more about our dreams and goals before enjoying dinner in the classiest restaurant we've been to in our area.

What a great weekend we shared.

Jan and Nora on November 19, 1983

"I've gained new power. I don't know where to begin. Everything is falling into place and I feel great! (Big sighs.) The Woman-to-Woman conference was outstanding. The positive energy from my various sessions was synergistic! Vibrating! Awesome! Bea hesitated about going, saying there was nothing new for her. I told her that I'm going all three days and she can come along if she wants. We went together to Sunday's last session, a culmination of genuine, positive energy for us. I was so desperate in September when I needed help from you, and now I feel that all is working out so beautifully."

"What happened, Jan? I'll have to try that on others."

"The peak of the entire weekend was our being at the Hyatt House and our conversation while circling around on top of our universe. We were to go to the English Room for my birthday supper, but it was too early so we went to the Hyatt and talked so intently that when the waitress would come, I was sure she could feel the energy aura around us. Bea and I seemed to draw closer and closer toward positive goals together. What totally incredible energy!"

"You can't prescribe that for everyone."

"And Nora, Bea told me for the first time—she revealed that she had listened to these tapes every Monday and had processed the whole thing."

"What a delightful disclosure."

"When I asked her how she felt, she answered, 'First I was angry and incredibly hurt and felt that your perceptions are all wrong. They're not real. And in the analyzing, I looked at it from your point of view. I'd been looking at me in my mirror and you were viewing you in yours.' (Pause. Sigh.) She told me that my perceptions are my perceptions and they can't be wrong if that's how I perceive them. 'Yet I can be sensitive about your perception of reality. You're entitled to the validity of it, and I certainly have different recollections of many incidents. But I'm not going to plead my case. I know that often I block it out when it's counter-productive to protect the fairy tale.'"

"How insightful she is, Jan."

"Then she asked herself if that was the way she wanted to be perceived? No! She said she could visualize my sitting next to her every night."

"Devotion."

"Nora, she said it was as if I were sitting next to the bed of a sick person and— 'You stayed there,' she said, '—and I'm sorry it took me so long.' (Groan.) Then she knocked on the huge windows circling next to our table, the windows that overlook the city. 'Rather than mirrors, I'd rather see our world through the clear window glass looking out to our future.' She doesn't offer apologies often and then this image of hers was so beautifully spoken, perceptive and positive."

"I've got goose bumps, Jan."

"She didn't say she was sorry for being a weak person or having problems. She didn't excuse herself for having emotional or drinking problems or being sick. Yet this was a heartfelt apology, something for me that truly makes a difference."

"I hear a strong statement of appreciation."

"I floated in an aura above the city. I'll never forget this awesome experience. And, Nora, she complemented me on the creativity of taping our sessions. She said as a person in her situation, coming here would put her on the defensive. This way she had the option of participating or not. It gave her an option of how to respond."

"That's amazing."

"And I didn't know if she was listening to the tapes. I didn't ask and I didn't care. I needed your help so much."

"And she listened to them all."

"She said she might want to talk to us sometime and give her impressions of what happened."

"I'd welcome that—anytime."

"And we've become the most amazingly resourceful people. And it's my birthday! We've had a whole week of donating all our bookstore books, almost $2,000 worth to our church, the Women's Bureau and more. There's nothing left for sale. And after her interview with H&R Block, she got the job. The person who interviewed her said, 'I know what it takes for this job and you've got it. I've got others to interview, but as far as I'm concerned, you've got a job.' And we'll sell my father's house to our renting couple that asked to buy it—and we got what we asked for. What a relief from tons of pressure, and we now have some money for security or to invest in us. Everything's turning around."

"Are you sure that everything is getting better?"

"I'm charged with positive mental energy. One of the courses I took on Saturday was 'Your Heart Is in Your Mind: Visualization and Energy.' I was meant to find it. I first went to a session on dreams and then on 'Money, the Last Taboo.' Hah!

That's not correct. 'Lesbian' is the last taboo, but this session was on evaluating your financial expectations, creating energy, creating self and money issues. The speaker explained how we set up our own negative imprints and project them, and then we expect negative imprints to be fulfilled. It's what I've been doing for the last five years—letting myself open to being a victim and not reinforcing what's positive. I was open to the victim role and was blind to reinforce what was positive. Visualization. Realization. Our speaker was personally vulnerable when she spoke of details to illustrate her own evolution. My heart went out to her."

"You're such a wonderful mother."

"Right! Always! Ha! She had us meditate. The room was quiet. I was tired. I visualized Randy King standing up behind his desk to shake my hand. I'm standing. The whole vision turned blue, a comfortable sky blue light lit up the room."

"Jan. Think of that often and see that."

"I will. I'll work on that! What's positive will gain control. I'm not going to be a victim. Instead of thinking that I'm going to the principal's office, my voice will say, 'I am wisdom. I am intelligence. I am PR. I am communication.' I was projecting, 'What's he going to criticize me for now? What did I do wrong?' Hell, I'm setting myself up to get shot down. And that's not going to work anymore. I feel so great. I feel like I can take all those other people who have been victimized and turn it around and make them feel better, too. I'm working on those goals. It's awesome!"

"What a delightful fantasy around Randy—and how you are going to project yourself to achieve that result?"

"I knew it all along. The best I can do. I was so tired and have experienced devastating events, one way or another. I can stand up and walk out, and in the process of my nurturing, life can be so fulfilling."

"How many fronts can you wage, Jan? Focus on this work thing now."

"—And on our relationship. The whole thing—together. We haven't stopped. It's growing."

"Sounds rich. There's a lot of talent and creativity together."

"It's taken a (Pause. Breathes.) long time and that's all right because we've been through so much for so long."

"I remember what you said, Jan. 'This relationship is so important to me. I'm not leaving this. I'll study it and see what I have to do.'"

"And then in June when I thought horrible things were happening between and to us. Alcohol, insecurity between us, desperate needs, and to have this all turn around! It's because I could communicate with you, Nora, and you helped me keep focused."

"Give some credit to yourself. There's no difficulty with drinking? You can comfortably have drinks when you want?"

"Absolutely, Nora."

"Getting on top of things is wonderful."

"Having others make decisions for you is frustrating. Deciding for yourself is the key."

"I believe in that, Jan. Dictations are damaging: how you must behave and must be; never do this or that; here's your type and these are your rules. That's the nasty part that goes with any kind of labeling."

"This whole lesbian burden adds a distorted dimension when you have to survive in this homophobic world. But we're congratulating ourselves on our decisions to have been smart enough to know and brave enough to take it on. And Bea said she going to Lakeshore Med Christmas party with me."

"Great. Are you pleased?"

"We're going to say, 'Here we are. We're victorious.'"

"You're going to scare some people."

"Other women come as couples and we might scare them as well. And that means that Bea's not going to be a Lakeshore Med victim anymore either."

"My fantasy is of your being there together. It feels so good."

"And her being there isn't going to hurt me either. I'm proud of us." (Quiet.)

"I was impressed, Jan, with the information you've provided me about people struggling with their sexuality. I thought a great deal—about your boss."

"I've known that—intuitively—but I never filled in the blanks."

"That's his job and I hope he gets done with it for the benefit of the rest of the people who are there."

"I'm more understanding of it and how to overcome my hang ups. I almost feel sorry for him, Nora—almost. I'm light years ahead of him."

"I imagine he's scared. You have not demonstrated any kind of fear about your sexuality. You're clear, comfortable and joyful."

"Yes."

"Your joyful relationship—now and in the future—looks very, very good."

"You can see the visualization tomorrow night when you come to moon group. We've worked a visualization of our future."

"How have you done that?"

"Oh, you'll see, Nora. I looked at our collages that we made during a past moon group. I forgot that I'd tucked them behind the sofa to get them out of the way. Last weekend I pulled them out and both of ours are visually negative. It was something I experienced and now it's behind me."

"I think that's marvelous. I remember it was fun to do, cutting and pasting images from old Life magazines. I'm excited for myself to do another and compare and applaud each other. I'd like to do mine over too. So grim. Broken legs. Ugh."

"It's going to take a long time to share everything that's happened. Pat Durovny is charismatic, fun and challenging.

Durovny spoke of the same books we've read like *Creative Visualization*, *Wishcraft*, *Mother Wit* and we had them at home sitting on our bookshelves."

"Lot of integration going on that was confirmed before but now it's being on top of everything—on top of Milwaukee, coming together."

"Like our house. It needs lots of work, a new furnace (Sigh) and closing Mother Courage Bookstore. Bea is free now. And we closed it together. At one of my workshops on the topic of being free from worry of money, we made a list of what we do for free. Making love is first on my list. And instead of shouting my anger, I'm singing—singing! And I haven't done that for a long time. Instead of finding a place to scream in anger or agony, I can sing. I'd almost forgotten how to sing."

"Energy is moving. So healthy. Such a wonderful alternative to screaming. And what are you singing these days?"

(Sings.) "'The Bells Are Ringing for Me and My Gal' and 'Everything's Coming up Roses.'"

"Just beautiful. And does Bea get to hear you sing?"

"Oh, yes. And what to do without money: making love and gardening and singing immediately popped into my mind. At the workshop when we were asked what we'd do with $100, I wrote that I'd give $100 to some woman's issue or throw a big party. Anyone can invite people to a party and they can bring a dish to pass. And then last week we gave all those books to the Woman's Resource Center, a grief support group, the Gay and Lesbian Union, Family Planning. We also gave $300 worth of books to Orphan Critters for their fundraising. We're to have simple goals. I'm able to do that. I'm erasing what's holding me down. It's not a loss. 'The bookstore is not a loss,' said Bea. 'It's a positive step.' Our published book is doing well. We're going to take on more subjects. We're going to invest in ourselves. Mother Courage is still alive. Bea's being positive and supportive. And I'm going to take time for my creative self for projects over and above Lakeshore Med."

"What are you going to write, Jan?"

"Hah! I'll write internationally famous and valuable pieces of literature that's going to unify all by sharing the deepest feelings and positive harmonies. I want to revolutionize the English language with neutral pronouns. It doesn't matter what gender you are. It's one-third written plus my *Feelings*, a book of poems, and "Your Days Are Numbered," a humorous piece. It will be small book that can be absorbed in a universal way like Herman Hesse's *Siddhartha*.

"Hum. You set high standards for yourself, Jan."

"I was taking a shower and I realized I have all these stories going on in my head, and why I haven't concentrated on them. It's because I haven't liked where I've been in my soul. If I'd written those stories, they would have been negative—and they're not going to be negative. Instead of being a victim, Nora, I am a warrior!"

"And those ideas have been germinating and now they're stronger. You've won again, Jan. I'm impressed. It's a constant theme in your life: solving problems and discovering good, positive energy. Then you take that piece of action that says, 'Now I'm going to share it with other people, and in doing so I'm going to make the environment around me more positive, delightfully creative.'"

"That's real. I've experienced that consistently but haven't identified it."

"As long as I've known you, your ability, almost the drive to do it is, 'First I'll find it and then I'll share it. I'm going to make this world a better place.' That's how I see you, Jan."

"I'm going to be focusing my goals. Pat Durovny said goals are streets on the Highway of Life, points of reference. All your goals fit to make your purpose come true and be the key element in your life. I created a purpose out of this: to increase in positive and compassionate understandings and then to share it. Life is to increase positive perceptions because everything I've done is coming together to do the right thing at the right time in the right place."

"You're a fully integrated human being at that time, Jan, a teacher or writer, and it all seems like it's on purpose."

"I'm happiest when I have a positive orientation and bring people along. When Bea was negative, when she was hurting so badly, it was painful, so painful—"

"But you have convictions and a history to support your convictions."

"I don't give up, Nora. I've had enough experience and I won't give up."

"I doubt it. And you're right to walk to Randy's office saying, 'I am wisdom.'"

"Carolyn called me at home this week with a big sigh. What's the problem? The School of Nursing called Randy about a problem. He said, 'Let the Communications Department take care of that,' and Carolyn complained that here we're stuck with more work again. 'Carolyn!' I blurted out, 'That's what we've wanted him to do all along. And we'll fix it.' It's working—and I'm not even at work."

"Forward! March! Damn the torpedoes!"

"If she or I make a mistake, it's no worse nor different than administrators making a mistake. It's going to work out and we'll all be all right. In addition we've had excellent press relations. St. Agnes is getting stepped on now. The reporter called and got to Nick, and she said she likes to work with us because we help her get the answers. Nick and I talked about it for a second when we passed in the hall. That makes me feel good. We have integrity."

"Yes, I would say that you do. Are you able to speak with Nick often?"

"No, but catching a comment from him is usually affirming or he wouldn't say anything. He passes reprimands to others to do that. And if a reporter said that to Randy, he'd fault me for being a reporter instead of a PR person. There's no other way to be. If something horrible is being hidden from the media, they'll find it from other sources. Randy wants a hack, like the Three-Mile Island person to cover up problems. I would like to tell Nick about my frustrations myself so he may understand, but Randy would fire me for sure."

"That's a job I couldn't live with, betraying the public to protect the government or a corporation when lives are in danger."

"Integrity is my most priceless possession, Nora, and I don't feel that I've compromised that. I won't get rich, but I act responsibly. I have strong convictions about that. (Pause. Sighs.) Bea and I each wrote our fantasy goals to reach by 1988. I wrote: one book published and making an impact in the world; checks coming in; financial independence; I'm still at Lakeshore Med and enjoy my positive leadership role. I don't think I'm going to solve problems there right away. (Pause. Sighs.) I love my hospital and—"

"That's clear, Jan."

"Bea and I made goals in thirteen areas and I started my LOG. I'm feel like I'm flying and it's fabulous having a whole week off to do this. I'm ready Monday to go back to work. I would have been a wreck processing all of this if I had to jump back to work right away. We took care of tons of reorganization."

"Lots of positive energy."

"And good health. (A sigh of relief. Pause.) I want to show you my LOG collage with 'to dos' for today—and my reinforcing graphic images like 'How to improve on a rainbow' and cartoons: one of two clams talking on the beach with one saying, 'I can't clam up. I've got a pearl in here the size of which you wouldn't believe!' Another has Ziggy standing before a collection of smiling people and a sign saying, 'Home for the Incurable Optimistic.' Another is from *The New Yorker* with one woman as Don Quixote with lance in hand and her short sidekick, like Carolyn, poised on two tired horses, me in armor holding a lance and staring in awe-filled determination at the windmill that I will try to conquer. Of course, I've images for material things—and travel too."

"And I'm so tickled to be a part of this, Jan. MyLOG's cover image has a monarch butterfly landing on a golden flower plus two Shakti Gawain's mantras. 'Every moment of your life is infinitely creative and the universe is endlessly bountiful. Put forth a clear enough request and everything your heart desires must come to you.' My favorite one is, 'This, or something better, now manifests for me in totally satisfying and harmonious ways for the highest good of all concerned' I will repeat that every day as often as needed, Nora."

"And I'm getting nice warm feelings from all of this."

"Don't forget our full moon gathering tomorrow night. It starts early at 5 p.m. so we'll eat supper first and then have our gratitude circle."

"And I'll bring steaks. I have collected several of them and they're waiting to be taken from my freezer, so fire up the grill, Jan."

Chapter 18

Bea on November 20, 1983

I broke my ankle today! I was running errands when I fell next to my parked car at the mall. I sat there, embarrassed, of course, until I realized there was no one around to see me, let alone help me, so I managed to pull myself in the car, set my foot with the broken ankle on the gas pedal, drove home, hopped in the house and called Jan. She came right home and rushed me to Lakeshore Med.

When we got there, a practice disaster drill alert blasted throughout the hospital so a nurse stuck me in a chair with my foot up on a stool in a corner of the ER for a couple hours while everyone was scurrying about with fake patients wearing ghastly fake wounds being triaged through the ER and sent to appropriate areas. Jan had to take photos, of course. But she checked up on me often until a kind nurse apologized, my bones set and my cast applied. It's heavy and I'm trying to get adjusted at home. It's a science to go up and down stairs, and it's painful. TV helps pass the time, but now Jan has to do most everything.

Bea on November 30, 1983

I'm getting organized and scoot around on a wheeled secretary's chair so I'm more useful. My ankle is still painful and my hip hurts, too. I'd only stepped on a stone and look what happened. I'm realizing I'm crabby. I guess my restrictions are dawning on me.

Jan on December 6, 1983

After my apprehension and lots of hard work by my committee and me, our "Bravo Lakeshore Bay!" reception turned out perfectly. Of course I was nervous first because I didn't know what to wear. I'm always in slacks and blazers at work, but I borrowed a long skirt from our closet collection and a new silky white blouse with ruffles that Bea acquired for her upward professional working-woman status. I was the perfect hostess with my Public Affairs committee members and my Carolyn successfully completing all their assignments. Each committee member was responsible for printed materials to fundraising, room arrangements and photo displays, refreshments, media, finances and thank you responses. Every aspect was well-organized and friendly.

I looked stunning during cocktails, which I avoided to keep my wits about me, but I ate some of the uniquely presented and delicious hors d'oeuvers created in the crisp, new kitchens of our recently constructed first class Lakeshore Bay Hotel complex. And I was stunned when I took my place at the podium and looked down to see Nick Dixon sitting directly in front of me next to the St. Agnes hospital administrator.
Undaunted, I called the program to order with the grace and confident spirit of a seasoned emcee. It isn't often that a woman addresses a majority male audience, but our women's numbers are growing as is indicated in this group of involved citizens. When the audience was seated, I looked eye-to-eye at individuals in the crowd and began speaking.

"Greetings and Welcome.
"As I look through the listings of organizations and activities we honor tonight, those names recall memories of pictures that I see in my three generations of family photo albums—attending parades and picnics, buying pottery and

pancakes—minor happenings and major milestones, proud events and fun.

"Images roll through my head like a mental movie, a slide projection of memories that make me so proud of my community that I invite out-or-town friends and relatives to join in sharing of it and I write to others to celebrate it.

"When I lived away from Lakeshore Bay, these were events I bragged about and missed a lot. When I returned to my hometown to live, I was happy to participate in them again.

"While I was away, I missed the lake, the changing seasons and the other natural elements of my hometown. But most of all, I missed the 4th of July fireworks and floats, the drum corps and the County fairs, ethnic and church picnics, the zoo and all the events that were created by people for people to enjoy, people who, as volunteers for the most part, worked hours and weeks and year after year to provide these wonderful activities set in our beautiful city right here in Wisconsin.

"Each of you represents something significant in the life of this community. Each of you has helped to enrich the quality of lives of hundreds and thousands of people who live in or visit Lakeshore Bay County.

"As an individual citizen of Lakeshore Bay County, I thank you for providing these memorable occasions in my personal life.

"As a person who has lived elsewhere, I thank you for making Lakeshore Bay so valued that I chose to return here years ago and have made a good life here for a long time.

"As a proud advocate of Lakeshore Bay, I thank you for giving me the long list of praises to use when I'm with other people who are not as fortunate to live here.

"And as a representative of the Public Affairs committee of the Business and Professional Association, I thank you for sustaining our community's traditions year after year and for initiating newly emerging events to add to those traditions.

"With this reception at our sparkling new 255-room Sheraton Lakeshore Bay facility, you're helping to serve as an all-County catalyst for a greater spirit of positive, cooperative energy. We affirm the quality of life that is present, a spirit that manifests itself in totally satisfying and harmonious ways for the highest good of all concerned.

"With this affirmation in our hearts I ask you, "How do you feel about Lakeshore Bay right now?"

(The audience responded with cheers.)

"Let's carry that feeling forward with contagious enthusiasm and share it with others.

"Let's Bravo Lakeshore Bay!—Where community pride is justified."

"Let's take time right now to acknowledge each other's contribution to Lakeshore Bay. Look to the left and look to the right. Look to the front and to the back, and see all of the other valued people here who are also looking at you as a valued person.

"Let's shake hands and say "Thank You" to each other."

Immediately the friendly response of Thank Yous filled the room as people shook hands all around, including Nick and his competitive St. Agnes cohort. I stepped down and shook each of their hands too before mixing it up with others in front of the room.

After I introduced the next speaker, I went over to the bar and ordered a martini.

My committee members congratulated each other for a successful evening. We all were aglow, including the new director of the Greater Lakeshore Bay Tourism and Convention Bureau.

I'd arranged for my talk to be printed as a commentary in today's *Bay View Times* and concluded by restating, "Bravo Lakeshore Bay!—where community pride is justified." A longer article was printed in Lakeshore Bay's weekly paper, with its editor serving on our committee. Also, *Bay View Times* Corporation, up to now was not known for donating money to community events, donated $500 to toward financing our reception.

Excerpts from letters responding to the reception include:

To Jan Anthony, Chairperson:
From Lakeshore Bay County Board of Supervisors A. Brian Calhoun, Ph.D.
"...The Greater Lakeshore Bay Convention and Visitors Bureau Board looks forward to continuing to work to make Lakeshore Bay a better place to live and work. We are certainly at the beginning of a new era, and we thank you so much for your contribution."

From W. D. Gittings of Gold Medal, Inc.
"On behalf of the Business and Professional Association's Board of Directors and officers, I would like to thank you and your Public Affairs Committee for the excellent job you did in planning and executing the "Bravo Lakeshore Bay!" program.

From Fran Weaver representing the Town of Mt. Pleasant.
"Bravo Lakeshore Bay!" was a warm and sensitive gesture on the part of the Public Affairs Committee to extend a welcome to Carol Wenter and to introduce her to the community...We are indeed fortunate to stand at the crossroads of time when momentum is gathering for a better Lakeshore Bay. I'm pleased to be a part of that momentum. Again my personal thanks for your ongoing work to make our communities take on a new life. Sincerely—"

From my co-hort Carolyn Schafer's greeting card showing line drawings of four adults wearing colored shoes and sox:

"Congratulations on your many feats! She wrote, "and knocking their socks off...Bravo Lakeshore Bay! You were, terrific! Thanks for inviting me along to share in the planning, execution and fun. I loved being a part of the whole thing."

Did those community executives know that an in-your-face lesbian organized this event? Did they care as long as someone did the task?

The plans for the new Lakeshore Bay County magazine are still in limbo.

Jan on December 16, 1983

I made tons of positive points for my work with the reception. We made everyone feel proud about being in Lakeshore Bay County. I had a great time chairing the event with eight important Lakeshore Bay PR leaders. The mayor and other dignitaries were most appreciative, and other hospital colleagues were there to witness and enjoy the evening.

Jan on December 16, 1983

Dear Matt,

Christmas is turning into a series of wonderful happenings. First of all, we've rented Mother Courage store and offices to Reindeer Rainwear, owned by no other than a man named Rudolph. He called us on Monday, we showed him the store on Tuesday and there was a rent check in the mail on Thursday. He operates a mail order men's clothing business advertised in the *Wall Street Journal*. His business is growing rapidly; he will advertise more and his home-based company is getting too big. He loves the location and the size of the store and is a fine gentleman.

Our hospital Christmas party last night was extra fun and extremely political for me because Bea came as my guest and we cheered for Carolyn's five-year-pin award. It was a wonderful evening with warm acceptance from co-workers.

On December 12, Bea slipped and twisted one ankle, tried to catch herself from a fall and ended up breaking the other ankle. Still we've moved her office materials out of the store and into the house so Rudolph could rent the space. Carolyn's son helped us. Doing all the shopping, errands, Christmas stuff, I'm realizing what a wonderful team partnership we had before this.

Our transition from the store will not be difficult. One of our bedrooms is now Mother Courage Press. Bea finished her H&R tax course on crutches and will join the staff after January 1.

Our Christmas plans are busy. Jenny will probably join us for a while after church. We'll miss you, but when you're away from home, you can enjoy yourself with those you choose to be with.

Oh yes, we mailed an order for *Something Happened to Me* to The Republic of South Africa this week.

And through an extraordinary sequence of happy insights, study and perceptions, we've integrated my therapy with our new job and security attitudes, plus a new awareness of an exceptionally positive future and other wonderful attributes into an absolutely grand anticipation of a most happy life.

How's that! And it's all true! And I love you!
Happy Holidays,
Mom

Bea on December 17, 1983

For today's final tax class, I achieved an overall course grade of 98 percent on the three-hour final exam. Obviously I got an A with my certificate and perfect attendance, especially when Jan drove me there every Saturday and even brought me my lunches.

I have a lot to celebrate.

Last Tuesday I closed the deal with Herb Randolph to rent the shop for his mail order business. He said his wife wanted his business out of their house.

Last night I went Lakeshore Med annual Christmas party. I was nervous, of course, with all our history there together. But I had a grand time. Jan arranged for a wheelchair, we ate lobster and people were very nice to us—to me.

Somehow after the awards ceremony, Santa Claus, in the guise of Dr. Jerome Glasner singled me out to spend what seemed like an hour with me in a magical after-dinner conversation. He neglected all the others—and the big shots—and sat next to me in a quiet hallway area where we could talk without music and other noises bothering us. Perhaps his ex-wife had mentioned my name and told him about a conversation she and I had a year ago. I actually didn't even know him, but we became instant soul mates, it seems.

Tomorrow we'll be exchanging gifts at Jim's house for the Lindberg family Christmas gathering. It will be fun with his little kids opening their presents.

Jan did all the shopping, including our Christmas tree, but I set up our little train to circle on its tracks beneath the tree.

Jan on December 21, 1983

I attended another of Dixon's extravagant, two-tiered Christmas parties, the first for hospital staff, managers and head nurses, the later guests were for important friends, so the heavily laden tables of gourmet food and beverages set under holiday boughs and bells would be consumed eventually by both parties. I'm sure what's left over will be taken care of when Nick and Diana's large families come to their home on the actual Christmas Eve and Day. (I wonder if Nick worked out a deal for all this through the hospital's Food Service providers.)

Of course I went on the first shift with the Lakeshore Med staff to pay my holiday respects in a self-assured yet cautious manner, mindful that I must protect myself from making any social or political blunders, however slight. So what's new?

I enjoyed sharing the spirited company of my peers without challenging my hosts. Some of the first shift had started leaving when I heard the piano in the music room of the large vintage house, and I knew Randy was again using his musical magnet to attract people around him. Of course, most of the party moved to sing his jolly Christmas music and carols and, for sure, that wouldn't be me following his lead.

It was a shrewd time for my exit. I found my coat and searched for my hosts to politely express my holiday wishes and farewells, and when I looked for them in the music room, I saw Randy's snippy young secretary leaning in toward him to take the soprano lead.

I opened the heavy front door with the view of the lake and stepped onto the wide front porch. Soft, abundant snowflakes had been falling to blanket a sparkly, fresh layer on the piles from our previous record-breaking storms, and I stopped, holding on to the top of the stair rail, to look at the floating ice riding into the dark horizon on Lake Michigan swells. The snowflakes melted as each landed on my face while I carefully crunched my way down the steps and brushed away the fluffy white mounds from my sporty old Toyota so I could drive home to be with my lover. Mother Nature's winter's snow warmed my spirit as I realized that from this day forward onto this Summer Solstice, each day's light would last longer and be brighter.

Bea on December 31, 1983

Our holiday season started with our full moon group on December 19 with more snow, but that kept no one away from our Solstice ritual. We had asked that we bring each other an imaginary gift and we had a merry time singing alternative pagan words to the standard Christmas carol tunes. Carolyn came directly after work with Jan and we had supper together that I made while hobbling about on my walking cast.

It was a good thing that we celebrated with our moon circle when we did because our Christmas Eve temperature slid down to fifteen degrees below zero. We were surprised when Carolyn and her daughter Jane dropped in for a visit while Jan wrapped presents. We felt warmed by their visit that truly felt like family. Jan told me she hadn't realized when she hired Carolyn that her daughter was such an accomplished attorney and a positive and dedicated role model. Carolyn then invited us to her little duplex jammed with her six almost mature children. One had a private, cozy sleeping nook under the stairs to the basement. The greatest gift was when Carolyn's kids and guests held hands and sang Holly Near's song, "We are a gentle, angry people" for our dinner prayer. It ends with "We are a gentle, loving people," which ultimately and sincerely, we are. Blessed Be!

On Christmas Eve, Jan rescued Jenny who had a flat tire coming over here for an early supper. Matt and Jenny stayed to play a few board games, and when they left us, they joined her father and other friends at the annual Letscher party that we used to attend. My kids came over on December 27 for drinks and snacks and we recorded our first Beta tape off of HBO.

I've been working hard and getting so damn frustrated solving our Vic computer problems. I worked two hours and couldn't get it to record data, but I finally got the computer to work after realizing something was wrong with the dumb tapes I bought the day that I broke my ankle. All Jan can do on it is play Pacman. I wish she would learn to program herself into solving minor problems rather than asking me for help all the time.

Technology challenges continued when I ordered a VCR for Jan's present and had a BetaMax delivered by mistake. I think it's meant to be. All the smart people we know have Beta, but Josh told me that Beta is already on its way to be obsolete. Hell. So am I.

Speaking of technology, the water line on our upstairs toilet froze up because it's on an outside wall. We tried to heat it up with blasts from our hairdryer, but before we did any damage, the toilet finally thawed out by itself.

We've just received our second manuscript to consider publishing. It's from Lynn Daugherty, Ph.D., a therapist from Roswell, New Mexico, who discovered *Something Happened to Me* and liked how we've handled that book. I'll consider it more carefully after the holidays.

It's good to walk again, sort of. I'm using various canes, but my favorite cane is the brandy cane that Jan gave me on my fiftieth birthday with tubes inside to carry liquid supplies. On New Year's Eve, we went to a movie to see Barbra Streisand's *Yentil* and I brought along my brandy-filled cane for the holiday and to warm us, of course, in this dangerously freezing weather. Two of our older Lakeshore Med's School of Nursing faculty friends, who, incidentally, seem to be another long-term, closeted couple, caught us with our test-tube flasks, thought the cane was delightful and wanted to know where to buy one.

Bea on December 31, 1983

Jan must have scrawled this note, I found it next to my chair on New Year's morning. "My children I love, but Bea Lindberg is my legacy, my soul mate. Happy New Year!"

Chapter 19

Jan on January 13, 1984

Our most frequent customer, Mary Virginia Devine, or as Bea calls her, The Divine Virgin Mary, hasn't lost contact with us because we've closed the bookstore. She sent us Solstice gifts and I've finally found time to send her a belated thank you. We invited our Ph.D. friend and author of Mexican-American folk magic to come to our full moon group but she said her parents wouldn't allow it.

Dear Mary Virginia,
    Your pentacles gifts have brought us great strength and power to enhance our New Year's goals of positive energy and success. Bea and I will share the wearing of them and I hung the large one in our window next to the crystals so we can see them each the morning. I hope we haven't lost contact with you. I'm sending you our moon group calendar and you're welcome to join us at any time.
    We would also like to drive you to some of your places and contacts outside the city if you ever need transportation and/or company, or if you want to have us join you for a visit.
    I'm looking at your unique unicorn card that is pinned carefully on my office bulletin board. I identify with that uniqueness and with that glow and, in this patriarchy, I need that extra reminder of what is possible in a better environment that acknowledges and reinforces creativity and uniqueness.
    Blessed Be, Mary,
Jan and Bea

Bea on January 18, 1984

We're on a roll starting out the New Year. I began working at H&R on January 7, but the office is in Elmwood so I hauled my weighty plastered-casted foot and ankle into the car to drive for the first week. I hadn't driven in five weeks and I was going stir crazy plus hating depending on others to get around. I had the cast sawed off last week and there was my old friend—my foot. It was scaly, swollen, misshapen and stiff. I came home to take a glorious shower and a soak bath! Then I dressed and went to work, using one crutch and my brandy cane to help me from the parking lot up the entrance stairs to our office building and then to my desk. One day, my brandy cane broke while I was leaning on it and I called Jan to make a crutch run to my office. Using the brandy cane to lean on is not its function. It's to be used in the future when I ask one of my sons to "Fix it!" and sneak brandy into my nursing home facility.

I'm reading Lynn Daugherty's manuscript, *Why Me? Help for victims of child sexual abuse (even if they are adults now.)* After Jan approves, I think we may publish a second sexual abuse book. Mother Courage Press may have found a niche to become a successful publishing house. Or as Jan keeps repeating, "This, or something better, now manifest for me in totally satisfying and harmonious ways for the highest good of all concerned."

Jan used comp time so we could go to Milwaukee to find printers who do bound paperback or hardcover books in small press runs. We visited four plants but it was useless. And of course these guys wouldn't recommend anywhere else to go. If we do more books, we'll have to use a different format than *Something Happened,* which is designed for easy printing and collating with simple staples holding it together. It's a real puzzle to find a printer to meet our requirements, as if the printers didn't bother to take two women and a press named Mother Courage seriously.

It's another full moon ritual tonight. I've been reading *Medicine Woman,* the book Carolyn's daughter gave me. I meditated and envisioned my animal totem name, Grey Owl.

I'm reminded of the couple getting my tax advice who asked me if the necklace I was wearing was a pentacle. I'm so comfortable in my role as our moon group leader that I forget how fearful others are of beliefs other than theirs. Their first fear is homophobia, second is pagan customs and witchcraft. Eh! Eh! Eh! They don't realize that their religious beliefs come from pagan and mythical traditions. Moments after they asked me if I was wearing a pagan symbol, I responded, "No. That's just a star. See? There's a star in the circle." After their tax forms showed that they would be getting a refund, they didn't care what jewelry I wore.

My tax expertise is helpful for us too because I figured Jan will get a $3,000 refund! Plus we've started negotiations on selling North Main Street for around $33,000 with give-and-take for FHA approval. Our tenants called to tell us they've acquired a loan for the property and we'll make an appointment with an attorney to start our part of the process.

After hearing all that, we went to bed early to celebrate with an amazing passion.

Jan on February 9, 1984

Happy Valentine's Day, Matt,

The time is spinning by and the days are getting longer. It's so good to leave work late and still see some sunlight. Our hospital twenty-six week TV series is about over and we've done an excellent job. It will be a relief not to worry about meeting those weekly deadlines. It's quiet in my office and I have been waxing creatively on five different projects.

Bea is spending many hours at H&R and is enjoying the challenges of solving people's tax problems. It may lead to other job options. She interviewed and passed a test at Advantage as a future estate planner and retirement counselor. She said the only weak point she has is the lack of greed. Their response has been positive so far.

Our 2nd Street tenant loves the shop. It's given him new life, he said, to have a store and business to come to rather than work out of his home. He is a gracious person too—and pays his rent on time. We've signed an offer to purchase with our tenants at Grandpa's house.

It's been a long time since everything has been so good and so economically secure.

Whoopee! And Blessed Be!

Jan on February 12, 1984

We've both been consumed with work and taking care of each other. Bea is courageously struggling while recuperating from her broken ankle. She's working more than from 9 to 5 at H&R on many days and some weekends, plus handling orders for the press, running errands and keeping up with entertaining families and friends. Last week she brought gray wool suit and fantastic coat, plus boots—exactly what she wanted, and she told me, "Yippee! I'm going to impress Advantage Insurance with the fact that I'm a first class broad and I deserve a high salary."

I'm now reporting directly to Chuck McCarthy, our young new marketing and planning administrator. Chuck has also inherited Laura Williams and her lineup of community support groups so she no longer reports to Nursing. That also includes our TV programs. I continue sending my weekly reports to Randy as well as Chuck. I wonder if they read them. And I wonder how my strong-minded colleague and friend Laura will respond to Randy's clone as a "function" of their "marketing plan" rather than her having total control of her work that she had while she reported to Nursing administration.

Bea's Josh seems so happy with Kim, his fiancé, and we showed them our Florida slides to prepare them for their trip. Josh also wanted Kim to see the family slides that Bea made for them and those that I made for Matt and Jenny, as if he could use those photos to orient his soon-to-be bride into his family history.

After they left we went to bed with a noisy and needy passion and woke again around 5 a.m. for more. Together we again entered our own world, a state of being in lusty exhilaration and joyful giving, a state of blessed harmony that is essential to my well-being and—hopefully to Bea's.

Bea on February 12, 1984

We woke up around 5 a.m. to make love again after making love before we fell asleep in each other's arms. Seems like weeks, even months in between, but we're working so hard. All this labor better let up soon because I don't know how much longer I can keep up this grueling pace. And days off are spent doing Mother Courage and property management and stuff. So I'm on practically all the time. But it will let up soon. And I need to get at my *own* taxes."

Bea on February 15, 1984

Last night I came home from H&R and we savored Valentine drinks, chili supper and then to bed for a wild Valentine buzz. We exchanged our gifts in bed. I gave her the cuddly white Sniffles Bear she had made such a fuss over at Marian and Sharon's. She gave me a "Lady Bull" stuffed animal for our new stock market bullish optimism, especially after I had Jan put $2,000 into the Fidelity Freedom Fund today. And I'm taking an investment class starting February 22.

Bea on February 19, 1984

Last Tuesday, I finished work on time and made it home to a living room full of full moon women. They talked calmly in the circle and we kept that up to meet everyone's need to express herself. It was a long circle service lasting until almost 11 p.m. It was good! Everyone feels strongly that our group meets our inner needs, is uplifting, nurturing, tremendously valuable and with conversation and eats after, we're all nourished, inside and outside our selves. We went to bed after 1 a.m.

I've had a strange out-of-it feeling. Perhaps it's a sinus infection, but I felt like I was half out of my body—or brain. I'm depressed too. It might be the ancient echoes of PMS. I haven't had a period since a surprise one in December and now it's our windy and gloomy March, usually a dreary time for me. But it shouldn't be. I'm studying to take the insurance agents state exam and my tax work is taxing but stimulating. I've even had time to do our own individual taxes and that of our partnership. I've transferred my $1,121 Mutual of Omaha money market to Fidelity Select Technology Mutual Fund, so now I'm involved personally in the investment game and the stock market. How about that!

Lynn Doughtery answered our offer tentatively to publish her *Why Me?* manuscript but she wants more information from us. I'm so busy sending out *Something Happened* orders and taking care of our properties.

The offer on North Main has gone through. We'll close on March 27 or earlier. I called my broker today and ordered twenty shares of Ameriteck! Ha! Jan and I came home and celebrated at the bar, talking up a storm and celebrating again in bed.

The Goddess is surely sitting on our shoulders—or wherever.

Bea on March 16, 1984

Jan did her two days of a two-and-a-half-hour class teaching journaling at UW-Oshkosh's good, old Capsule College. While she was setting up all her visuals on the first day, she turned around and was surprised to look down to see her mother's dear friend Rose Robsen and Rose's friend Marie sitting in the front row. Those elders keep active attending many classes around town, but Jan said they beamed at her, happy about being able to take a class from her. Her other students' workshop evaluations showed they were motivated to try journaling and that was exhilarating but mentally exhausting for Jan.

I studied for my Advantage tests and went to my last investment class that morning, but I sat in Jan's second journaling class. She was great, as usual, but more energized even though she complained afterward that the group wasn't as up as the day before. I could almost see the crackling interchange between her and her students—her golden glow.

Jan on March 16, 1984

I reached a genuine high teaching journaling at Capsule College. The committee asked me to repeat my program from last year, but I've studied, learned and practiced journaling even more since then. Capsule College has influenced me since my first attendance with Bea when it started—and when we "started" in 1974. My Goddess, we've been lovers for ten years! No wonder I'm high.

I wrote a lot of details on the chalkboard and handed them a survey of Ira Progoff's work on "the diary route to self-discovery" that included Intensive Journal information and literature. I passed out information on Pat Durovny's LOG: Life Organization Game that inspired Bea and me at Milwaukee's Woman to Woman's conference in November.

I read them a section from Adrienne's Rich's "Transcendental Etude" from *The Dream of a Common Language,* quoting "No one ever told us we had to study our lives,/make of our lives a study, as if learning natural history/or music, that we should begin/with the simple exercises first/and slowly go on trying/the hard one, practicing till strength/and accuracy became one with the daring/to leap into transcendence…"

I read a bit from *The Diary of a Young Girl* by Anne Frank using the copy we bought during Bea's and my visit to the Anne Frank House in Amsterdam in 1976.

I gave them Abraham Maslow's "Hierarchy of Needs" chart leading toward self-actualization, and a bibliography that included Diane Mariechild's *Mother Wit*, Lillian Hellman's *Pentimento*, Muriel James and Dorothy Jongeward's *Born to Win*, Shakti Gawain's *Creative Visualization*, George Simons' *Keeping Your Personal Journal*, Robert Akeret's *Photoanalysis* and Ruth Kanin's *Write the Story of Your Life*.

I thought I'd given them valuable handouts. My talking with them was fun. And I told them not to worry about following rules—except to put a complete date to every entry.

"It's amazing to find a valuable piece of writing and have no reference to where you were and when you wrote it. Listen to yourself and speak intimately to your journal as someone who listens and doesn't interrupt or tell you all her problems that are much worse than yours."

Somewhere I quoted—or made it up myself—that the lack of intimacy with one's self, and consequently with others, is what creates the loneliest and most alienated people in the world.

I told them to save calendars, photos, tapes, artwork, collages, letters, even relevant cartoons. But I spent most of the time going through Progroff's logs, his Stepping Stones and Dialogue practices. My listeners liked the idea of meditating on another person's stepping stones in their lives and then having a dialogue with that person—alive or dead.

All were absorbed when I read again the closing stanza from Adrienne Rich's "Transcendental Etude."

> "Vision begins to happen in such a life…
> only with the musings of her mind
> one with her body, experienced fingers
>   quietly pushing
> dark against bright, silk against roughness,
> pulling the tenants if a life together…
> slicing light in a corner, dangerous
> to flesh, now the plentiful, soft leaf
> that wrapped around the throbbing finger,
>   soothes the wound;
> and now the stone foundation, rockshelf
>   further
> forming underneath everything that grows."

It was so quiet when I finished the entire stanza, and then several started to applaud with others following. I was thrilled at having my soul-spilling thoughts truly accept.

Jan on March 25, 1984

Taking my own advice to reinforce positive attitudes by writing five good experiences that happen each day, my supercharged electrifying LOG datebook has five faithfully listed events for each day. How can you be positive about a funeral?

Well, I can say that I wrote a beautiful letter to my gym teacher, Miss Beth Lakely, on the death of her longtime partner, housemate, friend, (more than a friend?) Miss Ruby Patterson. Miss Patterson's obituary listed all of her family and then at the end of her survivors' names, "grand-nieces and nephews, and her old and dear friend and companion, Beth Lakely."

March 24, 1984
My dear Miss Lakely—Beth,

Life constantly changes and we continue to grow. My life changed ten years ago and for the last six years, my friend, Bea Lindberg, and I have been living at our home on Westwood Lane.

I know now how wonderful it is to have a dear friend who shares my soul, and I can only begin to imagine the sense of loss that you must feel now.

The segment from Adrienne Rich's poem, "Transcendental Etude" may express something of this.

> "Homesick for myself, for her—as after the heatwave
> breaks, the clear tones of the world
> manifest: cloud, bough, wall, insect,
> the very soul of light…
> articulates itself: I am the lover and the loved,
> home and wanderer, she who splits
> firewood and she who knocks, a stranger
> in the storm, two women, eye to eye
> measuring each other's spirit, each other's
> limitless desire,
> a whole new poetry beginning here."

Your lives have been new poetry for hundreds of us-—your loving student daughters. Our memories of seeing you in happy times gave us great strength and joy. May the memories of that joy in your life fill your loss quickly and fully in new strength for yourself.

Love,
Jan Anthony

Bea on March 26, 1984

I studied insurance all day before Jan and I went to the bank to join the North Main Street tenants and our attorney and the mortgage rep where we proceeded to close the deal on selling the house. Jan said she loved watching our young couple going through the excitement of buying her dad's house. It's another of "This or something better is now manifesting for me in totally harmonious ways and satisfying ways for the benefit of all concerned." Yahoo! We walked out of there with a check for $22,292 and went right to our bank and deposited $12,300. The other $10,000 went to settle Jan's mother's hospital bills from years of her being institutionalized. Jan's father would be proud of what we've accomplished. That's a big load off of our minds, but her dad carried that financial burden since Jan was ten, worrying about the cost of Mildred's care and then what the State would take from his inheritance for Jan to pay for her care even though she has died.

Jan then surprised me. We went to classy J. Trump's and enjoyed martinis, oyster on the half shell, swordfish for me, a special crab dish for Jan and German wine. It was superb. Wow! We're on Easy Street! I'm a "Thousand-aire!"

Bea on March 27, 1984

It's lucky that I wore my new grey suit for my Advantage insurance training appointment because two photographers took my picture in our training class with Stan for a recognition presentation of the insurance agency.

I shipped twenty-five *Somethings* to Calgary, Canada, after I went home to change and shop for an hour before going to work on taxes from 4 to 9 p.m. I checked ten tax returns and did two more. They were fairly easy, but everyone else is complaining about the horrible ones they're getting. Dear Goddess, please stay with me until the end of the tax season!

Last Saturday, H&R treated its district tax staff to a free dinner at The Wharf. I actually brought Jan as my date, though, of course, we didn't act like we were on a date. Jan's better at mixing with people and making conversation than I am so we—at least I—had a nice time.

I told our table the story of preparing taxes for the crabbiest man in the county with my most complicated return yet. It took almost two hours and he left before I could run a check tape. Then I found an error on Schedule A. That meant he would get money back instead of having to pay. I was shaking for an hour while one of the supervisors checked it before I could tell him. We all shared stories about our stressful clients who come in with their important papers in shoe boxes, the grueling pressure, challenging and complex tax forms and building camaraderie with staff and supervisors. The waitresses kept pouring wine in water glasses while we were exchanging stories, and you get thirsty when you're talking and laughing. I worked from 9 to 1 the next day and was I hung over.

Bea on March 29, 1984

I was home studying all day and inadvertently fell asleep after supper. Oh well. It was my first evening off in eons. Today I studied as usual until it was time to go to work from 4 to 9 p.m. I got two hefty returns and was feeling paranoid, but I'm talking myself out of it. I need confidence and courage, not paranoia about "What ifs?" countered with "Well, what's the worst that could happen?" And then I feel a bit better. Sometimes I think I start to get that way when things are going too well. Old scripts. Witch ones. "Sing before breakfast, cry before dinner." Junk! The Goddess will give me what is best for me.

Bea on March 30, 1984

Stan gave me an encouraging pep talk at 11 a.m. It looks like I'm actually becoming an Advantage agent. I'm going to have my picture taken for a promotion piece, business cards and a financial needs analysis sales tool. I'm moving right along, like I'm in now. He also signed me up as a charter member of a new Toastmasters Club that meets on Tuesdays. One of our Women's Resource members is in it too. It's a good thing I've been finding professional looking clothing to wear at all these events.

Jan on March 31, 1984

Bea bought a beautiful gray, pin-stripped suit, several skirts and blouses. She radiates positive power and self-assurance. She's glowing and happy—which makes me happy. I bought daffodils today.

Chapter 20

Bea on April 2, 1984

Our friends helped us celebrate our sixth anniversary owning this house together and our tenth anniversary as lovers with a party to remember! We both looked terrific.

We created invitations with whimsical clip-art clown jugglers dancing across the page that said, "On April 1, 1974, they began singing together "What Kind of Fool Am I'' and on April 1, 1978, they began living together at 2026 Westwood Lane. Bea and Jan invite you to sing along with them on April 1, 1984. What kind of fool can you be? Dress as your favorite fool and share you most foolish feats, fates, feelings and phenomenon. 4.p.m., Sunday. Respondez s'il vous plait 344-9109."

Jan dressed as the Tarot Fool carrying a white flower in one hand and a hiker's knapsack symbolically holding all of her possessions. She wore a yellow floral blouse and a yellow hat with a long feather. Of course, her faithful dog, our Luv, is supposed to warn her not to step off the hazardous cliff while she's dreaming of her potential successes. I draped a Stars and Stripes banner over the white dress I always wear to my kids' weddings and was Miss America. Unfortunately the bouncing golden stars bonging from my headpiece kept sloughing shiny sparkles into my drinks.

But the best costumes were Rita and Tim's Adam and Eve.

Our guests came from several circles of friends: church, Lakeshore Med, the bookstore, men and women, straight and gay. The only relative there was Jan's niece Kathy who keeps a close connection with her. Jan seems to be Kathy's mentor, including taking the job at Methodist College that Jan turned down because of the poor salary. Kathy has to work long hours, cover all the men's athletic events too—on weekends.

They left their inhibitions at home. Some of them left their husbands at home too. Pat Holmen came dressed as Wendy because she never wants to grow up but she imitated Lily Tomlin doing Ernestine, the bra-strap grabbing, snorting telephone operator, and that inspired others to show off their singing and acting antics—nourished by all the great booze, tasty food and good humor.

A wonderful success. Cheers! Cheers! Cheers!

Jan on April 2, 1984

I feel as if we're starting a new era, a wonderful new beginning again!

Fortunately, I took a day off from work so we could rest after our party by remembering the fun that everyone brought with them, along with lovely gifts and bottles of wine. Bea said she felt hung-over from yesterday's gala fest, but she pulled herself together to have a professional studio photo taken for her future as an insurance and financial advisor sales person, and she's studying hard to pass that state exam when she's not working or playing or sleeping. Her insurance job will start as soon as her H&R tax preparations are over on April 15. When she's not reading, she's listening to cassette motivational tapes or watching videos at the insurance offices with other trainees. She's even been talked into joining the Toastmasters group—and she's enjoying it. At her initial meeting, she was called on to do a 60-second impromptu speech on "Death and Taxes" in front of what she called "a high-powered group." She went in "green" and came out enthused and on a high until she resumed the H&R routine for two more weeks.

Bea talks about our taking a trip to Egypt so I had a new photo taken at AAA and renewed my old passport in case we need it. I wonder when we'll work that in?

I'm lucky to be able to drive to work. We've been looking at used cars but we still can't find one we can afford. My Toyota is dangerous to drive with rusty holes in the wheel wells sending fumes into the car. I cleaned out the area and devised a sandbag solution to spread out over the open spaces. I've noticed that rust is starting to etch its way around the windshield wipers. I'll have to drive it only on sunny days.

The press business continues as well. We received an enthusiastic response from Roswell, New Mexico's Lynn Daughterty, the author of *Why Me?*, and we may have ourselves a real publishing house with two books. Daughterty joked with us about Rosewell being next to Texas and close to God; it's also known for UFO legends. Good thing we sent out another fifty-book order of *Something* to EduPress to bring in some money for Mother Courage's new project with new typesetting and printing expenses coming up soon.

Bea on April 8, 1984

Two bits of news: Josh's little red Escort is for sale, and Jenny told us that Alex called her from Reno and is selling the huge house on South Main Street. He will buy Marge's house and Jenny will move in there. Crazy, man!

We took care of lots of good business this Sunday. Good thing I worked hard to be sure we received our tax refunds. Jan got $2,000 plus. We paid off all our attorney bills to settle Jan's father's estate and Jan sent Matt $1,500 plus $150 in interest to repay a loan he'd made to her.

We had fun at the church's annual dinner in the new hotel's ballroom. Those who were our party guests thought our April Fool's gala was great. Several said it was the best party they ever went to. Wow!

And Jan was buzzing with her political cronies about attending the Democratic caucus yesterday where she connected with lots of UUs and other liberal friends. She settled herself in the district's uncommitted group that swayed the 1,050 or so Democrats to put Jesse Jackson up for nomination.

Jan noted the creative program design of the church's pledge drive and dinner program and asked who did it. Brad Nordstrom used to do that and so did Jan, but Nordstrom hasn't been around for a while and Jan's been too busy. She found out about Kay Larson, a new church member and a freelance designer who did some Manpower and Milwaukee work from her home. She'll meet with Jan next week. Kathy said she left teaching in Lakeshore Bay to follow her dream of being self-employed and independent. Jan said Kay Larson could benefit Lakeshore Med in a cost-effective way. At least she'll be less expensive than Nordstrom, and she's a UU too, and a woman—someone Jan feels she can trust.

I also wrote a nomination paper to submit Jan's name for the Communications Award for UW-Oshkosh's Accent on Women conference and while I was at that I also wrote my bio for my Advantage promo piece.

Jan on April 9, 1984

Dear Matt,

I'm happy to be able to return the loan you made to me to pay for the furnace on 13th Street. I'm happy to be able to add some interest to it too. Those funds I borrowed from you originally came from a joint, long-term savings to help you and Jenny. Little did I think that I would need that help from you. I hope now that you and Jenny can benefit someway for something worthwhile. It's always good to have a nest egg and watch it grow into something even more beneficial.

With this, I clear the slate on the few debts. It's a great feeling. I'm stepping out of a poverty mentality.

That's not been the best for me and I'm making excellent strides toward economic security. With both of us working and managing and saving together, we should not need to be dependent on anyone. And that's a good feeling too.

More good news: Bea's start is assured at Advantage Insurance with good vibes and affirmations from her male supervisors. I looked for flowers for her but found freshly cut asparagus instead and added pussy willows to complete a bouquet until we ate the asparagus for supper.

Love,
Mom

Bea on April 15, 1984

I took the insurance exam yesterday morning! It wasn't easy and I did the best I could and I hope I passed. It was like taking the bar exam.

In the evening we met Josh at his soon-to-be new in-laws' house and I drove home in our Escort that we bought from him with Jan following for one of her last trips in her beloved but battered Toyota Celica. Yeah!

Always on guard with in-laws, we made a hit with them. Jan joined in with the "Dads" for a while and we touched base with everyone there. Josh and Kim's wedding will be on May 19.

Fortunately, we both took a sweet, loving nap together in the afternoon and released much of our tension before resting in each other's warmth with the spring breezes blowing across us from the open windows.

Our moon circle this evening lasted over three hours and I was ragged by the time we got to eat and totally exhausted by the time everyone left. Jan was pooped too, but I produced a fine ritual and celebration filled with caring and high hilarity, as usual.

I will start my Advantage job tomorrow at 9 a.m. and continue working the last few hours at H&R from 5 to 9 p.m.

Bea on April 18, 1984

I was surprised at the lack of surveillance at my new job with my own desk spending an eight-hour day like regular people do, except that I'm watching training and motivational videos on my own in my new office. I was kidded by another agent who told me how I must have had struggled to pass the test. "You only scored a 98% on the complex exam."

I joined my H&R tax gang for the last hour while they waited for the final "suitcase" pick-up of tax forms before we all went out to Nino's for drinks and a celebratory sit-down dinner.

In the middle of Tuesday night I woke up disturbed. I'm having qualms about this whole insurance thing. I simply do not like this first selling push I must make or I won't get on their bandwagon. They want me to make a list of all my friends and family and start selling insurance policies to them. I can't do that! Then I overheard a supervisor ask my boss where he expects to put all these new people and Stan responded, "It's my job to fill the stable with horses." Now I wonder what the turnover is and is this initial push some grand selling scheme—and whether the dogmatic leader like the Rev. Jim Jones would suddenly pop up and say, "OK. Now drink the Kool-Aid."

After some soul-searching and meditating on Wednesday, I made up my mind. When I woke up to the reality of what I actually would be doing, that I would have to sell myself, change my whole personality, compromise my integrity, it's not for me. I don't fit the Advantage picture and it doesn't fit with me. I can't give sixty hours a week to them, no matter how much they pay. It would interfere with my relationship with Jan. I wouldn't be able to handle the press business and that's something we both want. That is our purpose and it's too important to let that go. That's when I decided to concentrate on Mother Courage Press

So tomorrow I'm telling these guys goodbye. It's been a tremendous learning experience and I know the Goddess had me doing it for a good reason. It's built my confidence and taken me a long way. Now I have taxes and probably an insurance license to offer for the next job opportunity.

The Goddess will show me what's best for my purposes and for Hers.

Bea on April 19, 1984

I got up early and went in and told the boss I'm quitting. And I felt terrific. Then I went to UW-Oshkosh and reactivated my placement file and spent hours at my computer store to learn about Macintosh's new Lisa and the Apple IIe.

Jan's a bit baffled by the abrupt change in my career plans but during our cocktail hour when I explained that I felt as if I were one of the pieces of a pyramid game, and when I told her we could do more important work as publishers, she came around to my way of thinking.

Jan on Easter Sunday, April 22, 1984

With Bea preparing to have a reasonable, steady salary, I thought I was free of the worry of supporting the both of us, but within a day or two she abruptly decided to quit—after she invested all that intense study time, seemed so positive about a new career and bought all those dress-for-success clothes. I must admit I was stunned when she told me about her concerns. I hope that I showed her that I'm sympathetic about her quitting. I think I did OK. Since then she's been eagerly throwing herself into fixing her car, gardening, shopping, cooking and boiling eggs for us to dye for Easter baskets for her grandchildren. She's happy and that makes me happy.

<<<>>>

    We woke early with Bea's body rolling against me gently but firmly indicating what was on her mind as my mind sent electric shock signal spazzing through me like a mini-seizure. My body always reacts like that when our naked bodies find each other. When she envelopes me to indicate that she wants me, if she didn't hold on to me, I could almost flap right out of bed. That is until we find our lips upon each other. My outside tremors turn to intense pleasuring, concentrating on touching and feeling toward inside spasms of release. Rebirth! Renewal becomes our resurrection this happy Easter Sunday morning before church service. Spontaneously begun, we then delighted in a leisurely hour or more of lovemaking on multiple levels of intensity, to taste and nibble gently toward serious wanting, then coming together before calmly, knowingly changing our focus to delight each other—to reach more peaks of joy within our imploding valleys. It's been a long while. It always seems like a long while. It completes me.

    We may have been a bit late to church, but despite the drizzling, spraying snow and sleet, our faces glowed with happiness beyond our colorful congregation's family springtime ceremony of gratitude.

    Later I fussed in the kitchen. Jenny and her young man came for supper and we devoured thick steaks, potato salad and zucchini. Our conversation was honest and sincere before they left together heading for more changes in Jenny's life. She will be moving soon into Marge's house. And Marge will be moving to, of all places, Reno to work for Nevada's human services program.

    During our before-bedtime glasses of wine, Bea and I questioned the wisdom of taking off for Egypt, and we decided to keep close to home.

Jan on April 23, 1984

A document at church caught my eye, "Are Homosexuals 'Normal'?" It's by the Rev. Robert S. Lehman and published by the First Unitarian Society of Minneapolis in Minnesota. Rev. Lehman is challenging New York City's Rev. Dr. Donald Harrington's opposition for our UU denomination to establish an Office of Gay Concerns and the Rev. Dr.'s criticism of the materials in the About Your Sexuality course and the filmstrip "The Invisible Minority." Both include homosexuality and the Gay life-style in our church school curriculum and assume that same-sex relationships are a legitimate, acceptable alternative to other sexual relationships. This debate has been going on at the UU General Assembly for two years, and perhaps this spring's General Assembly will make the deciding vote.

Any persons who oppose issues on homosexuality in our blessed church have departed long ago and, with our Rev. Dr. Tony Logan as a role model of a beautiful soul and an intelligent and gay human being, we are free to seek our fulfillment, the realization of our own selves, and seek it in whatever way seems right for each of us in our congregation—and hopefully within our UUA denomination.

Chapter 21

Bea on April 28, 1984

We bought the Apple Lisa today at UW-Oshkosh's computer fair!

When I woke Jan this morning, she said she had new motivation and rejected the poverty mentality. We will dedicate the time from work toward our personal and creative projects.

I'd been up earlier, as usual, and meditated over my first cup of coffee. We took a shower together and made sweet love, then dressed and drove the Escort to the university. I felt glorious. The warm sun shone on us riding in our non-rusted shiny small red car.

We looked at various displays, learned a lot in Max Morrison's workshop demonstrating the Mac and rushed to the retail display to study the equipment and buy a Lisa II512X. Jan was in shock, but she knew how much research I've done to reach this point. The timing is perfect.

And I was officially notified that I hit the bull's eye on the insurance exam.

Bea on April 30, 1984

To prepare for Lisa, we gathered all the office paraphernalia to create workspace in one of our three bedrooms. It was long overdue because we've been so busy taking care of every other place we've owned, and now the two of us have time together to fix our own home and office.

Big boxes of our Lisa came at 5:30 p.m. with Paul, our installer. After supper, I was waiting for him and Jan was waiting for her high school reunion committee to meet at our house too. I'll bet they'll be surprised at my nude paintings of headless Jan hanging in the living room.

I was filled with excitement and trepidation. Paul got it going and was giving me a quick personal course in what it could do and how. Jan's friends began to arrive at the same time. When Paul started to print, it didn't work! He tried several options and still no go, so he took two disks and went back to the store. Meanwhile he left me with the program he had copied and I started to play around. I got a sample document started and gave the print command—and it printed! I did it!

I showed Jan's friends my samples and joined them for some sloppy joes that Jan offered because she doesn't like to bake desserts—and hasn't since she stopped cooking for her family when she "ran away from home" in September, 1977. I was so excited that I forgot I had not eaten supper—I didn't even snack.

Jan on May 2, 1984

Dear Matt,

This is my first attempt to use our Lisa Apple computer word processing system.

(I forgot to date this historic event, so I'll ask my friend and partner, who's been working with this machine for several hours, to help me scroll up to correct this important factor. She suggests that I add the date to the end of the letter because at this point in her vast experience, she has not had to do this step either. That's called "creative problem-solving.")

Having this word processor is another great leap for womankind and a positive step forward for Mother Courage Press. This process is awesomely easy to make corrections! I don't make too many mistakes because I'm free to concentrate on what I want to say instead of the mechanics of typing it. It's especially important now with concerns at work. I continually have to prove that I do have the skills and the credentials to do the job that they want me to accomplish.

I love this machine. I must practice with the "mouse" to get it on target.

Here's Bea with more details about the computer.

Hi Matt.

Lisa is the Lisa 2. She has 512k of memory. She has this brand new format using Macintosh software. It's so simple to operate, we were off and running with an hour of delivery and set up. Right now we're only using one of the built-in fonts in one size. Wow! Look at what I can do by changing the style and size just by moving the mouse down the menu. (Type format and sizes vary and then Bea added a fish.)

I got this fish into the text by taking it from a scrapbook. It started out as a crappie and ended up elongated into a northern pike, I think.

Here's your mother back again.

Matt, you're the best person to experiment with because you still remember when you were a learner. But, philosophically speaking, we're always learning—even your old mom.

Bea on May 8, 1984

Looking back at our Creative Visualization pages in our daily logbooks, I see that I must change our Treasure Map already because so much has been manifested. We have the computer, the great office, more money, more time, and for Jan, a better car. One would be inclined to think this stuff works! And it does! Creative Visualization, Manifestation Management, Life Organization, even Bea Sher's Wishcraft workshop at the ABA in Los Angeles in 1979—we've been applying them in earnest since November and the Woman-to-Woman conference.

Bea on May 12, 1984

Jan's been working late again for this morning's run. Great! Her hours have been cut, but they still work her like crazy. Hours schmours! It's her salary that's been cut. Absurd!

Because I offered to help, I became the run's official photographer. We got up at 5 a.m. and I had all my camera equipment ready to leave for the hospital. All the "old" faces I knew were helping people and they knew me, too. I took back my photographer role from when I worked with Jan at Lakeshore Med and loved it. My favorite part was shooting the hectic tote board area with Carolyn and Laura posting times and winners in all the categories. People are so fussy about gaining or losing a second or two, and our two friends were at their most patient best coping with all the runners breathing down their necks.

After the awards, we went to Jan's office and I took more photos before I left them working, then left to have the film processed. When Jan finally called home to say she was done writing up the media release for the event with all the scores, etc., I went to pick her up and she and everyone there loved my photos. That was the best part. When she studied them at home, she kept raving about them and how well I'd done.

I heard her on the radio twice today. She's great! Then she called and said she would be late and would bring Laura and Carolyn home for the spaghetti supper I cooked for them. We had fun talking—and drinking, of course. They left after supper and we crashed, but I woke up about 9 and fooled with Lisa. That's better than boring TV.

Matt on May 6, 1984

Hey Mom! Happy Mother's Day!

Everything's cool here in Reno. It's been an interesting year thinking back on how my folks have influenced me.

I guess in the past this kid has been kind of reckless with relationships, traveling and communications. With respect to relationships, it's been kind of a foot-loose time—meaning how should one know what to expect of another person when one doesn't know oneself? You've taught me how to empathize with people I'm interacting with, so I almost know what it's like to have a big family like some of my friends have. It's traveling—a chance to experience peoples' lives.

Remember the back roads when we drove through Florida and saw poor Black families working in the fields and living in shacks? Now, in being more selective in how to travel, I can empathize with people in Nevada. I'm meeting people from all over. Not all want to share their experiences and I can appreciate that. Most do if it's not threatening. And the more transient people are, the more difficult the communications. I'm constantly learning to cut through the crap and communicate.

In terms of settling down, living with Dad has taught me how to live with another person. He's pretty patient with me, but within bounds. He asks me what he needs to know. I'm used to thinking only for myself and it was hard to coordinate a dinner, etc., and have one of my computer systems fail at 10 p.m., and I finally eat dinner at six in the morning.

(I smile when he gets mad that dinner is late and my being held late at work and that I didn't call. He's the way you probably were when he was working such long hours and you were home with us kids.)

The lessons I learn from him are how to be Armenian: i.e., never volunteer anything, but I have instilled from you the idea to look and explore everything. Alex refuses to be theoretical, but that's partly because of his computer profession. In trying to merge people with computers, there is little room for delay; people get frustrated if it doesn't work for them, and they don't want to hear or know why.

You've given me the ability to think and explore without bounds. It's a creativeness that applies to system design and life in general. Sure there are a couple rules out there—like you don't try to fix a system without unplugging it, but rules may be guidelines as to how far a person can safely stray.

I guess what I'm trying to say is that Mom, you and Dad are a lot different and I try to integrate his business tactics, when necessary, and your inquiry methods, when possible. I guess a kid is a combination of his or her folks. I guess I'm not totally inconsistent in the way I think—I think.

Bea on May 20, 1984

This has been some weekend. On Friday I picked up Carolyn at 6 a.m. and we drove to Madison for an all-day workshop called "Getting Started on Writing Your Romance Novel." We both gained some valuable tips and it helped me with scripting my musical about my dad and me. My working title is "The King and I" and my songs are flowing from me—and my Lisa computer.

We returned at 7 and Jan and I were due at the Methodist Church in Elmwood at 8 for Josh's wedding rehearsal and, after a quick drink and some fast food, we made it just in time. The bride's family hosted the rehearsal dinner and the two of us socialized on politically correct topics with my soon-to-be in-laws of my oldest son.

On Saturday we got to the church at noon and all the women in the wedding party were dressing for the ceremony. My gown is the one I always wear and I'm happy it still looks good on me. Because I was nervous, I played the grand piano at the church hall while they all got gussied up.

We did the whole wedding thing and all went beautifully. After picture taking, Jan and I zinged out for home, changed clothes and went to a graduation party for Carolyn's son Ben and we were surprised to find Anna Spence and her daughters who are also Ben's good friends.

We went home again to change for the wedding reception where I sat with my ex- and his wife, my old friend Angie, but Jan perched in the back at the bar and entertained my two energetic grandchildren. She maybe was sensitive about being stuck away from everyone else and minding the kids, but she didn't say anything. She would have felt awkward sitting at the front table anyway. She discovered that some other reception guests were relatives of her ex's sister-in-law, so the word went out about us, I'm sure. So what the hell! Jan and I danced together several times and my sons danced with the both of us. That made it all great at last.

On Sunday morning I awoke filled with a sense of well being and we shared some dramatic passion. After working in the yard, Robin picked us up and we went with her to Naomi's, Ben's, and my Jill's husband's painfully long graduation ceremony at UW-Oshkosh, especially painful when Randy King was honored as UW-Oshkosh's Distinguished Alumnus and offered words of wisdom to the class while Jan and I grumbled quietly to each other.

He was honored "for his service as the founding president of the Alumni Association and organizing its first fund-raising campaign for university scholarships and library acquisition, his deep commitment to Oshkosh and its mission as well as his professional achievement and community service."

We recovered with our quick cocktail hour before we joined Jill at her in-laws' home for Jill's husband's graduation party. We gobbled up some food, took a couple pictures, chatted the prerequisite amount of time and cut out to come home to crash.

Bea on May 22, 1984

I was in a black mood yesterday and didn't know why. It's as if devils were sitting on my shoulder giving me bad messages, witch messages, but "witch" is a good word for me now.

One thing's been bothering me—those damn tapes Jan recorded when she went to see Nora! I couldn't believe that the first thing she wanted to do with Lisa was to transcribe them. I can't believe it! I would like to destroy them. As far as I'm concerned, they are an ugly distortion of events and happenings of our life. Jan was having a terrible time last year and it wasn't me causing it. She was drinking heavily. She was having weird control problems. She also went a little crazy. But in those tapes, I'm her problem. And I hate it!

Betty called right at cocktail hour and she had devils too. I went to get her, dazzled her with Lisa, fed them, and Jan made a big bonfire. We talked the devils away. My mood is better today.

Print-Line delivered fifteen boxes of *Something* and I assimilated them into my office and sent off a carload of orders through UPS with more orders waiting for me for tomorrow.

I also spent time locating and reading my Progroff journal and was surprised to find it had a great deal more substance than I remembered. I also read last year's diary to gain some perspective and it helped me move along.

Chapter 22

Jan on May 24, 1984

Dear Mindy,
　　One of our hospital's neighbors, a reporter for the *Bay View Times*, called me to ask for help in freeing the space in front of the homes on her street. She said it was difficult to park her car and inconvenient to unload groceries, etc., because of Lakeshore Med employees taking the spaces in front of her home. She reminded me that she and her neighbors could only park on one side of the street.
　　I told her that I parked there myself and liked the corner for the beautiful Lake Michigan view to start my workday. But when someone left a note on my car asking me to park elsewhere, I quickly decided to park in the hospital's new ramp. Moving my car helped Lakeshore Med's good-neighbor relations.
　　I hope that you would consider moving your car, too, and helping Lakeshore Med keep up our positive good-neighbor-relations with those living around us.
Sincerely,
Jan

　　A few days later I got this response from the neighbor: "Just wanted to drop you a quick note to say thanks. I appreciate your intervention in the parking problems and am happy to report that the problems have been alleviated.
　　"Thanks again for everything and thank your employees for their understanding in this matter.
　　"Sincerely—"

Jan on June 3, 1984

Randy phoned me with muffled rage and insisted I meet with him. I reminded him that he'd agreed to have someone with me at all of our future meetings. I would arrange for a colleague to meet with us before we set a time and place. I told him I would contact Joanne Zekas, who is working on her Master's degree to be a therapist, and then we'd set a date. I could almost hear his teeth grinding.

By the time we met, a bit of steam may have escaped from my adversary, but not for long. His devious parry-and-thrust manner was evident to both Joanne and me. She kept cool and didn't say anything to interrupt this interrogation.

Randy heated up. "Who do you think you are that you can tell people where to park their cars?" And he shrewdly proceeded to ream me out, to squash the essence out of my surprised spirit as he threw my memo to his secretary across the table toward me. My feminist cohort gave me some strength to politely defend myself, but after a few minutes, we both knew that my good intentions for the hospital's neighbor-relations were distorted.

Finally I took a deep breath and responded, "It's unfortunate that my neighborly relations efforts are misinterpreted, but nothing more will be accomplished by subjecting myself to this harassment." The word "harassment" must have hit a vulnerable spot, especially after Joanne had won her own harassment suit against her boss. She got some money but she lost her job and her ability to be hired in her home town.

Randy nodded his head with a spastic jerk as I stood up to excuse Joanne and me as we left the executive board room. When we walked past Mindy's office, she gave me a sanctimonious smirk.

Joanne and I shared this absurd situation briefly with Carolyn, then she gave me an enveloping hug and told me she'd have to find quiet space to process what she just witnessed.

Wednesday's full moon group gathered outside to cast our circle around our bonfire. Joanne told the women of our meeting with my boss and she shared her pain over the experience, her own harassment struggles and law suits that she won, and her memories resurfaced with empathy for me.

To honor the deep feelings with our need for a healing atmosphere, we switched to creating some irreverent hexing with the magic of a flaming fire to exorcise away any harm or pain to our coven women, to nature and to offer me support under the glowing full moon.

Bea on June 6, 1984

All would be well at St. Agnes Health Fair with Carolyn as a Cabbage Patch doll and Laura, Pat, Mark and Jan managing their "For Your Life" wellness video show and popcorn stand. Carolyn and Rita used their artistic skills to paint and cut out Carolyn's outline as a full-sized Cabbage Patch doll displayed outside the video movie room marquee with the popcorn machine billowing out bags of the aromatic freebie that lured St. Agnes fans in to sit and watch the show. Carolyn then mingled about the fair crowd in a Cabbage Patch nightgown, a heavy mask and an orange mop-headed wig as Baby Gretchen, giving away chances to win a Cabbage Patch doll and tickets to Lakeshore Med video theater featuring Lakeshore Med Birth Center.

While they were promoting Lakeshore Med, I reluctantly checked the empty apartment on 13th Street to determine what needed to be fixed and I ended patching up the backyard fence in weird sections by nailing the whole works together.

It wasn't as bad as I thought after I filled six trash bags and bought paint to redo the little upstairs apartment. On Monday I gritted my teeth and went to work patching and washing the kitchen walls and before I was ready to go home, I wanted to try the paint. I got fired up and pushed myself to finish the job with two coats. The worst is over.

On Tuesday, Jan and I cleaned and painted the apartment's living room, bedroom, closet and bathroom. We put a For Rent sign in the window. While we were there, a woman came up and said she wanted to rent the place. I pushed myself the next day too, painting the second coat in the bathroom, installing carpet and bathroom tile and throwing it all out the window to place on the curbing for tomorrow's trash pick-up day.

I was absolutely wiped! But when Josh called, we talked about this weekend's rafting and camping trip. Jan made supper and I crashed after that, completely out of it!

Jan on June 7, 1984

My Day of Infamy that I'd waited for this since 1978 when it became known that I was a lesbian.

Randy ordered me to stay in the board room alone after a group meeting and attacked me, endlessly listing all of the time he spent trying to work with me. I did not respond. It's hopeless. Finally, he announced that my department will be eliminated; no department, no Jan Anthony. Carolyn will report to Chuck McCarthy, the new marketing director.

"Rather than have you humble yourself for unemployment compensation, it's been decided to show you some compassion and allow you to stay in your office and continue to on the payroll while you aggressively seek another position."

Carolyn's sisterly love and grief for me was unmistakable and her concern for herself was stubbornly defiant when I told her she would report to Chuck'

Bea could tell that something was wrong as soon as I entered our home. "What happened?" Bea asked anxiously.

"I lost my job," and I finally cried. Without grounds for my dismissal, our abuser/harasser finally forced me out with a cunning move. He eliminated the hospital's PR/Communications department.

Bea on June 8, 1984

Jan woke me at 5 a.m. this morning. She was restless and when her skin touched mine, I knew that a gentle time of lovemaking would be welcome. Then before she went to work, we opened our camping trailer. I made to-do lists for our press business, for finishing touches needed on our 13th Street property, and then prepared our gear and provisions for our Wolf River rafting trip with my kids.

I'd settled in with my afternoon drink when Naomi came for our key so she and Robin could stay in our house for the weekend and care for Luv. Jan came home—broken. I was glad Naomi was here and could help me comfort her.

We ate supper and talked a lot before we went to bed. Jan woke and I got up to kept her company. Then I suggested we have ourselves a healing party back in bed, and I held her as we fell asleep.

Bea on June 8 to 10, 1984

With those lovely sleep disturbances behind us, we proceeded to organize our camper and head for the second annual Lindberg family Wolf River rafting adventure. We were the first to arrive and set up camp with family spaces all around the fire pit and we celebrated when each couple joined us for tomorrow's rafting.

After a hardy breakfast with my Joel frying bacon over the fire and Jill's husband scrambling eggs on the camp stove, we signed up at the raft barn and were bussed to the rafts that held only two people this year. That meant that we missed the large group spills and squalls of last year even though we'd meet up for a raft rodeo from time to time. This year's river was less awesome as last year's currents. Even Pismire Falls rapids at the end didn't scare us this time. Though idyllic, we just didn't enjoy the same camaraderie. Jan missed last year's fun, and this year her thinking and planning was for when we returned home and what would she do next.

Our barbecue supper, beer and trading lots of good jokes were great until it started to rain and we retired early.

I'm so proud of my kids. And I love it so when we're having a good time together.

Bea on June 15th-17th, 1984

It's a waiting game now. Wait, wait, wait to see when it will be Jan's last day—if she even gets a job. Heavy with apprehension about our future. Will we have to move? Can I ever get a job? Right now it would be counter-productive if we would have to move if Jan gets a job elsewhere and then we would be going in opposite directions. Drinking too much too. But what else is new or secure in our future. My trip to the settlement brought me some gin to sample.

We signed up for the Midwest Women In Print Conference in Madison this weekend, and Jan gave me a royal tour of her favorite University haunts after we checked into the Agricultural dorm room with metal bunk beds. We had a better room in an Indiana dorm. But UW-Madison serves beer at the Student Union where we sat outside overlooking Lake Mendota.

The all-women conference offered workshops on future trends in technology, on periodicals, mailing lists and distributors, publishers and bookstores, printers and publishers. Jan even attended one on burnout.

We learned about the political as well as practical matters of publishing from this small number of intense women, mostly lesbians from their appearance—and from their dedication. Some women own and operate their own printing presses because male printers won't produce their books. It's amazing how systems get organized to fill a need. Here we were with our one little book and ready to go for our second, and we find women who are determined to print their issues, stories, and histories. We did a lot of networking in the evening panel session but didn't go to the dance they had scheduled.

Because I've been studying contracts and author law, I fired up Lisa and worked all day drafting a contract we could send to Lynn Daugherty for approval. Lisa and I did it.

Jan on June 17, 1984

A truly valuable response to my letters came from less competitive, more compassionate professional colleagues like Dee Springer from the Milwaukee Regional Medical Center (MRMC). She told me that John Jackson, the new administrator of the Milwaukee County Medical Complex (MCMC), was looking to create a new PR position. He wanted his own hospital PR person, not one from another county office who had recently hired a newspaperman to cover all the Regional Center's healthcare institutions.

(This county-owned "county hospital" is now named the "Milwaukee County Medical Complex. How complex is it?)

Chapter 23

Jan on July 2, 1984
Gate Pass for the 4th of July Fireworks

After I wrote my "Bravo Lakeshore Bay!" newspaper commentaries in the spring, the Fireworks Committee Chair Mike Madden invited me to help with this year's fireworks.

Dear Jan,

I've been on the Fourthfest board for a number of years and visited with you and your father working on the floats, and I'm inviting you to be part of the fireworks crew this year…Your job is pretty easy. All you need to do is show up at 6:15 p.m. on the 4th, ready to work your butt off, hauling gear, sand, plywood, mortars and shells a half-mile out onto the pier. You must be smart enough to be able to read the wind, waves and thunderclouds, to be able to insure that the 100,000 people waiting for the show will be properly entertained. The grand finale will be shooting off 150 rockets in honor of the Lakeshore Bay's sesquicentennial.

As a rookie we will assign you to the sand detail; passing shells and loading mortars will come later. As a fan of our fireworks, and a vocal fan at that, you have earned a place on our committee. Remember, our committee isn't big on praises. When the show is over and we have picked up and packed up, you'll hear a lot of 'Good show,' 'Nobody got hurt,' and 'See you next year.'

Thanks for the 'BRAVO.'

<<<>>>

So this 4th of July we'll work under the fireworks after watching the parade with family and friends at my father's house that we sold to the tenants with visitation rights to the front lawn during the parade. Our new owners' family and friends fill up the rest of the yard and serve beer from a cool keg that we also are invited to enjoy.

Our new owners added a priviledge written in the sale that says that Jan, her family and friends will always have space in front of the house for each 4th of July parade, space in the back for parking and access into the home to use the facilities.

Bea on July 6, 1984

Yesterday my doctor told me to take Metamucil and calcium tablets for stomach problems and he checked out all my parts. I made a trip to the settlement and bought me some gin, which I sampled immediately. So did Jan after work. Then she drove us to Greek Fest to cash in our anniversary present from Martha and Fran. I can't help but remember the stressful time when Alex wanted me to meet him there—and we split a gyros sandwich while debating about Jan and who would get her. The ghosts that haunt that place were exorcised by talking about it now in light of our happy times together. I felt no pain with Roditis wine, saganaki and gyros in my ailing gut when drove home.

Jan wiped out on our couch while I had this strange experience as if entering an altered state. I was crying and I remember stepping close to an edge. My mother, father and my brother appeared and they didn't like me, not welcoming me with open arms. So I came back. That's when I moved close to Jan so she could hold my hand as in the *Altered States* movie where John Hurt, the chemically over-dosed hero, is saved by his woman lover, Blair Brown, from dissolving down a drain— to be lost forever. We held hands for a long time, tears running down my face and holding on tightly like two souls adrift in time. I told Jan of the odd experience I seemed to have had and of the feeling that my family never seemed to like me, and she said, "Oh, Bea. Not your brother too!"

They really did love me, you know, but this experience was a tremendous release for me and I woke up in the morning feeling much better—inside and out— with my pent-up rages and fears laid to rest for a while.

Jan on July 10, 1984

Bea's creating and mailing résumés as well, including a perfect position for her at the nationally circulated *Sailing Magazine* in Port Washington. I love the way she adapted her cover letter. She wrote:

Dear Ms. Hutchens,

In the middle of a brainstorm, it's valuable to have a seasoned hand at the helm to inspire confidence and reach the shore. Establishing a responsive climate for client or staff to create, coordinate and unify the energy of the crew has been one of my major strength throughout my many professional experiences.

My other strengths and skills are listed in my résumé, which I have enclosed for your review. If you think, as I do, that I could contribute new insights as well as proven experience to your crew, I would sincerely appreciate the opportunity to meet with you soon.

Bea on July 16, 1984

I worked on Lynn Daugherty's contract for three hours and I ran off a final draft to publish *Why Me? Help for victims of child sexual abuse (even if they are adults now)*. I worked out a great way to computerize my invoices to make the job less tedious.

The Shannons invited old friends to see Camela Parson and her husband who were visiting from Seattle. Joyce showed me their IBM and Lotus computer set-up and I'm convinced we did the right thing buying Lisa.

Many friends from past sauna and skinny-dipping parties joined in active pool games—a new Olympics, but quite not up to the standards of the upcoming one in Los Angeles. We played water volleyball, did handstands, synchronized swimming and had fun—like teenagers. Somewhere in playing Jan's favorite underwater game, Baby Seal, I bumped my head on the side of the pool.

Bea on July 24, 1984

My *Sailing Magazine* interview with Micca Hutchens in Port Washington went well. It's surprising that this young woman is responsible for this beautiful magazine.

Dear Ms. Hutchins,

Thank you for yesterday's interview. I thoroughly enjoyed meeting you and talking about *Sailing* and sailing. I drove home with my head in the shrouds thinking about the possibility of working for you. If there was any one qualification I lacked, I thought it might be enough experience of the right kind. Then I remembered that Naomi James had only had two years of sailing experience before she undertook to sail around the world single handed, and not only did she succeed, but she broke Sir Francis Chichester's previous speed record for the same voyage.

One thing we didn't discuss about my availability for the position is that I'm unencumbered by family. I'm divorced and my children are all grown with families of their own, and although I own property in Lakeshore Bay, I'm not adverse to relocation.

Again, I thank you for inviting me to be in the race for this position. I would hope that I could bring energy, enthusiasm and my own excitement to your fine magazine.

Most sincerely, etc,

Bea on August 1, 1984

During a cocktail hour this week, I told Jan I didn't want to go to the Michigan's Women's Music Festival so she's going without me. This upsets me but she's so stubborn and I don't want to go. I guess this is how it stands. I must not let her drag me into yet another thing I don't want to do. I made my own bonfire in our yard after supper for my evening's entertainment.

She'll be going with Robin and Naomi with Robin's ex-husband's van pulling our camper. According to hearsay, those two have been creating a lot of noisy fun together in their little downtown apartment.

At 4 a.m. this morning, Robin backed the van into the driveway with Naomi to hook up our trailer for their trip. I'm going to miss Jan but I'm not going to miss Michigan. The rest of the day was a zoo! My daughter and granddaughter came with blueberries for me and played in our tiny plastic pool that we bought for us adults to cool down a bit ourselves.

Carolyn called, all excited about her MATC interviews for the two jobs. \

Betty called and said, "I need a safe place," meaning she needed to drink with me, but I said I was baby-sitting. I even got a call from Pete Letscher. I haven't seen him for a couple years. Did he find out I was alone this weekend? I got rid of him quickly. The boob tube and the bottle may comfort me—yea though I walk through the valley.

At 7:10, Jill called. At 7:30 Marian and Sharon dropped by for a chat and didn't know Jan had left for Michigan. At 9:20 Jill called again. Shit. I turned on the answering machine. I was hoping for a few days of not having to be responsible to anyone. Whew!

Jan on August 9 to 12, 1984

My second trip to the festival gave me the know-how to help my two Festie Virgins adjust to the festival challenges, and we barreled through Chicago and Indiana loop traveling as Bea's father would say, "Like shit through a tin horn." I suggested to Robin that we volunteer to shuttle with the van for our festival work shifts. Naomi chose to be close to the performers so she signed up to guard the night stage during the day. But Robin and I had more fun making the rounds along the dirt roads and loading grateful women in various stages of bareness from all over the country, Canada, Germany, England and France.

We sang and laughed for each of our four-hour shifts while the van's interior and exterior grew dustier and dirtier in the hot, dry wind. I wondered if the motor would heat up while we bumped along the primitive paths on Lois Lane from Loud and Rowdy to Bush Gardens camping to the Cuntree Store and beyond. We transported a community of women in a land of Paradise.

We listened to Sonia Johnson, an ex-communicated Mormon lesbian running for president of the U.S. as a radical feminist. Other workshops we attended were on incest/sexual abuse, earth-healing rituals, sharing our anger, anti-victim training, and communicating love.

Sports events with nude women were especially interesting, plus music and dancing, a day-stage, an acoustic stage, night-stage, late-stage and midnight film screenings to celebrate women's lives. We enjoyed Kate Clinton's humor and performances by Ferron, Cris Williamson, Tret Fure, Bea Higbie, Teresa Trull, Alix Dobkin, Casselberry & Dupree and Australia's Judy Small,

The three of us had our fun together—but I enjoyed being on my own, too. I knew when I should stay out of the camper tent because it was rocking and rolling from my friends' passion of their first months of love. On this women's Garden of Eden for lesbians' loving and caring, they're free from the dread of being discovered and punished.

In the Marketplace, I could linger at my own pace and interests. I sought quiet space in the Oasis emotional healing tent, sitting, breathing and quietly unbinding my worries of being unemployed, victimized by heterosexism and prejudice, concerned about Bea and our future. I could have talked with a counselor, but I chose to be in this place where I could further the process of healing myself.

I felt free being without Bea, yet she was with me in my thoughts, wondering how and what she would say, enjoy—or reject.

When the three of us packed our trailer to leave, we drove along the distressed dirt path toward the exit. We hit a bump, dislodged our poorly connected hitch and dug a trench with the chains pulling the trailer's tongue through the soft, sandy road. We strong women promptly fixed that and headed for home only to get lost in the night on Illinois toll way interchanges, making the trip hours longer than on our way there.

Bea on August 13, 1984

I picked garden produce yesterday, made gazpacho and waited for Jan. I expected her home late, but not at 2:30 in the morning! I'm angry but I'm trying to control that I'm flaming mad. It's like when your kids would go out past a reasonable hour. Worry and anger gets you. And I'm angry with Jan for not showing better sense than to toddle in at that hour when she has a Milwaukee appointment the next afternoon. It's crazy irresponsibility! Then she expects me to be open-armed and all jolly when she finally comes home.

I was angry from the night before too. I cleaned up the house for our full moon women, even scoured the stove. I needn't have bothered. Nobody showed! Betty came around 7:30—sober, stayed an hour and left. Fine friends!

Jan on August 16, 1984

Bea went to the Milwaukee Zoo with me last night for a supper meeting to network with other PR colleagues and to hear the zoo director describe his aggressive marketing plan. Linda Edwards and I talked about my job search and I told her I was interviewing with John Jackson tomorrow.

"It's a miracle," I proclaimed in quiet terms. "We went to a house party and met a *Milwaukee Journal* librarian who brought two want-ad clippings for Martha, our hostess, about possible jobs at MATC and at MCMC: two positions at the technical college and one at the hospital. And there's also an opening at the Zoo!"

Martha said she didn't have that kind of expertise and actually offered the clippings to me. And I shared the info with Carolyn and we both interviewed for both MATC positions, and Carolyn got one of the jobs and I didn't get either job. That was quite an experience having a panel interview me and then they sent me off to a room with a pencil and paper to create a favorable media release about to cover up a problem, the old 'shit into sunshine' deal. This was tense. And I couldn't think without my typewriter, and I made a mess of it. Besides, Carolyn is probably relieved to be on her own in this new environment.

"What about MCMC?"

With more volume I announced, "I'm meeting with MCMC's John Jackson tomorrow!"

Linda looked about to see if anyone was listening besides Bea and pointed out that a *Milwaukee Sentinel* reporter was just hired to do PR work for the Department of Health and Human Services on the County grounds.

"I've no idea what's going on. John Jackson's relatively new too. Who knows what he plans to do. Please don't say anything about my interview."

Just east of the zoo, across Interstate 45 and north of the jumble of highway interchanges is the county hospital, now the Midwest Center Medical Complex (MCMC).

When Bea and I left the zoo to search for the hospital, we stayed off the highways and headed east. When we turned north on 87th Street, we found ourselves driving on a narrow, tree-lined residential street for one block before stopping on Wisconsin Avenue.

There it was, looming down on us like Daphne du Maurie's Mandalay mansion in the movie, *Rebecca*! The columned entrance to the old County General Hospital was stained, its concrete trim jagged and weather-beaten. Filling a monumental silhouette in the twilight sky, its faded yellow bricks encase what seems like forty windows set in least nine intimidating floors that must be hospital wings spread out and rising on each side of its neglected entrance. As if brooding over acres of landscaped park with a murky lagoon languishing at the ground's lowest level, ancient weeping willows dipped their branches toward the water, softening the sharp, severe concrete edges of this once-proud building and grounds.

After we responded to the green light to proceed, we stopped before crossing a bridge to take in the view and catch our breaths.

What am I getting into? Starting in the 1940s when my dad and later my family would drive north to see my mother at the Winnebago State Hospital, we would travel on Highway 100.

Many times, we'd pass the County Mental Institutions west of where we were then. That building looked something like this building, and each time we passed it, I would wonder what it would be like to be a prisoner in those ghostly gothic hospital wards semi-hidden behind trees and tall, chain-link fences with barbwire coiling across their top edges.

Would I be stepping back into a hospital of those haunting decades of my mother's institutionalization? I could almost sense her hospital ward odor from visiting my mother during her years of captivity.

Undaunted, we traveled further up 87th Street to a newer front entrance, even though the address is 8700 W. Wisconsin Ave. Good thing I wouldn't play the fool and march up the old sidewalk into that ancient front door. What we found on 87th Street was an expanded structure north of the old building—with a massive marquee with glass doors opening into a black marble entrance leading to a more contemporary hospital wing. At least it looked as if it belonged in this decade. It appeared as if it had a capacity of over one thousand beds but my research indicated that the current hospital capacity was for 500 beds. Much of what was visible must not be utilized.

And what the hell are all these other buildings around us as we made our way through the grounds?

When we returned home, the message on our answering said tomorrow's 9:30 a.m. job interview was postponed until September 6 and that I should formally answer a want-ad in tomorrow's Milwaukee papers for the MCMC position posted by the Milwaukee County Personnel Department.

How many hoops do I have to jump through?

And speaking of hoops and jumping, the Olympics in Los Angeles entertained us through these stressful times.

Jan on August 24, 1984

What a jumble! Yesterday I wore Bea's, now my "dress for success" outfit and walked confidently into choice offices for an interview with Ben Barkin, the partner of perhaps the top PR firm in Milwaukee. Wow! Would I be in the big leagues working here! Our polite exchange ended up with an offer to freelance occasionally when the firm has a hospital client, and I declined. I need all the security and benefits of a full time position so I drove home disappointed and depressed.

But before my 3 p.m. meeting with Barkin, I returned to MATC to claim my red portfolio for the Barkin interview and for the one I've been promised with Jackson. A clerk called a panel member that I faced last week, but he said he couldn't interrupt the meeting in the room to retrieve my precious collection.

"You can't miss it. It's a fat red ring binder," I exclaimed; and getting red myself in a slow burn, I refused to back down, insisting that he wouldn't disturb the meeting by softly walking into the room and retrieving the invaluable proof that my work is critical to whomever decides to hire me. He finally gave in, entered the hallowed sanctuary, snatched my portfolio off a table and handed it to me.

Bea told me she sent out a 200-book order of *Something*'s to the Indianapolis Human Services last month and put all that on the computer invoice. She also wrote five cover letters and sent out résumés for herself in answer to ads for positions in the Milwaukee area.

Bea on September 4, 1984

I applied for nearly twenty communications positions as editor, magazine copywriter, artist, audio-visual, bookstore manager and I tested and interviewed for many of them, but today's interview was unique. I answered an ad with Edstrom Industries for a graphic artist and communicator in the animal care field with research on swine and cattle, rabbits and guinea pigs.

I looked and felt smashing for my interview with my new jacket, new shoes, even new underwear. I had a long interview with the company owner. They make animal drinking units and pig showers. I toured the factory and they have everything needed to do in-house publications, but I don't think we have a need and skill match here. While driving home, I nixed it.

Jan is planning our Seattle trip this evening. She'd send two letters to Tacoma and Seattle hospital openings listed in the *Wall Street Journal* and is considering stopping at their Personnel offices while we're there on our two-week vacation.

Jan on September 6, 1984

My career depends on John Jackon's impression of me, humble in the presence of this charismatic person. I'm sure that he's aware of his charisma, yet he seems to want to soften his strength to put me more at ease

I started off by handing him my red portfolio that he accepted it, pretended that it was heavy for him, raising his formidable eyebrows on his broad, brown brow. I think he was impressed. I did try—desperately inside—to be his chosen one, and handed him a lighter offering, my recently received reference letter from my respected leader Clark Young.

Mr. Clark Young on September 1, 1984

Dear Jan,

You can be certain that your record of accomplishments while Director of Communications at Lakeshore Medical Center is not only outstanding but may not be surpassed except through you. An examination of your award-winning accomplishments in special events, publications, media relations, public relations, and television programming also reflects your extraordinary sensitivity and comprehension of the complex works of the hospital organization. Your knack for finding the right phrasing and pictorial depiction of the hospital world portrayed appropriately for the public, the community and all levels of government has no equal in my 44 years of hospital administration.

I wish you continued success in your well-chosen profession and I know that Lakeshore Med Hospital, Racine, and I are very much better for your contributions.

Very sincerely yours,
Clark H. Young
F.A.C.H.A.

"That's impressive," Jackson nodded as if to be tipping his hat. "Jan. Are you sure you want to come to work here for a starting salary of $28,500?" (As if he were apologizing about its small amount.)

"Yes. I am."

"And are you sure that you'll want to move to Milwaukee County within six months after starting the position?"

"Yes. I am."

"Good. Now you go and make a good impression on all these assistant administrators on this list I've made for you. Each one is waiting to meet you."

Meeting each man was confusing, and the administrator who had handled what PR work was done had left the hospital so I had no idea what happened except that an agency, Joseph, Sigman, Somebody, had designed the hospital logo and developed some brochures. From their individual inclinations. They tried to describe what they each wanted from me. They also tried to educate me on how the hospital was connected to all other government and private organizations.

The Milwaukee County Medical Complex is truly complex.

When I got home, exhausted after the interstate drive and the interview tension, my priority was to mail a thank you letter to Mr. Young: "Your letter was the frosting on the cake when I left the interview with John Jackson. It was truly a tribute and an honor to be so warmly and considerably praised. Thank you. I'll treasure this respected affirmation. Gratefully, Jan"

Bea on September 12, 1984

Carolyn returned from her vacation and we gave her a party at Laura's home with good eats, drinks and lots of hospital people. I took a phone message for Jan while she was helping Laura at her house with party preparations. I called her there to tell her she should stand by at 4:30 for a call from Jackson, but it didn't happen and she was strung out when she picked me up at 6. One of the reasons she so worried is that her age will register with Jackson and he'll think she's too old. She'll be 53 in November. But Carolyn's age didn't seem to be a factor for her new job. And they both look and act much younger than they are.

I bought Carolyn a leather briefcase as our group gift.

Our rummage sale last weekend was wet on Friday and my arthritis was bad but I sold $250 of stuff. Jan helped on Saturday and we sold more, including our beloved camper that we moved to the front of the driveway, opened it up and used it for our rummage sale office and refreshment center. Getting rid of the old was great to prepare moving to a new house.

Robin wants to buy our house later for her, her kids—and Naomi. That would be a great solution for all of us. She could rent our house and buy it later. Naomi will stay with our Luv while we're off to Seattle.

Jan on September 13, 1984

John Jackson finally called me early this morning to say that I'm the person he wants for the job. It's a promise to be in an important position in the Milwaukee health care arena with a vastly improved salary. I'll be working for a man who seems to be a blooming humanitarian, a liberal and dedicated person who says that "I am the right match to work with him to effect change and to care for people." His powerful voice nails me to the floor.

We're elated, but without the job being signed, sealed and delivered, we don't want to jump for joy yet. This is not for other's ears either because I expect to be terminated immediately after Lakeshore Med administration hears of this job. This "verbal handshake" over the phone is so genuine, but if he doesn't follow through, I know I'll feel like the bride left at the altar and want to sue for breach of promise.

He said my starting date might be October 15. I told him I'm heading to the Great Northwest for a vacation until September 28 and will notify his secretary when I'm back.

Finally Bea and I must deal with this reality. It's hard to finally digest the news, and we have overwhelming feeling about moving, but reality is sinking in hour by hour.

Ironically, I also received an encouraging letter from a Tacoma hospital vice president and an interview with Milwaukee's Visiting Nurses Association. I cancelled the Zoo and Nursing interviews because of our much-needed vacation and my great expectation of John Jackson keeping his promise.

Bea on September 18 to 28, 1984

We flew over our nation's sacred Northwestern spires, Mount Rainier and Mount St. Helens in clear weather, until we neared Seattle proper where overcast skies cleared finally to blue. After picking up our Dodge Aires, we were surprised by the steep city streets when we found our hosts' neighborhood where Camela Parson and her husband live. I don't like to stay at people's homes. Never have and don't want to this time either. My independent parents never stayed with relatives on their trips either. But Jan insisted we see her dear friend Cam and her husband, so I went along with it. After we learned where we would be ending our day, we drove back into Seattle's center, parked our classy car, and headed, as is our custom, to the top of the places—The Space Needle. After visiting the buildings and shops created for a World's Fair, we boarded the monorail to downtown for a visit to the Public Market at Pike Street. We checked out the fresh fish markets, troubadours playing hammered dulcimers, art and crafters and American Indian stalls.

On our way back to Cam's, we bought our liquor supplies and a hostess gift. After a couple wrong turns up and down Seattle's hills, almost like San Francisco, we found Cam's home where we talked and caught up on all our news. They offered to show us Seattle, but we had already seen the best of it. Instead, Jan and Cam shared old stories so her David could hear about her adolescent days living with her talented Unitarian family who rented Jan and her husband's lower flat when their Matt was in Montessori School and Jenny was a toddler.

We went off to sleep around 10:30 on our first futon. It was 12:30 a.m. our time and we'd been up since 5 a.m. Despite our obvious exhaustion, Jan woke me in the night with her sneezing and she finally stopped being brave and admitted that she couldn't breathe. She seemed to be having an asthma attack so we sat out on their porch for more fresh air until she settled down enough so we could go back to sleep again.

Violinist Cam and her trumpeter David play with the Seattle Symphony Orchestra so they had time to spend with us during this leisurely morning. When we told them about Jan's attack during the night, Cam said, "Oh! Right! You must have been sleeping on the cats' pillows. I forgot you have allergies, especially to cats! I remember now hearing you sneeze when we lived downstairs of you."

"And when I was pregnant," Jan said, "I couldn't decide whether to cover at my nose or grab my crotch to keep my baby from falling out!"

When we described our plans of driving along the coastline, they raved about Kalaloch Lodge overlooking the ocean in the Olympia National Park. We stopped at AAA to get more maps before leaving them until the last night of our trip before flying home. We headed south to our Ocean City destination around the tip of Puget Sound through Tacoma. Jan quickly cancelled her interest in stopping for a job interview at one of Tacoma's medical centers because of the area's putrid smell.

We drove south, then west toward Olympia National Park and toured the historic Ellison Oyster Company oyster farm with its bins of unopened oysters, each quickly being shucked apart by weathered old hands sliding the slippery contents while sorting them into cool, clear baths, then quickly packaged into fresh oyster containers, a strangely entertaining experience. Of course we had to buy a pint of fresh, raw oysters packed in ice. We stopped at a few stores in Aberdeen, bought ice and a large foam cooler for the car and found an ice bucket at a rummage sale that would be perfect for future ice cube needs. We discovered a motel in Ocean City that had a kitchen where we savored our martinis and ate some of our raw oysters that were classified as extra small but were huge. Jan had a problem downing them, but she did manage eating four. Her mom and dad loved to eat oyster soup and crackers and raw oysters when she was a kid, but oysters are about the only food she doesn't care for. She loves the crackers.

The broad rolling waves and the roar of the surf drew us out of the motel to walk to the Pacific Ocean. After crossing a rickety bridge to the beach, Jan began running across the sand to get to the water's edge while I stayed resting on the roots of a giant driftwood log as big as a bus. Jan called to me, proclaiming that she was having a spiritual experience and she will stay on the beach until the sun sank in the ocean.

The restaurant next to our hotel served us a steamed clams supper and we cooked the leftover clams for breakfast and made oyster stew to save for lunch. We were to drive right past the Kalaloch Lodge and made reservations to treat ourselves by staying there tonight.

Wow! Our room in this luxury lodge offered a breathtaking but overcast ocean view with driftwood the size of boxcars jumbled about in all directions, entire trees with their roots twisted along the high water line near tall grasses holding together sand dunes. The giants from the rainforest behind us are torn away from the land by soaking rains that weaken their roots and they topple over and slide into the ocean. When stormed-tossed on the beach, they bleach out on the sand near to Mother Nature's majestic rock outcroppings that stand as Her temples.

Sipping beer from our stash of cans in our backpack, we trekked up and down the wet and windy deserted beach, taking pictures, climbing logs, picking up rocks. Jan again ran about to touch the next monumental rock formation she reached, each set like a primitive shrine in the shifting tides upon the earth and ocean horizon.

After watching her flit around like a dragonfly, she finally came to rest next to me, thoroughly chilled, landing on my small rock outcropping perch, its dampness taking warmth from our bones. We trudged the sandy shores, climbing over and around the driftwood to our lodge and to our room to savor our martinis or brandy. We moved a loveseat in front of the open window and we snuggled together under a blanket. Jan ordered from room service, which is rare for her to do, and a woman delivered absolutely delicious salmon and cod tempura that we fed to each other as we waited for the sunset. When the room server opened the door to bring in our supper, she looked surprised at our sitting there—so close.

Still ready to celebrate, euphoric on the ocean air and heady ozone atmosphere, Jan maneuvered the table with food and our drinks close to me so I didn't have to move. The talent for our evening's entertainment flew to our windowsill to perch and watch us eat. We feed these few hefty seagulls with imposing beaks the remaining oysters that we warily placed, one-by-one with a fork, on the porch roof outside our open window. Using the not-so-fresh oysters to feed our seafaring feathered friends pleased Jan because we didn't throw them out—and she didn't have to eat any more of them.

The sunset slipped into the ocean without much fanfare on this blustery gray day. While keeping the window open, I dozed on Jan's shoulder until we moved together to make love amid our cool, fresh and billowy bedding. Still invigorated by her ecstatic experiences prancing among Mother Earth's imposing power and beauty, I lay naked under feather quilts and surrendered to her naked self. Her enveloping, all-encompassing aura surged above me, warm now and free, a oneness melding with tidal sounds of swelling waves, lush smells of damp, forever green rainforest and pungent tastes of salty breezes blowing over us through the window until Goddess-given climaxes and peaceful cuddling brought us sunshine in the morning.

While devouring a shrimp and cheese omelet breakfast while overlooking the ocean from the lodge restaurant, we heard stories of the tides and driftwood logs that had caught beachcombers unaware and crushed them against other logs and rocks. Thanks for the warning now that we're leaving.

The morning beaches were even broader under a warming sun and puffy clouds, and we walked on Ruby Beach, then drove up the Hoh River Valley with beautiful vistas of the ocean and the forest primeval. Often, we tourists would be ready to drive off on to a wide spot in the road when logging trucks speeded too close behind us so we'd be intimated and move out of their way.

We walked almost a mile along the sun- and shadow-lit self-guided Hall of Mosses Trail in the Olympic National Forest studying flora and fauna with falling trees growing new life from mossy sprouts that surrounds their trunks. Jan acted elfish again, especially when she entered the center of the remains of a seven-foot moldy tree and stuck her head out of a hole with an impish smile. She's becoming a wood nymph as well as my personal and insatiable nymphomaniac.

We found a nice motel at Forks for $21, settled in and went off to LaPush, a Native American town on one side of a "cut" and Rialto beach, another magnificent Pacific-rugged shoreline with giant driftwood and craggy rocks in the surf. We hiked for about two miles, but hustled back because it was getting late and we didn't want any scary tide incidents to happen to us. Jan brought us hamburgers to eat in our little motel after our cocktails, and we crashed—a sound, uninterrupted sleep for both of us tonight.

I woke early and got caught up writing in my journal before we drove to Sol Duc Hot Springs, which opened at 9 a.m. The air temperature was 58 and we could smell sulfur as we drove into the area. We quickly changed into bathing suits and plunged into glorious hot mineral soaks and swims again and again. Three round pools are constructed so the hot springs flow from the hottest of 109 degrees and down to a lovely 73-degree pool with fresh water, all perfectly suited for us water gals.

After lunch we drove on to Port Angeles and the All View Motel with a view looking down on Juan de Fuca Straits and up to the Hurricane Ridge Mountain. We drove up, up and up to Observatory Point through dramatic clouds and drifting mist. The last curve to the Point surprised us. Snow! The evergreens became instant Christmas card pictures, and that's all we could see, so we enjoyed the drive down to town and devoured a huge crab supper at the famous Dungeness Three Crabs Restaurant.

The dock was our morning destination to board the M.C. Coho ferry for a chilly but delightful crossing to Victoria on Vancouver Island, British Columbia, Canada. We sat inside the bow of the ferry for the one and a half-hour trip and landed in the most delightful city I've ever experienced, surrounded by water, sailboats, a rocky coastline, parks and homes with flowers everywhere, like in England—only better.

Our visit started with Victoria's Seaquarium right next to our dock on a permanent barge surrounded by fish pens. We boarded it and descended below the water level to view through glass windows every sort of Pacific sea creature imaginable. In an underwater theater, a diver displayed the creatures including Armstrong the Octopus, the star of the show.

We found our motel, a super classy place at a bargain, so we decided to stay two nights to tour the city in our car, visit the impressive Totem Pole Museum and park, and savor tea, scones and crumpets at an English inn. After a rest at our motel and our traditional cocktail hour there, we savored sushi, tempura and teriyaki at a Japanese restaurant before heading downtown where the Parliament building was lit up like Christmas.

After a leisurely awakening in our queen-sized bed, we finally got ourselves going to enjoy breakfast at a cafe featuring spinach and feta cheese and brie-filled croissants. That fortified us when we found the maritime museum where I gave Jan a guided tour about the Trekka, John Guzzwell's boat that he sailed, single-handed, around the world. He was on the Tzu Hang where she pitchpoled off the roaring 40s. We also saw the Tillicum, a converted dugout canoe that sailed half-round the world with great fanfare around the turn of the century, but it didn't finish the circumnavigation. Jan thanked me for my nautical tales that I remember from my readings—or is it from my previous life as a sailor.

One of the best museums I've ever experienced was the British Columbia Museum that incorporates the five senses into most exhibits. The five-senses experience started immediately outside the entrance where we watched a man sculpting with a chain saw, chopping a totem pole into reality from a huge log. However, the fragrance of cedar chips flying and the roaring from the power tool couldn't recapture the hand-carved spiritual artistry of the original Northwestern tribes.

Jan's favorite place was the Bengal Room in the venerable, ivy-covered, brick-red Empress Hotel with its British Empire atmosphere reeking of the days of its historic colonial power with tiger skins draping the paneled mahogany walls, its upscale British bar and high-back bamboo chairs arranged in its spacious and airy hall with the afternoon sun shining on the room's elegant tribute to Victorian England.

Jan said she should be wearing a pith helmet and saber with white jodhpur pants, snug fit to the knee with flaring hips, and shiny black riding boots. Her jingling medals on her high collared white jacket would match the bold gold trim epaulets on her shoulders. She felt like Rudyard Kipling though I think she's been imprinted by too many movies of that era as we sipped Canadian ale rather than English lime and lager.

The rate of exchange here is three to one so we're in good shape, especially after stocking up at the liquor store. We rode up Beacon Hill and enjoyed a drink with the expansive view of snow-covered mountains across Puget Sound back in the U.S. We agreed that Victoria would be an ideal retirement location.

The weather is perfect as we drove north to Nanaimo with fiord-like views. We stopped at a petroglyph park with primitive rock carvings before we loaded onto a three-level ferry big enough to transport huge trucks to the mainland and the city of Vancouver. The ferry went at a good clip and, of course, we sat in the bow, but this time we were sheltered behind huge glass windows keeping us warm and snug over calm waters.

We headed toward Vancouver on the Interstate but impulsively turned off to discover what was on Grouse Mountain. Wow! The Skyride, North America's largest tram system, goes practically straight up for a mile of breathtaking views of the city, its shore and the Lion Gate Ridge way below. After lunch, Jan said she was eternally grateful for my backing down about taking a helicopter ride off the mountain because she still hasn't recovered from one helicopter ride she took with Jenny years ago when their tourist helicopter ride almost nicked George Washington's ear at Mount Rushmore. However, she relived that scary thrill with me on the way down on The Skyride as we went straight out over the edge with the two of us standing against the front windows as the gondola went out into space with nothing below us. Yips!

We had reserved our motel back on earth, but it took us hours to reach it as we drove south past the main part of Vancouver. We thought we could drive back to see the city, but it turned out that we were too far away and too tired to tackle city traffic again. Plus that, we didn't know what to do or where to go when we'd get there, so here we were in a strange motel with nothing to do and no place to go. But we discovered the motel's indoor steaming heated pool and after a drink or two we went swimming.

With windows fogged by steam and having the pool all to ourselves, what's a person to do? We abandoned our suits and played Jan's favorite Baby Seal caper, swimming under the water, floating, touching, kissing and splashing together playfully and naturally as we had done on our 1976 European honeymoon, swimming nude at a secluded pool at a Black Forest inn in Germany. What delightful joy it is to play.

We swam in the hot pool again in the morning, took our wine with us and got nicely laid back. Again we were alone, playing baby seal. Who knows how many watery mammals we can think up? We finally checked out of the big city of Vancouver with the longest seaport on the Pacific Coast, which we saw only from its interstate highway and from this steamy motel pool. But what memories we have of our visit.

Before crossing back into the States, we bought two pairs of moccasins and two warm Indian knit hats at the duty-free shop. Then we drove down the coast along Puget Sound to Whidbey Islands' Oak Harbor and found our motel, ate lunch at the Two Sisters near a windmill in the town. We were so tired, we started slowing down, drove to see the sun set in the west across the beautiful places we had experienced in this fabulous sea and land paradise, and we went to our motel for a blessed sleep.

Our Whidbey Island sojourn had us stopping at Holmes (my maiden name) Bay where we beach-combed for shells that were covered with barnacles. We built sand castles until it was time to reach the end of the island and board a short ferry and ride under cloudless blue skies to Seattle. We stopped several times along the waterfront for chowder and fish and chips, fed the gulls right out of our hands, and examined piers of tug, fishing and ferryboats at their berths.

We joined again with Cam and David who took us to dinner at the Fisherman's Terminal Wharf restaurant. Wow! The view unfolded as a forest of fishing boats returned to port while we relished in our seafood sampler supper that was deliciously perfect for our last night in the Great Northwest. To our surprise and with lots of fun, our professional musicians took us to their neighborhood bar and we shot pool until 11:30. Cam took up the game when she needed hand and finger exercises to strengthen her violin playing. I think they were surprised that we could hold our own with our billiards expertise.

We enjoyed our last chat with Cam in the morning as we packed for our flight home, flying first to Portland, Oregon. We passed tremendous mountain views, including flying right over Mount St. Helens! I spent most of the time looking at the country unfolding below. The clouds looked like chunks torn from wool fleece with paw-print shadows tracking them on the Earth's surface below.

It was sunset when we landed in Milwaukee and our house was fine when we came home with our dog to greet us and piles and piles of mail. We made our calls to our daughters, and my Jill announced that she is pregnant and due near my birthday in May. Yeah!

Chapter 24

Jan on October 2, 1984

John Jackson called saying he is interviewing five people in the next two weeks and that I'm still the top candidate. He talked about a November 5 starting date and will mail me a written offer after completion of the interview process. This is too intense.

Bea on October 4, 1984

Jan's verbally been offered a job to start on November 5. Now we have to sell our home within six months to live within Milwaukee County—a rule. Rummage sales. Uncertain times. Feel like Margaret O'Brien's Christmas Eve scene in *Meet Me in St. Louis*. After that, the stress of planning our future, painting rooms to sell our house, hiding all our nude paintings in the attic.

Two days ago after packing loads of orders including four boxes with 25, 50, 80 and 100 copies, Laura came to talk about her problems at work. Today, Carolyn at MATC came over to commiserate because she made a big goof at her new job at MATC and was shaky about it. Also her new Nissan sedan is having adjustment problems and is in the shop. Oh well. Roses do have thorns, don't they?

Jan carpooled with Ken Voss to the HPRW meeting in LaCrosse and she called while Carolyn was here. It's great to hear her voice. I miss her and I mostly ate all day. So much for the diet.

I've lost my lean and hungry look and with it, my appetite for life. I waited for Jan all day. She said she'd be home in the afternoon, but she's riding with Voss and has to adjust to his schedule. After pacing the floor, I went shopping. She finally phoned at 6:30 from a gas station west of Milwaukee and showed up later, all bright and bushy. We had a row about her being late and I'm to blame somehow. How is that?

A bit of helpful information from HPRW is that she discovered that Mark Massoni, a former HPRW colleague and someone she likes and trusts, is now connected with Worzalla Publishing Company in Steven's Point and we're asking for a bid to produce *Why Me*.

Bea on October 11, 1984

I watched the first American women walk in space. Kathy Sullivan and Sally Ride are part of the seven Challenger crew. In the evening we watched the debate between VP's Bush and Geraldine Ferraro. You'd think women were finally getting a piece of the pie. Hooray for Kathy, Sally and Geraldine!

Two days ago, I took the civil service exam again in Elmwood for their bookstore manager. I did OK but with a lot of ambiguous questions, I don't have much chance of getting anywhere. The last time I took the test brought me absolutely nothing, but I'm still responding to ads and applying for part time teaching.

Betty Hanneman had a party for Anna Spence's daughter Elisa—not to be a baby shower, the invitation said, but it was. It was more like our full moon women's spirituality gatherings and Betty did two meditation exercises. Our old UU and folk dancing gang was there—and Marge, our former best friend who's now Jan's ex-husband's wife. That's not easy.

Tomorrow we're off to the Woman-to-Woman conference, which is good because that should take the pressure off of our long ordeal of waiting about jobs. Jan told me it's the hardest work she's ever done.

Bea from October 12 to 14, 1984

Anne Wilson Schaef, the first day's keynote speaker, empowered us to be aware of the white male system that encourages addiction and addictive relationships to keep us out of touch with ourselves. Yet if we get in touch with ourselves, we can't tolerate the system in which we live. It's an either/or situation where there are no winners. She described:

1. The Reactive Female system based on superficial male validation;
2. the White Male system that is power; and
3. today's Emerging Female system.

"Only a zombie survives by choosing neither to live nor die," she said. Being addicted to powerlessness and death produces diseases, and she stressed, "Addiction is anything you feel you have to lie about—and sobriety is living in process, living with totally free will and acting out of our own spirituality."

I listed her characteristics of an addictive system:
1. Male self-centeredness, "for or against me," defining everything in terms of "me."
2. Illusion of controlling the feelings of others. Religions and psychotherapy facilitate the system. We must shift to another way of "being."
3. Denial is to refuse to see what's going on.
4. Dishonesty is a requirement to lie where dishonesty is the norm.

5. Women are being removed from true spirituality. Our "Life Force" counters with not being dead, not being alive, merely survive to fit in the system.

Jan and I, in inspired anger, realized her point that understanding will help us work within and change the misuse of the white male power system that oppresses us.

Of course we bought her *Women's Reality*, and we'll read and learn more right away.

In relation to that topic, we went to "From Dreaming to Doing" with a dynamic duo of June Kroniskey and Susan Winecki who call their motivational agency "Athena."

One said, "We are like sponges filled full of negative messages and we need to be squeezed out. We have a sense of not being lovable, not loving all of our parts, not loving ourselves. We're operating at half-mast. We must look at ourselves in a different light."

They asked what is your mental picture of someone you would like to be and I wrote their list in my LOG: success, attitude, money, energy, freedom, mental ability, guts, poise, beauty, confidence and/or a strong sense of self?

What do you have within you to help fulfill dreams?
 1. Name three successes you have achieved within the past year.
 2. Which one is the most significant? Applaud yourself. If you feel good about yourself, you spark others.
 3. What makes it meaningful? To stir up trouble, we need fire in our lives, be hungry for fun and adventure and want to be wild and free.
 4. What obstacles did you overcome to achieve success?
 5. What qualities, skills and abilities within you helped you: quick wit, good nature, something intrinsic to you.

"Programming a computer," I whispered to Jan.

6. What resources outside of you did you use to create this success?

"H.R. Block. Stock market. Insurance exam," I continued.

7. How did you celebrate your success? "Probably with a couple of good, stiff drinks," I ended.

At the end of several inspiring workshops we met Carolyn and Joanne Zekas at the convention cocktail bar to listen to a choir of women from Madison. Lesbians? When we came home, Jan turned on PBS and Virginia Wolff's *Mrs. Dalloway,* which put me right to sleep.

The next day I went to workshops that were more of the same for me, one telling me to get in touch with the other half of my brain. I'm integrated and was comfortable with both hemispheric processes. Other claptrap that inspired Jan was what I already knew: "Small changes become endless possibilities;" and "Living on Purpose. Be an 'I can person' who also has the power to choose an attitude."

Our second-year workshop with Patricia Durovny seemed as if she were winging it with her "The Attitude of Gratitude" concept. "If it is to be; it's up to me. I can make a difference. Right livelihood. Win. Win. Win. Listen to the little voice inside." She stressed survival issues, which we know only too well: "Fear overtakes wants. Am I ready to do what it takes? The results? A high success potential ratio."

I think Durovny is overworked, being responsible for this year's conference. As Mother Courage, we had offered to help and went to one meeting last spring where a roomful of women brainstormed about keynote speakers. One suggested a dynamic TV newcomer, Oprah Winfrey. She has ties to Milwaukee and perhaps they should try to get her now when she's still an affordable speaker. But Gloria Steinman got the call in this important election year.

Good thing the dog barked on Saturday morning or we would have slept too long. It was so foggy we went past our exit but drove around and parked all right. We missed the "dynamic duo" warm-up speeches, but with all the successful woman routines we've experienced, we truly appreciated the impressive competence of women at the conference.

We met Pat Holmen and Laura Williams at the doorway to the Grand Hall champagne brunch buffet featuring Gloria Steinman. We had an excellent time and Gloria was inspiring! Unity to fight for reproductive rights and freedom was her theme. She got the biggest applause when she said that the power of government must stop at our skins. We have to redefine and revalue work—including all productive labor. Families must live within the democratic system with individual rights for each person and she compared our culture and our politics with women living in unfair power relationships, citing TV images of violence and sex roles as the deepest roots of personal and institutional violence. Of course, Geraldine Ferraro's name as the Democratic vice presidential candidate seemed second place to Walter Mondale in this audience's overwhelming applause.

After motivating afternoon sessions, we sat at the bar for a glass of champagne and while in the full flush of the conference, I wrote my affirmations with Jan leading me on.

Bea's Women to Women affirmations:

I now weigh 150 pounds. I look fantastic. All my clothes fit beautifully.

Jan has her new job at Milwaukee County. Jan loves it.

We found a beautiful new house in Milwaukee County that has everything we want.

Why Me? is published. It looks great! We're swamped with orders and business is thriving.

I belong to new networking organizations. I'm meeting new people every week.

We sold 13th Street.

We have more money and resources than we dreamed of.

We're now celebrating the best Holiday Season ever.

We're relaxed and totally comfortable. We're healthy and strong. Our love and strength spreads out from us in rippling waves to empower other people. Our prosperity is catching. Our love is catching. Our energy and creativity creates the good life for others and us.

Jan wrote her affirmations after being pushed into The Big Leagues. She'll be the first official PR person heading her one-person department of a 460-bed historic County-owned hospital with 1650 employees. Yikes.

She wrote, "I am the successful public relations director of the Milwaukee County Medical Complex and I want to be happy for what I can give, not just thankful for what I can get."

Jan mellowed out, leaned towards me and spoke in my ear, "We'll start this new week keeping the Woman-to-Woman glow. Since last year's Women to Woman conference when we talked above the city at the Hyatt cocktail lounge—whirling in an aura of love—it's been a year since we've evolved. That is truly wonderful!"

Meanwhile, a 128-car pile-up in the fog on the northbound lane of I-43 was being untangled. Fortunately we avoided that, thank the Goddess!

Chapter 25

Jan on October 20, 1984

Jenny came with Mondale/Ferraro yard signs, bumper stickers and buttons, and we ate Bea's pumpkin soup with Carolyn and her Roger before we watched the TV debates between Mondale and Reagan. We don't take for granted how great it is having family and friends—and most of our church members—in agreement with us when it comes to politics and social issues. One openly Republican woman, an active church member and attorney, vowed to stay a Republican because she hopes to improve the party

During the "Kate and Allie" TV program, Susan Saint James and Jane Curtin pretended to be lesbians! How affirming that was for us!

I'm preparing a Marketsearch application to begin immediately if there is any catch in my getting the MCMC position. Meanwhile I submitted my job search expenses to Randy of $21.40 for 107 letters mailed for job information and $3.20 postage for 16 thank you letters totaling $127.12 for travel and mailing.

We're dieting and restricting ourselves to two drinks an evening, either wine or beer, and walking and trying to exercise. Our new regime was successful and we're relatively peaceful. But waiting for The MCMC Letter grows more intense. Every day Bea waits for the morning mail. The Post Office could have changed this route. Once she went off to kill some time and when she got home, the mail still wasn't here—but I was. I couldn't stand it at work waiting for a call from Bea. The mail finally came after I went back to Lakeshore Bay but still no letter.

I broke down and bought some brandy. I'd missed a call from Jackson because the hospital switchboard operator didn't page me when I was out of my office, (She probably knows about my non-status status.) and also we had a message on our answering machine at home. I'd missed The Call again. I couldn't cope.

After cocktails and supper, we went up to bed early to give gentle love, to comfort each other with intimate touching, knowledgeable fingers, mouths and tongues in sensitive and supple places, breasts and labia, intensely bonding together in our own world to peak in harmony and rest together in peace.

From John Jackson on October 24, 1984

Dear Ms. Anthony
　　I am pleased to offer you the position of Director of Public Relations at the Milwaukee County Medical Complex effective November 5, 1984,
　　In this position you will provide leadership for the hospital public relations and marketing. This position may also include supervision of hospital information functions and other related internal and external communications systems.
　　Because this is a new position, and because of the hospital's unique position with Franklin Lutheran Memorial Hospital, the Medical College of Wisconsin, the Milwaukee Regional Medical Center and other County departments, you may be required to coordinate with a number of key persons as we develop our public relations program.
　　Your starting salary will be $27,500 pending review by the Civil Service Commission. I am optimistic that the salary can be increased as the program develops.

Attached is a statement of benefits. Please respond to this offer in writing as soon as possible.

Sincerely, etc.

Jan on October 26, 1984

Dear Mr. Jackson,

I am pleased and proud to have been chosen to join your staff as Director of Public Relations starting on November 5, 1984. I will be looking forward to meeting with you on Monday.

Thank you.

Bea on October 29, 1984

We woke early this morning, made love, and Jan went to buy this Sunday's *Milwaukee Journal* where we searched for house ads for two hours and marked what we wanted to see. After breakfast, we drove around Milwaukee for more than five hours and looked at probably fifty to sixty houses with Trick and Treat kids running all around each neighborhood and suburb. At least Jan doesn't have to x-ray those damn Halloween bags again. We learned about what's available and how much it will cost us. We drove home with mixed feelings, depressed by some houses we looked at and liked but couldn't afford and others we could afford but were old and tacky.

Another catch is our plan to sell our house. Once Robin Witte talked about buying our house if Jan and I moved, but now she's backing off because Naomi wants to get an advanced degree in San Francisco. Robin surprised Naomi by insisting on going to San Francisco with her. I don't think that's what Naomi expected, with Robin being older and having two kids, whatever. Robin will not buy our house.

Now we have to spruce up our house, painting and cleaning, scheming and calculating its selling points to get our equity so we can settle in Milwaukee. We tore up the place to paint the living room but we succeeded in making everything a mess. I took down all of my paintings and put most of them in the attic. This is a terrible job! Jan whipped herself into a cooking frenzy again with harvesting the last of the garden produce. She's a real pain when she does that because we never eat till late and if I want to eat earlier because I'm hungry, she gets pissed.

Then we got a call about something being wrong on our property on 13th Street. I hate rental properties! So I arranged for my son to go over there. I drank too much brandy. I hate tearing up our house, my bones ache and everything is so frustrating. I don't want to move. I don't want to change everything. But I don't have a choice. I don't like hiding my nude paintings. I miss them. It's like part of me must be hidden, as if Jan is ashamed of them and me. Our home that was so honest is no more.

<<<>>>

Jan on November 3, 1984

"Good luck." That's what my Transgressor said. Does he know something I don't know? I'm sure he does. "Good luck?" Is that what I need? No! I need courage. And as a new, one-woman PR person in this huge hospital, I need to build team support with staff already in a place to be successful in a system that I know nothing about.

I guess I was also a leader of sorts while being supportive in my most humble job—that of wife, though I loved being a mother. I asked for that, put my teaching career aside and did what every "normal" woman expected to do —sublimate herself for her husband and family, including in-laws. And I did that well until I felt lonely and finally so angry that I had to move on and out. I stepped out of bounds and became "crazed" enough to leave my home, husband and "heterosexual privilege" to start new adventures in unknown and socially unacceptable territory.

When I stopped being totally supportive of my entire family, they were confused. Some hated me. I stopped being their holiday entertainer, their moral supporter, the glue that held them together. Oh well. I had to hold myself together first in order to continue to work and support the financial and emotional needs of my lover and myself.

My work as a teacher, volunteer, my church, newspaper reporter and a hospital public relations person have always promoted others and the causes I've served.

I remember as a teacher inspiring high school students to love literature and language, to be creative, independent and responsible. I think I inspired youths as a church school worship leader and I sustained a strong base for the church school as it is today.

I loved the challenge as a newspaper reporter where I advanced awareness of alternative ways of thinking and acting on sexism, religious practices, the environment and feminism, but I hated the passive oppression I felt at home from a husband jealous of my success and the diminishing maintenance of him and his.

I loved working at my hospital, one of two in my small city, I fought for it through many conflicts including a six-weeks strike when I wrote a newsletter everyday—every single day. The newsletter gave information to hospital staff and strikers too that, it is said, helped to crack the strike leaders' credibility. I loved my co-workers and their work in serving others; I supported my hospital then even when administrators stopped supporting me.

In my new position in this huge metropolitan hospital and its clinics, I'll support and champion the staff and their work, motivate the public to choose our hospital for care, and with others, make this county-owned public hospital more successful and sustainable.

Of course, Bea and our Mother Courage efforts have always been to increase the self-esteem and strength of women in the battle against patriarchy. What a cause that is!

Through it all, my main effort, my highest priority, is always toward a happy and success-filled relationship with my lover and the work that we have accomplished together. At this stage in my life, I must focus on my keeping this complex new PR position to advance all our goals, to feel secure, to travel and to enjoy our lives together. While I support her, I need her nurturing love and her many talents to help me. Then we'll be more secure, successful and happy in our long lives together.

As a communicator, I will maintain a calm attitude, respect my colleagues as I would expect their respect in turn, and hopefully, add a tasteful bit of humor.

Finally after years of professional success in the midst of intense emotional harassment, I was accepted as the public relations director at one of Milwaukee's major metropolitan hospitals, the Midwest Center Medical Complex.

Jan on November 3, 1984

This morning I looked out our bedroom window at our once bountiful backyard full of vegetables that grew boldly in boxes of soil enriched by my compost. My yard was art for me. Like a jigsaw puzzle that's never finished, I'd find pieces to fit into the scheme of it. I wonder if I'll have a garden in Milwaukee.

I lost myself remembering. Even before WW II, my mother planted a victory garden and when she was sent away again early in her life, I tried to keep it up with its kitchen garden assortment and marigolds. I tell, when someone listens, about hauling my wagon full of buffalo dung fresh from the zoo but it was too strong for the garden growing right under our kitchen window.

I'm sure I'll never again live near a zoo. Or Lake Michigan beaches. Or public parks.

When my dad was in the Navy, I pushed the heavy manual lawn mower with its rusty blades to lop off the grass. The few simple plants along the south side of the house would dry up from neglect but the trumpet vine and that yucca plant that we brought back from our 1936 trip to California thrived.

In our home now, I planted a cold weather yucca perennial in a sunny spot next to our kitchen door. It took a year or more, but finally green spikes shot up five feet carrying a bloom base as huge as a large loaf of Wonder Bread that was covered with white blossoms with a foul scent that floated through the kitchen door and lured insects with its kinky fragrance more suitable to bloom in a deserted, dry desert.

My plan intended for the vine was to climb up an unsightly telephone pole, cover it and an attached white metal sign with red letters commanding everyone not to climb the damn pole. The hearty vine was to hide the old wooden pole in plain sight, attract hummingbirds and improve the view. Several winters of ice or climbing squirrels ignoring the sign must have weighed the vine down to become a fat, bushy base with a few red-orange trumpet blossoms to attract one or two hummingbirds for a few minutes.)

I hope all will survive when we sell our house.

When I was a teen, I never thought about gardening. I chose basketball and volleyball, but those games need a team to win and another team to lose. Playing baseball in right field was boring; I wasn't a good hitter. I loved tennis and played competitively for years.

I started to garden when Husband Alex and I bought a two-flat and I became a stay-at-home wife and mother. Late one spring day after completing carpooling kids home from Montessori School, Matt, Jenny and I rescued a large turtle from the center of busy West River Road.

I stopped the car and traffic, pulled an old blanket from the car clutter to spread over her, picked her up from behind and quickly plopped her in the trunk until I got home and grabbed our encyclopedia to discover her species. She became our Roxie, the Blanding's box turtle who loved eating my fresh gardens greens, juicy bugs on leafy weeds and Alex's fishing worms surviving in a covered tin in the refrigerator.

One summer day I answered the phone and the startled grocer on our corner declared, "Mrs. C! Your little girl is pushing a huge snapping turtle with a long neck reaching out of her doll buggy. You need to come right away. Other kids are teasing it with sticks Your daughter's not afraid, but I'll keep her safe until you get here."

Jenny had taken her out of the recycled chicken wire and lumber cage built from my dad's stock pile to make Roxie a pleasant pen in a shady spot among the bushes. Roxie survived many baby buggy and wagon rides and tolerated swimming with children in a kiddie pool until the time they forgot to put her back in her pen and she was gone.

I figured Roxie made her escape route under an old fence, crept across a neighbor's yard and down a steep, weedy, wooded hill to scurry some blocks toward West River Road where we supposedly rescue her. Did she made it across the street? Hopefully she escaped to live in the muddy banks of the Wood River where she belonged.

Digging in the dirt, spreading my compost and tending to plants is healing. I lose myself in it. I enjoy music through my earphones from the tape deck stashed in my jean's back pocket. I love music from our lesbian musicians plus Joni Mitchell, Cat Stevens, Carol King and hearing the words repeatedly of Jean Houston's taped interviews sharing her wisdom. As my hands and arms, back and legs move about nurturing the earth, music and ideas and creativity reach into my mind. It's a fabulous combination and it shuts out distractions like my otherwise quiet neighbor swearing at his sons. Hopefully our new neighbors will be friendly with us two women living on their block.

We will leave three evergreen trees competing each other in a small space. What a jumble the tree roots must make under the surface, all those roots stretching to find nourishment and space to grow. I read that tree roots nurture other tree roots. Bea's grandchildren are sprouting up like young trees. From our crone connections to Mother Earth and the Goddess, we may mentor them to accept our connection to the earth. Their roots are growing as their values form, their characters develop.

What a tree each will be. Our children and their offspring are my most precious plants. I love to watch them mature and gain wisdom.

What a challenge I gave mine when I walked away from their secure and safe home base—to be a lesbian.

This spring I transplanted tired perennials from the neglected garden that came with the little house my Jenny bought after Alex moved away. But it was I who cut myself from their established roots, took a traditional plant, our home and family, and chopped it into pieces.

For this plant, I combined two garden forks, their backsides against each other like a wedge, slammed their prongs into the top mass of earth, pulled the fork handles apart to break the soil, to split the roots. I touched taproot, the center stem that goes down, down, leveraged against those stubborn roots, axed and pulled until the taproot tore loose and gave way. I dug out that huge clump and unbraided the twisting and twined roots.

If possible, with gentle hands, I transplanted my Jenny and Matt's roots, as well as our own roots, to different places and added uniquely nourishing ingredients to soften the trauma of being so cruelly separated. Hopefully we all will make new gardens in good soil and grow—grow into vigorous plants—and bloom.

Chapter 26

Bea on November 5, 1984

On Jan's first work day on the job, she looked magnificent in my new red blouse, black pinstriped suit and my raincoat. She felt good too, she told me, except that she hated to have to shave her legs and pull on panty hose, but it's all for a good cause. This weekend while Jan worked inside, I scraped and painted the window stills and touched up the side of the house, trimmed the hedge and accomplished other heavy work. We rehung the draperies and replaced the furniture.

On Saturday night we dressed in our witches costumes for our church Halloween party. The gay gang was there, mixing with straight couples and older kids, all having a good time. When our little person friend Em Kuiper came with Betty Willing, they set off a riot of laughter. Betty dressed Em as a perfect Fred Flintstone, and of course, Betty was Betty Rubble.
Last night I was exhausted but Jan stayed up a little longer until she was really tired so she could sleep without worrying about today.

Jan on November 5, 1984 and beyond

I maneuvered my snappy little red Ford Escort through heavy morning traffic with huge semis belching exhaust and snapping their bare-lady tire mud flaps at me speeding along next to their huge spinning wheels. I made the correct turns to pull into the public parking lot and arrived at Administrator John Jackson's third floor offices at 8 a.m.

A primly dressed secretary told me to take a seat. I wore Bea's classy dress-for-success black suit, a skirt, of course, and a silky white blouse with fashionable frills and sensible, little-old-lady, closed-toed wedgie pumps. (I knew I'd miss the comfortable slacks outfits I used to wear.)

I hope I looked cool and calm on the outside, and I finally started to feel that way on the inside when John Jackson opened his office door to offer me his welcoming giant brown hand as I entered his office to begin my new career. My imposing Black boss with a great white smile ushered me into his office. I'd never shaken a hand like that, one that enveloped mine.

We chatted informally for a few minutes, but his time is precious and he gave me an agenda of people to meet. Each would orient me on their responsibilities and warn me what not to do, he joked. His schedule had him leaving early for the Court House. He pointed to my fat red ring-binder of all my hospital work sitting on the board table. "That's there for all my administrative staff to see, and they like it." He probably thinks I'm to do it all—but not immediately, I hope.

"Your first big project will be promoting and organizing an open house on January 12 for Wisconsin's first Magnetic Resonance Imaging Center to be here at our hospital. The MRI, built by General Electric, is being installed now. You can work with our Sig and the Medical College's PR guy John Turner. Dr. James Henderson is our medical director, and I asked him and Froedtert's PR guy, Jack Knight, about you, and Jack said you'd be the one for this job. You'll meet Sig today."

He led me to my office right around the corner from his administrative suite past the closet-sized copying and coffee room. My office door, directly opposite the men's room door, contains a desk and a chair, a couple of empty file cabinets and a table, no phone, no typewriter. Some daylight may shine through the two tall bare windows that face another yellow brick hospital wing of the towering hospital structure built in the 1930s. I'm in a 1950s addition.

He quickly walked me through my inner office doorway to another room that could be a reception area with space for a secretary. Opposite that is another office like mine that's to be filled by Administrative Assistant Bob Blain. As Mr. Jackson handed me my keys, I told him it seemed to be a comfortable set-up, but I would need the tools of my trade, at least a typewriter and a phone. All will come in time, he assured me, and he had his secretary guide me to Personnel to begin my rounds.

It took days to get my phone connected but I soon was shackled to a pager. The typewriter issued to me had keys missing. In time all was transformed into a warmer, friendlier place with clean office furniture, a corkboard wall for brainstorming and storyboarding. New draperies improved the stark view of a faded brick wall. Eventually a shared secretary helped me through the system after I plead innocent about bending some bureaucratic County regulations, for example: not becoming a County resident in six months and hiring my business partner, Bea, so she'd be the best, most convenient resource and get paid for the computer work she does as Mother Courage Enterprises.

I intend to be "in the closet" here. I won't repeat my openness that compromised me with Lakeshore Med administrators and who knows who else, but when the efficient Personnel clerk asks for the name and address of your beneficiary and you give a woman's name at your same address, she isn't stupid. I'm sure that by noon, if the name didn't imply a mother or sister, most of her lunch buddies will know of my ambiguous status.

Each assistant administrator I met directed me to the next starting with Personnel. He asked me when I would assume the responsibility of answering media phone calls from the busy nursing supervisors, but I don't even have a phone (nor would I know what to say). He led me to another County Hospital veteran Outpatient Assistant Administrator with over twenty clinics to tend to. He passed me on to Outpatient Services Department Nurse Mary Walker who ran me through the clinic's crowded, rather seedy waiting room and long, green-tiled hallways with many medical specialties.

Then I met directors of Volunteers, Patient and Community Education Admissions, and Billing, and Trauma and Emergency Medicine Nursing. They each tried to explain their part of the puzzle in this public and private political conglomeration, but I'm more confused as I stumbled my way through the maze. And this is only the first day.

Tomorrow, Johnson will introduce me at the Administrative Coordinating Council meeting of about forty department heads. After that I'm to meet MRMC's Dee Springer and I'll thank her for helping me find this position. Though I'm not yet spending time in my office, I would like to involve Bill Wells' secretary, Rosie Alders, whom I hoped would be my secretary with Bob Blain. Bill Wells had done some PR work before he left and it would be helpful if his secretary came to our area. Someone mentioned an agency and its PR rep, but I'm not clear about his role. Would I be able to use this agency? Also on tomorrow's agenda I'll meet the new Assistant Administrator, the Dietary Director and Communications Center who manages mail, switchboard and hospital receptionists.

There's an equitable mix of races and ages. I like that. And this is only the start of learning about this place and its people.

Just after 5 p.m., I staggered to find my Escort in the vast public lot and paid my way to exit. Dressy shoes with a bit of a heel and skimpy leather soles has never been my style. My outfit now includes a laminated photo I.D. that hangs from my lapel. Tomorrow it will open the employee parking gate where I'm to enter another building, walk in a long tunnel under the street and come up in the old building but close to the elevator. I'll get the hang of it all.

And what in Hell is in a Magnetic Resonance Imaging Center?"

<<<◇>>>

It was surprisingly dark. We've switched to standard time yesterday. Good thing Bea changed the clocks, as she always does, so I wouldn't be late on my first day. But is it dark! For many of the years I worked at Lakeshore Med, I lived either two blocks away from my hospital or a couple of miles west. Now I have to choose how to get back on the Interstate, make the correct lane choices so I don't end up going to Madison or mix into downtown traffic.

Yes, it's dark. I have at least twenty minutes of my commute to drive headlight to bumper in three to five lanes coming and going on this clear November night. Ahead of me I see snaking red eyes in the tail lights of my co-commuters, and in opposite lanes I see a python of white headlights twisting by me. My rear view mirror reflects the white light images that surround me like immense, roiling boa constrictors—and I'm a most insignificant part of the whole, moving with the masses until I find the correct off-ramp, leave the highway lights and continue following my lane in the country darkness, finally reaching my Lakeshore Bay business lights, turn at my corner, find my home—and my Bea waiting for me with a chilled martini or two that I so rightfully deserve.

Jan on November 16, 1984

My dear Matt,

Upon concluding two weeks on the new job, I'm happy to report that I'm ready to take on the whole Milwaukee environment with my hospital's M.A.S.H. trauma and emergency department and $110,000,000 budget. Unfortunately my salary does not reflect the total budget amount, but undaunted, I go forth. I hit the road early each weekday toward the more volatile southwest with high-rise expressways and potentially humongous audiences to please.

So far I haven't met a person I didn't like, but then, you know—old lovable me!

I said my farewells to friends at Lakeshore Med. They're having a party for me on this Thursday at Laura's. Clark and Betty Young will be there.

Our publishing business is growing.

Love,
Mom

Bea on November 20, 1984

Dammit! Even Jan's drive home in the dark is hectic. After she told me about it, I could see her, an insignificant segment of a dragon's backbone with its miles-long spine slithering swiftly along. Cars with red tail lights twist and turn, and in opposite lanes, a giant snake with glowing white eyes slinks for miles heading toward her. And they never stop until she exits the ramp for home. Whew.

But I still don't want to move from our home.

I told her she didn't't have to keep this job. She'd get another one. No. She said she'd make it work. Enough searching for another job with hours spent on our computer, writing over 100 letters, individual resumes to selected groups: hospitals, feminist-friendly organizations, general employers, and then subjecting herself to five or six interviews. Wearing panty hose and skirts. Overcoming nerves in strange office buildings with her enthusiastic sales pitch and a smile.

Music and song are therapeutic so I bought her a new invention, a singing machine with eight-track tapes, speakers, the whole shebang for background music so she can sing while reading the lyrics to match the music.

Fun from the start for Jan—and for all our visitors—and she really belts it out when she sings like Liza Minnelli, "If I can make it there, I'll make it anywhere! It's up to yoooou! Milwaaauuukeeee!" Milwaaauuukeeee!" Hurrah!

Jan on November 23, 1984

My mental and physical work wipe me out. I get home weary almost to tears, enjoying cocktails later than usual and savoring Bea's supper made with love. Though it's been another stressful week, it's time to go to bed with more than thoughts of sleep.

I could tell. I was aware of her gestures. Her hands touched me once as I passed her chair. She gripped my arm, hand over hand, to pull me gently toward her face and mouth to meet hers, soft and slightly open and moist. The kiss was perfectly gentle, sweet yet seductive.

"Hum," and she shook her head. "My eyes crossed after that one."

Because of her various ailments, I was remarkably cool about the possibilities that could be waiting for me. Was she just teasing me? I knew I could still be rejected.

After watching TV's *ER*, she touched my shoulders and my hair when she passed behind me in my chair.

"I love it when you touch me" I said to inspire more, but that doesn't always work. Many times I would hint about loving or I would comment, but not often. It's been a long while since we made love. This time I said nothing.

She went up to bed. I finished my wine and my routine with few expectations yet alert to the options ahead. I was thinking more than feeling when I went upstairs and undressed. Without hesitation I set my naked body fully against her half-covered body and wrapped my arms around her, embracing her gently. My intentions were clear, enough to risk rejection —but there was none. I felt an urgent passionate response to my embrace and her mouth, aggressive in its need for more.

My hip. My right hip was stressed. It's me this time in pain, but I moved to a different position around her as she opened her wintery pjs for my face to find her breasts. My mouth made my pain and brain relax and I encircled her body in love.

She wanted our Valerie, our vibrator—So soon? And we used it to reach orgasm together.

To give pleasure. To receive it. Embrace and two bodies become one. Breasts touch. Legs move to band together. Hips twist. Pubes meet. We rest like that and breathe. Backs strong now. Forgetting our weakness. Endurance. Words of love. Calm to passion. Exciting sounds. No one will hear. Oh Goddess. Our hands. Our fingers. Our tongues. Prolonging our pleasure. Tasting desire. Pulsing hard. Holding on. Shaking. Moaning. Clutching. Coming to climax. Together. Stroking. A sip of wine. Resting. Soft talk. Sweet head on my shoulder. Breath on my breast. Her hand on the other. Sleeping as one. Oh how grand. Thank you.

Bea on March 21, 1985

After months we took the For Sale sign down from our home and decided to be a two-residence family. What a relief!

We bought a cozy, two bedroom "im-mobile" trailer home, our Sweet Haven only five minutes from Jan's hospital. Our dog Luv and I go there at least two nights a week and Jan stays there during long hours and bad weather.

We eat supper at posh restaurants around our metro area or hamburger joints nearby with Luv loving the gourmet doggy bag treats that we bring to her. But most of all, we're relieved not to be in limbo about our real home.

Jan now qualifies as an official County resident. I hated even thinking of moving everything, including Mother Courage Press, and being far from our families, friends and our church. So we comply with a County rule and we solved our housing dilemma.

Somewhere between all that, I'm working on Jan's work projects for MCMC to produce printed-ready, designed brochures, newsletters, posters, etc. I guess I'm her PR agency that doesn't get paid well and gives her time for other work priorities. She brings lots of computer work home to do in the early morning or late night hours. She needs a Mac at work.

This letter is produced on our new computer and printer. This technology brings such creative power into our lives and freedom to expand our goals and Mother Courage Press.
Blessed Be!
Bea and Jan

Chapter 27

Jan on March 25, 1985

"You've been here before," I said to myself, "not knowing what you'll do, yet somehow you do it." That's how I'm surviving after five months in this job.

Every day, reporters call me so I must keep current on a list of our victims of mayhem. Fortunately, nursing supervisors handle that on p.m., night shifts, weekends. Each morning I'd check in with last night's supervisor de-stressing with other RNs in their staffing office near mine. We'd usually laugh together unless there's sad news. I love those women and men, the heart of our hospital.

We have to be careful and current with this information. Often we could not release a person's condition. Had anyone died? Were families notified? Was there a criminal investigation? At times, a celebrity is hospitalized like a race car driver, and their own press person responds to media. This is tricky business that may go on 'round the clock.

Media would sometimes slip onto a nursing unit to interview a patient. Supervisors would call me to escort them out in a diplomatic manner. I needed to be tactful on the way out so they'd remember and use our positive news and events. I think the three TV stations, their reporters and crews and two daily newspapers and their medical reporters trust me—I hope.

One afternoon after two months in my job, an administrator bolted into my office shouting, "There's gunshots between the hospital and the School of Nursing dorm!" Without thinking, I slipped by him and ran down the back stairs, out the door past a frightened woman in a Security uniform, and headed toward a tight circle of uniformed County sheriff deputies.

What the hell! Standing just outside their circle, I stared where they stared—between two cars parked in the crowded back lot. I saw a rumpled mound of coats covering what appeared to be two dead persons heaped together over blood on crusty old snow. A man lay humped over a woman's body. Bits of a faded hospital gown showed from under his coat. From gaps in her coat, we could see the white hem of a nurse's uniform.

Because I was new, it was politically correct to defer my responsibilities on this to the County PR guy who out-ranked me and took over. He, a former newspaper reporter, an award-winning journalist, should have known better. He assumed that the prisoner and nurse escaped from my hospital. And I was dumb too to check it out.

He screwed up the reporting, even OK'ing printing maps showing how the prisoner could have run out of our front doors and around our huge hospital to get to his car. No one ever asked if he could have escaped from another hospital like the one next door.

Nor did I, and I'll always regret that I didn't know better.

Deputies refrained from shooting toward our hospital because employees, nursing school students and faculty jammed window spaces to watch what was going on. Would our fugitive consider shooting into them?

The security officer that I passed when I ran out the door had fainted and fell face down on the ground when bullets zinged over the parked cars. She and other guards would get therapy counseling after all this.

I drove home late in the night and downloaded on Bea and martinis.

<<◇>>

(I learned the truth about this event years later from journalist Fox Butterfield's book, *Children: The Bosket Family and the American Tradition of Violence, pages 295 to 301,* based on interviews and an investigative report by the County's Sheriff's Department.)

Frequent convict Butch Bosket's plan was to swallow salt to make him cough up enough blood to look critical. He consumed 18 salt packets saved from his meals and was brought from the County jail to my hospital's radiology department for X-rays as an outpatient. After that, Butch was transported through the long tunnel connecting us to my sister hospital, Froedert, for in-patient admission and treatment in its gastroenterology unit.

Butch's girlfriend, Donna, convinced an accomplice to park her car to the right of Froedtert front entrance and wait. She warned the 18-year-old that there may be cops and shooting.

Disguised as a nurse, Donna entered Room 3158 and slipped two of three guns to Butch who had been considered a model patient. Butch's deputy guard sat at the foot of his bed waiting for her shift replacement. She looked up to see a pistol at her head while Donna took the handcuff keys from her and unlocked Butch's arm cuff attached on the bed.

They gagged the guard and handcuffed her hands and her leg to a bathroom pipe. Butch walked out with his "nurse" who made a right turn at the stairs rather than a left that sent them down the stairs to the rear of the hospital.

From his office window, my campus PR colleague saw a man in a coat and hospital gown running at the back of Froedtert with a nurse chasing him down the slight sloop toward the back of my hospital. "It must be someone from the mental health complex escaping medical advice," he joked to his secretary.

Struggling to be freed in the hospital room, the gagged and tethered deputy reached the emergency cord, waited about a minute or so until she thought people were clear of any violence, pulled the cord and "Prisoner escaped" alerted campus security and sheriffs who surrounded the trapped couple between the cars in my hospital's rear parking lot with random bullets flying.

Butch Bosket popped up and down "like a turkey firing his guns in each hand," an officer described. Butch knew he couldn't escape. He would go back to prison.

"Don't shoot! I'm a hostage," shouted Donna, now standing, looking like a nurse with her hands up.

Butch pulled her down to him and shot her through her temple. Then he shot himself in his ear.

Though newspaper readers assumed that the reporter's story printed the truth, and no one, especially my colleague from our sister hospital, ever offered to bring truth to light until this book was printed.

Bea on March 25 to 27, 1985

I remember that night. Jan never got home 'til after 9. They had a shooting on the grounds. A woman helped a man to escape and when it looked like they may be caught, he shot her and himself. J was right there and she helped with the media scene. She was somewhat upset when she told me about it.

Jan didn't get home again tonight until after 6. Supper's chicken's not quite done. Burned the steak yesterday. My culinary arts are failing. Lost interest.

The rest of the evening didn't go very well. I dozed off and woke but still super-sleepy to Jan's watching an old Judy Garland movie on TV. (I really wasn't up to that so I went upstairs to check on another movie.) J. was flying mad at me because I hadn't told her what I was going to do. I walked into Jan's crazy anger—Christ! I can't move without her permission. She started to throw popcorn at me. I got up and looked threatening and she stopped, but not until she threw more popcorn around the room. It's still here on the floor. I'm not picking it up. She was irrational. She made some illusions to my diary. I asked if she read it. She denied it, but kept talking about it. My writing seems a threat perhaps an account of events from my point of view? My feelings? Even as things happen it scares her. Hell. It sure scares me! This stuff is crazy and it's going on more and more. I'm really worried about her—about us—about me!

Everything's fine today. She slept 'til after 8. I picked up the popcorn. I wasn't going to talk about it. We gently eased into the day, went out for breakfast, then to the sports show. It was fun. On the way home we stopped to buy some seeds and she planted them and dug in the garden. Just what she needs for her spring fever. It was a lovely warm day.

Jan from May 1984 to 1994

Too many open houses and special events wiped me out.

We established the State's first adult bone-marrow transplant unit and built a new trauma center in a huge new outpatient services building. Other PR pros smarter than I am would have hired an agency. I had to do everything on the cheap, bargaining for free services, and they must be the best.

Three months after starting this new career, I planned my first event: the opening of the state's first magnetic resonance (MRI) imaging facility housed in a concrete basement area that could be available to our sister hospital but in a tunnel far from our hospital entrances.

With Bea and two other creative gals that I hired for this occasion, we used whatever we could to warm up the concrete tunnel site. We posting enlarged photos borrowed from the medical college, created and hung blue and gold felt fabric banners from the overhead pipes and ducts, and assigned administrators as welcoming hosts to guide visitors to the elevators and down to the new MRI.

What to do with visitor jewelry, watches and other objects vulnerable to MRI's magnetic hazards? We bought camera film processing envelopes to hold wallets and personal metal objects and tore off the tags for the visitors to reclaim their valuables.

Bea was my photographer for this. The bonus of my job came when it was over and the two of us reached my office. I collapsed in my desk chair. We were alone. She handed me a refreshing martini poured from her icy cooler. She had a tray of olives too and cheese and crackers.

One November weekend, an impatient line of freezing people stretched out in front of a State Fair building where we hosted a free cholesterol screening partnered with information and promotion via a local but major TV news channel.

When Administrator John Jenkins entered the building, he was surprised and pleased to see huge banners with MCMC's name hanging from each concrete column. He was impressed on how we organized the place with our volunteer nurses and lab staff drawing blood samples in a well-lit, clean area while Auxiliary volunteers served hot refreshments to our trusting subjects watching a MCMC promotion video on giant screen while they sat comfortably, waiting for their screening results.

I stood outside in front of the entrance door for hours being chilled to my bone marrow with a cold wind blowing under overcast skies. I tried my best to entertain the impatient crowd waiting for "now certified, cholesterol-free people" to leave and for me to let those next in line inside.

We tested over 7,000 people.

<<◇>>

I became a regular at the new County Paramedic Communications Base in our Trauma Center. That's where I'd get faster news on victims coming in on ambulances and helicopter. I could even watch events happening on TV sets installed above the vast communications electronics board.

In the old ER: Once I stepped aside of a bloody shooter strapped and secured on a gurney in the same crowded triage surgery while the lives of his two victims were being saved.

In Surgery: Trauma Center doctors and surgical teams labored to save two policemen from bullet wounds. The dayroom was filled with wailing relatives, and I was among those trying to comfort them as best we could. Wives begged to talk with a doctor and when the time seemed right, I walked alone down the hall to the surgery door and rang the shockingly loud, clanging bell.

Soon the door slid opened before me and I was stunned at the sight of our imposing Armenian trauma surgeon with a bushy moustache and burly eyebrows staring down at me. He was covered with blood from his shoulders to his shoes.

"They're dead," he said. "There's nothing more to do. Transfused blood just oozes from their pores." He read the urgent look on my face. "OK. I'll clean up and come and talk to families."

In Cardiology: Staff alerted me that a donor heart was to arrive this evening. My assignment was to keep everything secret or I was to keep media out of the way until we could announce a successful result. The last successful heart transplant performed at a hospital competitor happened two decades ago. She became a hero and lived to see her successful transplant hospital grow and become a major health care center.

A scruffy crowd of pushy news people was expected to get in the way when the helicopter landed at our heliport near the ambulance door. I found a small room in the ER close to the doorway that is used to tell family that their loved one or some other victim is dead. I pulled two twin-sized settees together to make a square plastic-upholstered box, fell asleep and woke when I heard the helicopter's rotators roar. I expected to protect a sterile masked team with a neonatal-type crib glowing plastic tubes connected to beeping monitors. I witnessed one nurse, swiftly but smiling, proudly climb out of the helicopter holding a small red Colman picnic cooler. Rather than going to a picnic, this simple container preserved a freshly extracted human heart to be installed in another person who will return to his normal life as a healthy and happy man.

It was not about Dr. Frankenstein and his monster.

I stayed through the evening, answering phone calls and dragging myself back and forth through another creepy tunnel with bare light bulbs hanging from exposed wires to meet with my academic teammates deciding on what to do next in their posh, wood-paneled offices.

I was on for 36 hours, finally with media people piling in with our secretary while the campus team squeaked through my back door across from the men's room into my small office to try to make the best of this dilemma. What do we say? How do we say it? When? It must be now.

Our first heart transplant recipient didn't make it.

In Orthopedics: Ronald McDonald asked me to escort him to visit with the five-year-old boy who, normally, would have been at our neighboring Children's Hospital. But he was an orthopedic patient in our hospital. The boy lost both arms in a farm accident. The clown gave him a soccer ball.

Throughout our campus and city: The cryptosporidium drinking water outbreak strained our office and campus phones: three hospitals, a regional blood center, several labs and pathology departments and the medical school. By initiating a coordinated response determined in a meeting at my hospital, we organized to give the media informed answers from one source, not me.

Later, I experienced my personal cryptosporidium outbreak while at the County's Art Museum negotiating to use one of their paintings for a more welcoming illustration for our new patient menus. Suddenly I ran to a women's restroom just in time. That's not what cool PR people are expected to do.

A serious cryptosporidium patient: a friend, a signing expert who answered for the deaf when they were arrested, put in handcuffs and unable to communicate, was a young guy who died in my hospital. He also had AIDS.

And Jeffrey Dahmer: Notes stuck helter-skelter on our elevator walls asked for information about a young Hispanic fellow who had an appointment in one of our clinics. He was missing. Soon his mother and sister met with nursing supervisors and me. We told them what little we knew about missing his appointment. They wanted an answer that we didn't have. Sympathy didn't help. Later through the news, we found out where he'd been found.

A news photographer friend quit his job after taking photos in Dahmer's apartment, including Dahmer's opened and exposed refrigerator.

I had to keep cool and controlled without official post-traumatic stress disorder therapy. No wonder I started having panic attacks with scary mental images, sweats, feeling loss of control.

Bea remembers the first panic attack

Jan shouted from her shower and ran to me naked with her robe in her hands. She said, "Don't be scared but —" She was terrified. Couldn't express herself but said, "Sharp head pain. Images. Pain's stopped now."

I helped Jan into her robe, we sat together on the couch in our trailer home in Milwaukee, our Sweet Haven only five minutes from her work. Jan calmed down after I held her for a while. She seemed to be OK, got dressed and convinced me that the best place was to go to her hospital and check in with the Employee Clinic doctor.

I drove home but drove back up to Haven early. Picked up gyros for our supper. I remember how we held each other on the couch and fell asleep and we were very peaceful when we went to bed.

I remember. Jan had another episode another morning at Haven. She screamed out like she had a great idea or was it pain? I don't know. That time she had a rapid heartbeat and pulse, was confused, inarticulate, and showing fear.

"It's like a guide wanting to tell me something," Jan uttered. "What's happening to me," she moaned.

After convincing me that she'd get help at work, I headed for home to be near the phone. Jan called and said she did get see him and got a meds to help. She drove home by 6. We played pool after supper and she trounced me. She seemed OK. We talked it through in the morning and she drove off to work like normal.

Jan remembers after the first panic attacks

When our employee physician examined me, I told him that it finally got me.

"What's that that got you?"

'Schizophrenia."

"Why' do you say that?"

"I've been waiting for years. Much of my mother's life was spent in mental institutions because of that. I heard it was inherited and I've had that hanging over my head for years. And I think about my kids having it too."

"Your medical record shows me your age."

"That should be right."

"If that's right, then you should have had schizophrenia years ago. You're too old now."

"Why didn't someone tell me!"

"You probably never asked."

I coped with panic attacks several frightening times. Once I was talking with my Black secretary, Annie, and heard myself quoting Jesus, speaking in tongues and spouting hateful racist slurs. She kept talking to me and in seconds she came back into focus for me. Shocked and scared, I asked her what I had said.

"Why nothing."

I felt as though I was the demented girl in *The Exorcist*.

While driving through the tangle of an Interstate exchange, the physical sweating and flesh crawls started and I shouted, "Not Now, You Bastard! NOT NOW!" The scary feelings stopped and I never suffered another panic attack.

Jan on May 1, 1994

Again after nine and one-half years, a second hatchet-man administrator in my career life traumatically forced me out, this time into early retirement. Who needs PR when your 135-year-old County hospital is forced out of business, is sold, and all but one or two newer building are demolished.

Our revered nursing school building refused to budge when one of the first wrecking balls smashed into her. Her faculty and I watched and cheered her grit. Highly skilled nurses left or transferred to other County services like its jails. Acute care specialties and remaining facilities like the Trauma Center merged with our "sister hospital" that became staffed by all of our campus medical school physicians and interns. Beloved broken hospital building spaces became parking ramps.

Would I miss its demands, the excitement, the bloody traumas, compassionate healing, long hours and stressful politics of the job? I loved my job, my hospital and staff, a diverse and open-minded group.

I was too young to retire. I would have stayed there for more. When I negotiated with personnel, I realized I had over 2000 hours of leftover sick leave and comp time. That's one year without compensation.

Bea's analysis of our situation became clear. Our Mother Courage Press, her widow's Social Security that she got when Jake died, and my small County pension would be our lifelines. I would receive no pension from Lakeshore Med.

When friends and co-workers asked what I will do with my time I answered, "My business partner and I own a book publishing company, primarily producing therapy books for the sexually abused." That impressed everyone and it made me feel better about leaving.

But I discovered on my last trip to my small-shop printer how I felt. Over my tenure and with Bea's Mac expertise, Bea and I produced a bi-weekly employee newsletter that was distributed every payday. That's almost 250 computerized double-sided pages that celebrated my historic hospital and its people.

I handed my last newsletter to my friendly printer and then, surprising him, I started crying. This was it. The end.

My hospital all but disappeared. My hometown hospital still exists but its Golden Years era that our team promoted stands almost unoccupied.

Afterward

Bea's notes and lists from May 1986 to 1999

Believe it or not—and here's a secret. With Jan's increasing MCMC salary over ten years, Mother Courage Press, real estate rentals and sales, and Jan's taxable income growing from $22,300 from her old job at Lakeshore Bay in 1984 to a max of $46,200 in 1992, $45,000 in 1993 and $41,300 in May 1994 when she retired.

Some years, I didn't make a cent, however, our inherited real estate values combined with our best Mother Courage Press sales in 1988 increased our joint income to $78,000 with a dozen books in print. Some years my Press earning ranged from $1,300 to two to four years ranging from $10,000 to $15,000 at the max for me. But I'm proud to say that I managed all the funds, taxes, royalties, printing and maintenance expenses, and when Jan was forced to retire, she kept on working with me and loved our travels.

I am not doing a "poor me" routine, but I'd like to tell you some of the financial facts of my life. For the last years of Mother Courage Bookstore, working five to six days a week, fifty-two weeks, all I was able to draw from the business was $1,753, and that included $708 to pay for my health insurance. If I had any sense and interest in it, I should have found a job with a regular salary and some fringe benefits. But I felt we must keep our women's bookstore open.

I accrued no Social Security benefits and contributed to no pension plan. I was considered a single woman with no husband to support me or to put me on his benefit plan.

One time I met with a Social Security woman to explore any options, and I had none. She sympathetically asked me how I was getting by? I actually started to cry then while I thought of how I'd answer that question. Finally I said, "I'm living with a friend who has a full-time job and she's letting me live with her.

Then *Something Happened to Me* caught on, sold over 20,000 books, and attracted other authors. Our second book, *Why Me,* won the Editors' Choice award for young adults books in *Booklist,* a publication of the American Library Association and we had eventually had twenty-four books in print to sell.

I framed one check and posted it on our office wall.

Commonwealth Bank of Australia, Balgowlah, NSW, 13 October1987
Pay Mother Courage Press
The Sum of One thousand seven hundred twenty-nine and 99 cents
Boobook Publications PTY LTD
Signed by S.A. Hayis

One big surprise came in the mail just before Jan and my unofficial marriage ceremony with guests and all by the Rev. Dr. Tony Logan in March 1999. An official-looking Social Security letter informed me that I would be getting a widow's monthly check because my ex-husband died. When I called to report that they made a mistake and that his wife was still living, the agent explained that both of us would get monthly benefits if we had lived as his wife for over ten years. Hell! I lived with him over twenty years and raised his four kids! Blessed Be! I'm now a Rich Widow.

When Jan retired, we thanked The Goddess for our joint increased incomes, our humble real estate earnings and Eleanor and Franklin Roosevelt and his Secretary of Labor Frances Perkins for our monthly Social Security checks.

<<<<<◇>>>>>

From Mother Courage Press

All Books in
The Whistling Girls & Crowing Hens Series

Book 1—*Not to be Denied* captures humorous, sad and scary family life between 1900 and 1970: The Depression, war, life at home, schizophrenia; tomboy girls and teen girlfriends, sexual encounters, children, husbands, and individuals' choices that shape them. Passion explodes for two women in their early '40s. Liberal religion and Transactional Analysis weekends bring them together. Their paths meld when these naïve lovers test their magnetic attraction after Jan asks, "What could it hurt if we just let it happen?" (January 2024)

Book 2—*Gullibles' Travels.* Divorced Bea tries not to be a lesbian and her lover Jan strives to keep her children, husband and Bea happy. Bea and friends test the Sexual Revolution of the '60s and '70s. Jan recalls living in Cold War Germany in the '50s and touring Greece, Leningrad and Moscow with her husband in the '70s. Jan defuses a labor/management conflict and Bea and Jan escape to Europe for a rowdy and risqué three-week escapade in '76. (April 2024)

Book 3—In *Secret Transgressions*, Jan's hospital PR job expands with Bea as her assistant. Jan's marriage turns raw. Divorce. Bea is subject to sexual harassment in the workplace, is fired, and Jan is emotionally harassed on the job. Travel helps them heal and they create Mother Courage Bookstore and Press. (July 2024)

Book 4—*Being Mother Courage* embodies a dream come true: creating a feminist bookstore and experiencing historic events and adventures in the women's movement and the gay/lesbian world. They extended their first American Booksellers Association (ABA) trade show in Los Angeles starting with San Francisco's gay scene, on a night unlike any other, and ending by sailing with Seaworthy Women on a 31-foot wooden ketch launched from the 5000-boat Marina del Rey to Catalina Island. Women's spirituality circles and lesbian support groups in Bea and Jan's home inspire and support women. Jan confronts job harassment and Bea faces the bookstore's demise. Their Cancun vacation fun ignores sun-bathing on beaches to explore Mayan ruins. Jan enters the snorkeling world led by scuba-diver Bea. At home, their full moon circles begin with feminist and original rites and rituals. Tension turns to courageous laughter when conflicts are overcome. Bea uses her skills to pioneer Apple's Mac desktop publishing and was a guest speaker/teacher at the International Women's Booksellers Conference in Spain. (August 2024)

Book 5—In *Grit & Gratification*, Sailor Bea commands the boat and Jan, her bungling crew. Bea and Jan muster strength after Bea's homophobe father and Jan's supportive father die and they rehab their inherited rundown properties. Their new Mother Courage Press creates a significant, successful book for sexual abuse victims. When their retail bookstore closes, they are free to travel. As lusty lovers, they tow their camper to New York City, Provincetown, America's Stonehenge and Niagara Falls. Then they experience Michigan Woman's Music Festivals. Jan accepts that her lost Door County acres can be found on women's festival land. (January 2025)

Book 6—In *Moving On & Up*, Bea rejects joint therapy sessions with their friend. Jan goes alone to heal her stress asking to use her uniquely devised feminist therapy regimen that eventually benefits both women. Jan's boss eliminates her PR department and job, but her reputation earns her a better one at a major metropolitan hospital. Bea and Jan stay strong together. Mother Courage Press begins to thrive. Surviving scuba diving and wild camping trips, sneaking into Disney World, being inspired at women's music festivals and gatherings, traveling through the Great Northwest makes them feel on top of the world.

Book 7— In *Close to Fine* (1984 to 1995) Jan moves up to the 'Big Leagues' of hospital PR in an exciting but stressful job. Mother Courage Press is thriving and they dare to publish Entity Jeni's channeling via a friend's New Age psychic energy messages. Seaworthy Women sailor friends sail together across the Pacific in a small sailboat and send Mother Courage Press their manuscript so Bea and Jan fly to New Zealand and later to Australia. More fun starts with a trip to guitar heaven in northern California, and at home, Bea starts a woman's kitchen band to entertain audiences and themselves.

Book 8—In *Intimate Passages* (1984 to 2013) Bea challenges the intimate aspects of their long relationship but Jan persists as a new friend comforts Jan. Goddess searching journeys to England, Mexico, Malta, Egypt, Scotland and France sustain and inspire them

For additional information on the series, contact:
Publisher Jeanne Arnold
MotherCouragePress31@gmail.com
MotherCouragePress.com

Books are on Amazon and Google Books as ebooks, Amazon and Barnes and Noble for paperbacks, and available through Ingram for libraries and all bookstores.

About Jan Anthony

Jan may brag about being a battled-tested warrior queen, but she's really an optimistic crone who blends truthful and imaginative words to recreate two women's audacious journey together. Their frustrated search for happiness as married women with teenage children fails. They fall in love, discover the depths of women-creative cultures and fight for successful careers while challenging socially acceptable norms. Jan's storytelling takes you into their intimate lives that enhance sensual and spiritual memories with their bodacious, risk-taking adventures.

Mother Courage Press
MotherCouragePress31@gmail.com

www.ingramcontent.com/pod-product-compliance
Lightning Source LLC
LaVergne TN
LVHW021802060526
838201LV00058B/3211